European Historical Fiction and Biography for Children and Young People

Second Edition

by

Jeanette Hotchkiss

The Scarecrow Press, Inc.
Metuchen, N.J.   1972

Library of Congress Cataloging in Publication Data

Hotchkiss, Jeanette.
    European historical fiction and biography for
children and young people.

    1967 ed. published under title: European historical
fiction for children and young people.
    1. Historical fiction--Bibliography. 2. Children's
literature--Bibliography. I. Title.
Z5917.H6H6 1972   028.52   72-1597
ISBN 0-8108-0515-4

TABLE OF CONTENTS

INTRODUCTION

Roads to the Past

The contribution of fiction and biography toward fostering enthusiasm for history can hardly be overestimated, especially when, as nowadays, top-notch writers are producing for children and young people a wealth of books so exciting and well-researched that their elders can share the enjoyment they provide. For this is truly a Golden Age of juvenile literature of all kinds, and in the historical field there are many forms: myths and legends (often with some factual base), novels and romance, poetry, and even some fantasy in which we pass freely through the boundaries of time and place. Text books stress dates and names and battles, but fiction and biography lead us by the hand into the past, remote or recent, in a way that makes us almost feel that we have lived in the time about which we read and are recalling our own pasts.

Historical fiction has formerly been defined as pertaining to events of not less than a century past, but the new Random House Dictionary of the English Language gives it a freer definition as "a narrative in novel form characterized by an imaginary reconstruction of historical events and personages." Surely to those born even a third of a century ago, World War II is an historical event and its leaders and participants historical personages. So does history creep up on us, crowding us toward the future.

Those who take more pleasure in fact than fiction will find biographies also "characterized by an imaginary reconstruction" of the lives and times of illustrious men and women, for, without going beyond the facts of the matter, a good biographer takes us into his subject's home and world whether it be large, as in the case of a Napoleon, or small, as in Jane Austen's England.

There is a dearth of stories and novels about certain times and places--Central Europe, for example--and there we must read biographies to show how people lived in the

6

small principalities and kingdoms of what we now know as
Germany. I hope that some author, leafing over the pages
of this book, will be inspired to write some exciting fiction
about eighteenth and nineteenth century Germany, Czechoslovakia or Hungary, or that other neglected area, Spain and
Portugal.

My purpose here has been to fit events and personages into their proper settings of time and place and often
it has seemed like putting together a tantalizing jig-saw puzzle. I would see a color and shape that certainly looked as
if it belonged near another like it, but finally discovered
that it was part of quite a different pattern in the picture.
Such was the case with the period of the Crusades. Should
Richard the Lion-Hearted belong in England where he spent
very little of his life or in France where he spent most of
it or even 'way off in Byzantium?

Another way, however, of looking at the shape of
this book is to consider it a roadmap atlas to the past. As
I said in my introduction to the first edition, I won't attempt to advise you as to which road you should take. There
are straight, smooth roads such as the Romans built (the
more factual books). There are shady, winding paths through
the Forest of Arden (romances.) And there are rocky, pre-
cipitous roads with hairpin turns that scare the wits out of
you but give you a spectacular view from the top and a long
sigh of relief when you reach level ground again (novels of
intrigue, adventure, escape). But this much I can say:
there are no dead ends in history. Every road comes from
somewhere and leads somewhere in time, and we ourselves
are travelers on them. By discovering how we arrived at
this place in the twentieth century and learning as much as
possible about those who traveled the roads behind us, we
may gain a clearer vision of where we are heading and of
where we really want to go.

How to Use This Book

I defy anyone to lump readers in neat little age
brackets according to their abilities or tastes, but we have
used certain symbols to give some indication of reading
levels and to prevent, for instance, a 12-year-old from
wandering into the picture book area of the library with its
playpen and stuffed animals. He will feel much less out of
place in the adult section, but if he is lucky, he'll find
some shelves set apart somewhere for young adults.

So here are the signposts: "E," for elementary includes not only beginning readers, but slightly older children
who read slowly or with some difficulty. "E and I" is a
symbol for the sake of those who don't stay beginners very
long and want more exciting books than the primer type.
"I" alone, for intermediate, suggests ages from eight to
twelve, while "I and YA" point to books for ages ten or so
up. "YA" alone aims to please the average (if there is
such) young person from twelve to fourteen, while "YA and
A" goes on up from there, even to college. "A," of course,
speaks for itself and includes many of the classics.

It will not always be possible to find all the books
you most want to read. Certainly no one library could con-
tain them all; none is as rich as that in either money or
space, and unfortunately some books become lost, strayed
or stolen, and others have to be discarded to make room
for newer books--always a sad situation. So become a book
hunter. It's fun. Visit neighboring libraries and search the
bookcases of your friends and relations. Sometimes church
rummage sales or second-hand bookstores yield surprising
finds.

I wish I could suggest bookstores, but the price of
all books including juveniles has soared so high that this
would not be a practical suggestion. Except for the paperback sections. In the past five years, I am happy to report,
there have been great strides in the publication of junior
paperbacks--not just the classics but also recent novels.

So good hunting and good reading and may you become real history buffs like me.

Sources, Methods and Acknowledgments

During the five years that have elapsed since the publication of the first edition of this work, I have discovered
new sources and some of my former ones have dried up.
The literary supplements of newspapers in my own area
used to pay much more attention to children's books than
they do now. In fact one, in particular, no longer has any
review of juveniles except for a special section twice a year,
while it used to have a whole page weekly. Another
crowds its juvenile reviews into the bottom corner of the
last of the pages devoted to literature.

Bookstores, like the newspapers, all too frequently relegate the childrens' department to a back corner of the shop with limited space. There are some blessed exceptions, but this is a fairly general practice. However many stores do carry the new good paperbacks which are coming out these days for children and young people and also the splendid new editions of the classics.

My best sources of information on what is being published and reviews of new books are Publishers' Weekly and the Horn Book. And always, always, public libraries—here, there and everywhere. My historical resources have not changed. Even before I dreamed of doing this kind of a bibliography, I had found an absorbing hobby in outlining world history, by countries, based on the Encyclopedia of World History compiled and edited by William L. Langer. Even earlier, I read, with my own children, Hillyer's Child's History of the World and we made our own historical map with crayons on shelf paper. When it came to doing a bibliography of historical fiction and biography, however, I decided that this was a bit too wide a scope and limited myself to the British Isles and Europe.

Now as to methods, young people with whom I have discussed the matter agree with me that authors are entitled to have their books shelved under the pen names they have chosen. I can understand why this is not done in some libraries; it's a matter of logistics, I suppose, but who ever thinks of Mark Twain as Samuel Clemens?

As to spelling, in every case I have used that which appears in the title or content of the book. Some of the legendary Irish names are spelled in many different ways as are the Viking ones like "Eriksson" and "Hakon." Rumania is sometimes spelled with an "O" instead of "U" and Yugoslavia with an initial "J."

My criteria for selection have been the same as they were for the first edition, namely, historical accuracy, literary merit, readability, and good taste. I am happy to say that I have had to limit very few for lack of these qualities. Editors have taken care of that, and I could only wish that they were as conscientious about adult literature. Juveniles have become more realistic in recent years, and there is a decided change in what is considered "suitable" for young readers, but this is all to the good in my opinion. Not all the books are of equal literary value, but few, if any, are mediocre.

I am grateful to all the children's librarians I have met in the course of my work and applaud them for their dedication in making readers out of television watchers. Very special thanks go to the staff of the children's room of the Highland Park, Illinois, Public Library, under the able leadership of Mrs. Jo Hemsworth, who have made me call that place "my home away from home."

To my husband who has all too often to listen to the typewriter even on holidays or repeat his questions and remarks because I am so deep into a book, my loving gratitude and appreciation.

PART I: THE BRITISH ISLES

GENERAL HISTORY

1.   Dickens, Charles.   A Child's History of England.   1852.
     A book to be read for entertainment rather than
     historical accuracy, as the great novelist was not
     a great historian.   (I and YA)
2.   Maurois, André.   An Illustrated History of England.
     Viking, 1964.   Translated by Hamish Miles, with
     a foreword by Sir Arthur Bryant, and revised and
     abridged from an earlier history.   (A)
3.   Stenhouse, Lawrence.   The Story of Scotland.   Watts,
     1961.   Ill. by B. Biro.   Good background for the
     many exciting novels set in Scotland.   (YA)
4.   Trease, Geoffrey.   Seven Kings of England.   Vanguard,
     1955.   Brief biographies of Alfred the Great,
     William the Conqueror, Richard the Lion-Hearted,
     Charles I, Charles II, William III and George VI.
     (YA)
5.   _____.   The Seven Queens of England.   Vanguard,
     1953.   Biographies of the seven queens regnant of
     England: Maude (granddaughter of William the
     Conqueror), Mary Tudor, Elizabeth I, Mary of
     Orange (with William), Anne, Victoria, and
     Elizabeth II.   (YA)

PREHISTORY, ARCHAEOLOGY, MYTHS AND LEGENDS

6.   Branley, Franklin M.   The Mystery of Stonehenge.
     Thomas Y. Crowell Co., 1969.   Ill. by Victor
     Ambrus.   The story of the age-old mystery of the
     great stones on the Salisbury Plain, upon which
     many novels and legends have been based, with
     drawings made on the site.   When, why, by what
     people, and how, were these gigantic stones raised
     have perplexed archaeologists even with the modern
     tools of radiology and computers.   (All Ages)
7.   Capon, Paul.   Warrior's Moon.   Putnam, 1962.   Ill. by
     Albert Orbaan.   A novel set on the Salisbury Plain

about 2000 B.C. about the builders of Stonehenge,
with King Arthur appearing long before his time.
(YA)

8. Colum, Padraic. The King of Ireland's Son. Mac-
    millan, 1916 and 1962. Ill. by Will Pogany. An
    Irish folk tale. (I)

9. Garner, Alan. The Owl Service. Henry Z. Walck,
    1967. A Welsh fantasy in which a legend is acted
    out through succeeding generations with brooding
    suspense. (YA)

10. Hunter, Mollie (McIlwraith). Thomas and the Warlock.
    Funk and Wagnalls, 1967. Ill. by Joseph Cellini.
    A fairy tale set in the Scottish lowlands at an in-
    determinate time, about witches and warlocks and
    fairies and a powerful blacksmith and his couragous
    son. (I)

11. Hyde, Christopher. Temple of the Winds. World,
    1965. Ill. by Joseph Cellini. The struggles of a
    poetic boy as he grows up expected to be a ruler,
    the building of Stonehenge, and the conflict between
    the Twelve Tribes and the "longheads" are the inter-
    woven strands of this novel. (YA)

12. Jones, Gwyn. Welsh Legends and Folk Tales. Oxford,
    1955. Ill. by Joan Kiddell-Monroe. Little-known
    legends retold. (I)

13. Kipling, Rudyard. Puck of Pook's Hill. Doubleday,
    1902. Fairy tales about the period around 300
    A.D. (I)

14. _____. Rewards and Fairies. Doubleday, 1910.
    More fairy tales of around 400 A.D. (I)

15. Leodhas, Sorche Nic (Leclaire Alger). By Loch and
    By Lin. Holt, Rinehart and Winston, 1969. Ill.
    by Vera Bock. Tales from Scottish ballads which
    were based on real happenings, enlarged and en-
    hanced in many retellings. (I)

15a. _____. Heather and Broom, Tales from the Scotch
    Highlands. Holt, Rinehart and Winston, 1960.
    Ill. by Consuelo Joerns. Stories which have come
    down through the centuries, first told by monks
    and sung by harpists, and later passed on by the
    "seanachies" (story-tellers). (I)

16. _____. Thistle and Thyme; Tales and Legends
    from Scotland. Holt, Rinehart and Winston, 1962.
    Ill. by Evaline Ness. Many of these tales, the
    author explains in her introduction, she herself
    heard told in Scottish Gaelic and translated in the
    cadence of that tongue. (I)

17. Lynch, Patricia. Brogeen Follows the Magic Tune.
     MacMillan, 1952. Ill. by Ralph Pinto. A continu-
     ous folk tale, full of Irish magic, with a glossary
     of Irish words. (I)
18. Neavles, Janet. Beyond the Mist lies Thule. Barnes,
     1961. Ill. by Arthur Zaidenburg. A novel set
     half in ancient Greece and half in Celtic Britain.
     (YA)
19. Nye, Robert. Taliesin. Hill and Wang, 1966. Ill. by
     Dorothy Maas. A story from a famous collection
     of Welsh legends, about the poet Taliesin, who had
     tasted three magic drops from the magic cauldron
     of a witch. (I)
20. O'Faolain, Eileen. Irish Sagas and Folk Tales. Ox-
     ford, 1954. Ill. by Joan Kiddell-Monroe. (I)
21. Picard, Barbara Leonie. Tales of the British People.
     Criterion, 1963. Ill. by Eric Fraser. A retell-
     ing of traditional stories brought to the British
     Isles by the various peoples who settled there:
     Iberians, Celts, Romans, Saxons, Danes and
     Normans. (I and YA)
22. _____ . Celtic Tales. Criterion, 1964. Ill. by
     John G. Galsworthy. "Legends of Tall Warriors
     and Old Enchantments" about the people of Dana,
     Finn and Fianna and a different King Arthur than
     the sixth century one. (I and YA)
23. _____ . Celtic Tales from the British Isles. Cri-
     terion, 1963. Ill. by John G. Galsworthy. A
     companion volume to "Tales of the British People"
     in four sections: England, Wales, Scotland and
     Ireland. Many of the characters from these tales
     will be met later in their proper time settings.
     (I and YA)
23a. _____ . Hero Tales from the British Isles. Cri-
     terion, 1963. Ill. by John Galsworthy. A com-
     panion volume to "Tales of the British People,"
     in four parts for England, Scotland, Ireland and
     Wales. (I and YA)
24. Pilkington, F.M. The Three Sorrowful Tales of Erin.
     Walck, 1966. Ill. by Victor Ambrus. These
     tales are more deeply mythological than most.
     (YA)
25. Pugh, Ellen. Tales from the Welsh Hills. Dodd Mead,
     1968. Ill. by Joan Sandin. An attractive book of
     Welsh folk stories as the author learned them from
     her Welsh grandparents, some eerie, most hu-
     morous, and all delightful. (I)

25a. Pugh, Ellen. More Tales from the Welsh Hills. Dodd,
     Mead, 1971. Ill. by Joan Sandin. A second collec-
     tion of folk tales told to the author by her Welsh
     grandmother, conveying the cadence of Welsh speech,
     and with a guide to the difficult pronounciation of
     Welsh names and words. (I)

26. Schmeltzer, Kurt. The Axe of Bronze. Sterling, 1958.
     Ill. by Mike Charlton. Fiction with a slight plot but
     a great deal of interesting information about the mak-
     ing of bronze and the building of Stonehenge. (I)

27. Sprague, Rosemary. Northward to Albion. Roy, 1947.
     Ill. by Kurt Werth. A novel based on a legend
     written by Geoffrey of Monmouth in the twelfth cen-
     tury, about Bryttys, Prince of Troy, how he sailed
     to Albion and founded Britannia. (YA)

28. Sutcliffe, Rosemary. The High Deeds of Finn MacCool.
     E. P. Dutton, 1967. Ill. by Michael Charlton.
     Retelling of tales from the south of Ireland. (I and
     YA)

29. _____. Warrier Scarlet. Walck, 1958. Ill. by
     Charles Keeping. A novel of the Bronze Age. (YA)

30. Treece, Henry. The Dream Time. Meredith Press,
     1967. Ill. by Charles Keeping. This last book by
     the prolific novelist, with an epilogue by Rosemary
     Sutcliffe, is more of an impression than a novel; a
     dreamlike story about the dawn of humanity as ex-
     pressed in cave drawings and about the first making
     of iron and the beginning understanding among people
     of different tribes and speech. (I and YA)

31. _____. Men of the Hills. Criterion, 1958. Ill. by
     Christine Price. A story of prehistoric Britain in
     all its primitive savagery, and how the small dark-
     skinned natives were besieged by the Sun King's
     men from over the sea. (YA)

32. Wilson, Barbara Ker. Scottish Folk Tales and Legends.
     Oxford, 1954. Ill. by Joan Kiddell-Monroe. A
     wide range of tales, legends and fables, based
     chiefly on a collection of Gaelic folklore, "Waifs
     and Strays of Celtic tradition." (I)

33. Young, Ella. The Tangle Coated Horse and Other
     Tales. Longmans Green, 1928. Ill. by Vera Bock.
     These episodes from the Fionna Saga, one of the
     oldest of Gaelic Sagas, require poetic imagination
     of readers. (I)

34. _____. The Wonder Smith and His Son. Longmans
     Green, 1927. Ill. by Boris Artzybasheff. Old
     Gaelic tales about the Gubbaun Saor, skillfully wov-

en into a continuous story by a woman who gathered
them from villagers in County Clare.   (I and YA)

FIRST CENTURY B.C.

35.   Polland, Madeleine. To Tell My People. Holt, Rinehart and Winston, 1968. Ill. by Richard M. Powers.
A strong novel about a young half-savage girl captured by the Romans at the time of Caesar's first
invasion of Britain and taken as a slave to Rome
where she learns of the civilization and power of
the Romans and tries to go back to Britain with the
second invasion to warn her people of the impossi-
bility of resisting Roman rule.   (YA)

FIRST AND SECOND CENTURIES A.D.
(The Roman Period)

36.   Faulkner, Nancy. The Sacred Jewel. Doubleday, 1961.
A novel in which history and legend are blended into
a suspenseful plot about the Druids and the people
they served in A.D. 30 when Cymbeline ruled over
southeastern England.   (YA)
37.   Gard, Joyce. The Mermaid's Daughter. Holt, 1969.
A novel about the Sea Goddess cult in the Isles of
Scilly two centuries after the Roman conquest of
Britain, the heroine Astria elected in youth to be
the mermaid goddess.   Historical evidence in a
folkloristic postscript.   (YA)
38.   Gray, Ernest A.   Roman Eagle and Celtic Hawk.
Barnes, 1959.   Ill. by Douglas Hall.   A tale of
three young Romans and their daring escape from
the King of the Brigantes A.D. 69, with an appendix
describing Roman military organization and camps.
(YA)
39.   Polland, Madeleine. Deirdre. Doubleday, 1967. Map
and ill. by Sean Morrison. The Tragic love story
of Deirdre of the Sorrows and Naoise who loved her.
(YA)
40.   Seton, Anya. The Mistletoe and the Sword. Doubleday, 1955. A novel about the conflict between the
Roman legions and the British tribes in 60 A.D.
Quintus Tullius, Catus, Petillius, Valerianus, Queen
Boadicea, Conn Lear and others.   (YA)
41.   Shore, Maxine. The Captive Princess, The Story of

the First Christian Princess of Britain.   Longmans
Green, 1952. Ill. by Kreigh Collins.   A story of
the mid first century A.D., the time of the Emperor
Claudius and the beginning of Nero's reign in Rome.
(YA)

42. Snedeker, Caroline Dale. The White Isle. Doubleday,
1940. Ill. by Fritz Kredel. A novel about a noble
Roman family finding a new home and religion in
Britain in the early part of the second century.
Names of cities and rivers on their journey from
Rome are listed in both Latin and English.   (YA)

43. Stephens, James. Deirdre. Macmillan, 1969? Ill. by
Nonny Hogrogian. First published in 1923 this version of the story of the "Troubler" of the sons of
Cuchulinn is presented as it might have been told by
poets in the halls of Irish kings.   (A)

44. Sutcliffe, Rosemary. The Eagle of the Ninth. Oxford,
1954. Ill. by C. Walter Hodges. A finely plotted
novel based on two mysteries: one the disappear-
ance of the Ninth Roman Legion about 117 A.D. and
the other the discovery, almost 1800 years later,
of a wingless Roman eagle dug up at Silchester. A
good map and place names in Latin and English.
(YA)

45. _____. The Hound of Ulster. Dutton, 1963. Ill.
by Victor Ambrus. A retelling of legends and history about Cuchulain, Deirdre, Queen Maeve and
other half-legendary, half-historical Irish characters.
(I)

46. _____. Outcast. Oxford, 1955. Ill. by Richard
Kennedy. A novel about a Roman orphan cast out
by the Britons and captured and enslaved by his
own people.   (YA)

47. Trease, Geoffrey. Message to Hadrian. Vanguard,
1955. A novel about Hadrian's visit to Britain
about 117 A.D., completely fictional except for the
character of Hadrian but based on sound research.
(YA)

48. Treece, Henry. The Centurion. Meredith Press,
1965. Ill. by Mary Russon. A beautiful book in
every way, first published in England under the
title "The Bronze Sword," the story of a retired
centurion of the famous Ninth Legion and the final
defeat of Queen Boadicea, with a glossary and introduction clearly defining the period.   (YA)

49. _____. The Queen's Brooch. G. P. Putnam's
Sons, 1967. Jacket by Brian Wildsmith. A grim

sanguinary novel of a young Roman tribune who sees
both sides of the struggle between the Celts under
Boadicea and the Romans under Suetonius and has to
make a choice. (YA)

50. _____ . War Dog. Criterion, 1962. Ill. by Roger
Payne. A fast moving story (as are all the books
by Treece) about a dog whose Celtic master is
killed and his difficulty in transferring his loyalty
to his new Roman master. (YA)

51. Walsh, Maurice. Sons of the Swordmaker. Stokes,
1936. A novel about Ireland at the beginning of the
Christian era when Conaire the Great was High King
of Erin at Tara. A fine mixture of legend, history
and Irish mysticism. (A)

THIRD THROUGH EIGHTH CENTURIES

A. The Death of Roman Power; the Dark Ages

52. Finkel, George. Watch Fires to the North. Viking,
1967 (First American). A splendid historical novel
(rather than legendary) with King Arthur as one of
many kings in Britain in the sixth century, the narrator being his young companion and later successor.
He goes with the king to the court of Justinian and
Theodora and is trained in horsemanship under General Belisarius, after which they return to Britain,
taking Thracian horses with them and fight many
battles against invading Saxons. Good maps and
glossary. (YA and A)

53. Gard, Joyce. Talargain. Holt, Rinehart and Winston,
1964. Jacket by Nonny Hogrogian. In the frame-
work of a few contemporary chapters, this is the
absorbing story of a seventh century lad, living with
adopted parents on the Northumbrian coast; how he
became part of a herd of seals living on a nearby
island, how they came to his rescue, and how he
finally solved the mystery of his parentage. (I)

54. Mayne, William. The Hill Road. E. P. Dutton, 1968.
Jacket by Krystyna Turska. For readers who enjoy
highly imaginative trips into time and place, this
"now and then" fantasy will suit perfectly with its
combination of the present and the Dark Ages. (YA)

55. Sutcliffe, Rosemary. Dawn Wind. Walck, 1962. Ill.
by Charles Keeping. A novel about the beginning

emergence of England at the time of Ethelbert of
Kent (560-616) who was converted to the Roman
Church by St. Augustine in 597.   (YA)

56. _____ . The Lantern Bearers. Walck, 1959. Ill.
by Charles Keeping. A novel about the last defenses
by the Roman-British leader Ambrosius against the
Saxons and the traitorous Vortigen in the fifth century. (YA)

57. _____ . The Silver Branch. Walck, 1958. Ill. by
Charles Keeping. A novel about a young surgeon in
the Roman army during the decline of Roman power
in the fourth century. (YA)

58. Willard, Barbara. Augustine Came to Kent. Doubleday, 1963. Ill. by Hans Guggenheim. The story of
the first Archbishop of Canterbury, sent to England
by Pope Gregory I to reconvert Britain. (YA)

B.   Fifth and Sixth Century Ireland
(The Golden Age of Irish Monasticism)

59. Cantwell, Mary. St. Patrick's Day. Crowell, 1966.
Ill. by Ursula Arndt. The story of the Irish saint
who was born in Roman England about 385, educated
in Gaul, and died in 461, with accounts of the cele-
bration of his birthday. (E)

60. Curtayne, Alice. Twenty Tales of Irish Saints. Sheed
and Ward, 1955. Ill. by Johannes Troyer. Told
with gentle humor. (I)

61. _____ . More Tales of Irish Saints. Sheed and
Ward, 1957. Ill. by Brigid Rynne. (I)

62. Lynch, Patricia. Knights of God. Regnery, 1955.
Legends, ballads, brief biographies and simple fic-
tion about nine Irish saints, some of a later period.
(YA)

63. Oliver, Jane. Isle of Glory. Putnam, 1964. A biographical novel about St. Columba (521-97) who
founded monasteries in Ireland and converted the
northern Scots to Christianity. Explanatory preface
and list of characters. (A)

64. Polland, Madeleine. Flame Over Tara. Doubleday,
1964. Ill. by Omar Davis. A novel of St. Patrick,
his conflict with the Druid priests, and the conflict
he caused in the heart and mind of a young Irish
maid. (YA)

65. Reilly, Robert T. Irish Saints. Farrar, Straus, 1964
(A Vision Book). Ill. by Harry Barton. Brief biographies of 12 Irish saints and saintly characters,

some of a later period.   (YA)
66.   Reynolds, Quentin.   The Life of Saint Patrick.   Random,
      1955 (Landmark).   Ill. by Douglas Gorsline.   (I)

C.   All About King Arthur and His Knights

The immortality of King Arthur is such that he pops
up in the most unexpected times and places.   Here is an attempt to gather all the stories about him into one section--
the late fifth and early sixth centuries where the historical
king seems to have belonged, but it is doubtful if he will
stay put here.

67.   Bowers, Gwendolyn.   Brother to Galahad.   Walck, 1963.
      Ill. by Don Bolognese.   Arthurian legend treated
      realistically with reference to the historical charac-
      ters, Hengist and Horsa.   (YA)
68.   Bulla, Clyde.   The Sword in the Tree.   Crowell, 1956.
      Ill. by Paul Galdone.   (E)
69.   Clancy, Joseph P.   Pendragon, Arthur and His Britain.
      Praeger, 1971.   Illustrations from a manuscript of
      Lancelot du Lac (fourteenth century French), now in
      the Pierpont Morgan Library.   This 1971 Book
      World Honor Book is so definitive and handsomely
      made, that it will surely be found on adult as well
      as juvenile shelves.   The author has much to say
      about the relationship of history and poetry and
      writes as both an historian and a poet.   As the
      former he gives us an unusual history of prehistoric
      and early Britain and the Roman period before the
      end of the fifth century when, he feels quite certain,
      Arthur was a real person.   A chronology of events
      from 600 B.C. to 634 A.D.--maps and a bibliog-
      raphy.   (YA and A)
70.   Curry, Jane Louise.   The Sleepers.   Harcourt, Brace
      and World, 1968.   Ill. by Gareth Floyd.   A fantasy
      of King Arthur's knights discovered in an archaeo-
      logical "dig."   (YA)
71.   Fadiman, Clifton.   The Story of Young King Arthur.
      Random, 1961.   Ill. by Paul Liberonsky.   A short
      book about the birth of Arthur and his becoming king
      at eighteen.   (I)
72.   Fraser, Antonia.   King Arthur and the Knights of the
      Round Table.   Knopf, 1971.   Ill. with full color
      paintings by the author's daughter Rebecca Fraser
      (at the age of 12).   The romantic world of Camelot
      recreated.   (All ages)

73. Frith, Henry. King Arthur and His Knights. Garden
      City, 1932. Ill. in color by Frank E. Schoonover.
      (I and YA)

74. Hieatt, Constance. The Joy of the Court. Crowell,
      1971. Ill. by Pauline Baynes. Possibly the oldest
      story of the Arthurian Cycle, this was translated
      into Norwegian about 1230, at the request of King
      Haaken, and is here retold from the French poem.
      (I and YA)

75. _____. The Knight of the Cart. Crowell, 1969.
      Handsomely illustrated by John Cretzer, this lesser-
      known story of Lancelot's rescue of Queen Guinevere
      from the evil Sir Malagant is largely based on the
      works of the twelfth century poet, Chrétien de
      Troyes. (I)

76. Hibbert, Christopher. The Search for King Arthur
      (consultant: Charles Thomas). American Heritage,
      1970. 124 illustrations, 48 in color. A book about
      excavations where, Mr. Hibbert believes, there is
      definitive evidence of the historical Arthur and his
      Camelot. (I and YA)

77. Lang, Andrew. King Arthur, Tales of the Round Table.
      Schocken Books, 1967. A facsimile of the early
      twentieth century version of the legends. (I)

78. MacLeod, Mary. King Arthur and His Noble Knights.
      Lippincott, 1949. Ill. by Henry C. Pitz. A simple
      retelling of the Malory tales for boys and girls. (I)

79. Malory, Sir Thomas. King Arthur. Dodd Mead, 1953.
      Retold in modern English by Mary MacLeod, with
      16 pages of introductory remarks and descriptive
      captions by Basil Davenport. A fine translation for
      old as well as young adults. (YA)

80. Mark Twain [Samuel Clemens]. A Connecticut Yankee
      in King Arthur's Court. 1889. The humorous but
      also reflective story of the contrast between the
      life and thought of the days of King Arthur and the
      machine age of the present. (A)

81. Newman, Robert. Merlin's Mistake. Atheneum, 1970.
      Ill. by Richard Lebenson. An original story, using
      familiar legendary material and written with wit and
      ingenuity, about two boys who go in quest of the
      great sorcerer, Merlin--the first to make him right
      a mistake he made at the time of the boy's birth,
      and the other to achieve independence and manhood
      after his sixteenth birthday. All this takes place
      in the period of the Crusades but involves the past
      and the distant future. (YA)

82. O'Meara, Walter. The Duke of War. Harcourt, 1966.
     A fresh interpretation of the legends in which Arthur
     is portrayed as a great general rather than a king
     and with the emphasis on military strategy.   Maps
     on inside cover.   (A)
83. Peare, Catherine Owens. Melor, King Arthur's Page.
     Putnam, 1963. Ill. by Paul Frame. A novel of the
     king as a thirteenth century character after the find-
     ing of the Grail by Sir Galahad, and of how his page
     boy grows in understanding and wisdom after con-
     frontation with evil.   (I)
84. Picard, Barbara Leonie. Knights of King Arthur's
     Court. Oxford, 1955. Ill. with wood engravings by
     Roy Morgan. A fine retelling of the legends with an
     especially good chapter on the quest for the Grail.
     (YA)
85. Pyle, Howard. The Story of King Arthur and His
     Knights. Scribner's, 1903. The following books
     were also published by Scribner and illustrated by
     the author: The Champions of the Round Table
     (1905), Sir Lancelot and His Companions (1907),
     and The Grail and the Passing of Arthur (1910).
     They continue to hold top place in all young peoples'
     stories of the king both because of the text and the
     illustrations and, though there are new editions with
     different illustrators, it is good to know that the
     original has been xeroxed.   (I)
86. Robbins, Ruth. Taliesin and King Arthur. Parnassus,
     1970. Ill. in four colors by the author. The young
     bard, Taliesin, travels to King Arthur's court and
     wins the king's favor with tales of the past and the
     future. (E and I)
87. Schiller, Barbara. Erec and Enid. Dutton, 1970. Ill.
     by Ati Forberg. An unusual bit of Arthurian lore
     translated and adapted from the original of Chrétien
     de Troyes. (I)
88. _____. The Kitchen Knight. Holt, Rinehart and
     Winston, 1965. Ill. by Nonny Hogrogian. An adap-
     tation, based on Malory, of the legend of Sir Gareth
     and Lady Lyoness. (E and I)
89. _____. The Wandering Knight. Dutton, 1971. Ill.
     by Herschel Levit. A tale of the early exploits of
     Sir Lancelot. (E and I)
90. Serraillier, Ian. The Challenge of the Green Knight.
     Henry Z. Walck, 1966. Ill. by Victor Ambrus. A
     tale, in lively verse form, of the testing of one of
     King Arthur's knights. (I and YA)

91.   Sobol, Donald. Greta the Strong. Follett, 1970. Ill.
      by Trina Schart Hyman. A new Round Table story
      about a female knight errant who, sixty years after
      King Arthur's death, goes in quest of the secret
      hiding place of his sword, Excaliber. (I)
92.   Sutcliffe, Rosemary. Sword at Sunset. Coward-
      McCann, 1963. A new conception of the Arthurian
      legends, based on archaeological and historical re-
      search, in a skillfully constructed novel with maps
      and glossary. (A)
93.   Tennyson, Alfred. Idylls of the King. 1859-85. In
      these ten books of poetry based on Malory, King
      Arthur and his Knights are presented from a Vic-
      torian viewpoint. (A)
94.   White, T. H. Arthurian Trilogy. Putnam, 1939-58.
95.   The Witch in the Wood, The Sword in the Stone,
96.   and The Once and Future King. Sophisticated, sa-
      tiric versions of the legends, anachronisms being
      the main source of humor. (A)
97.   Wibberley, Leonard. The Quest of Excaliber. Put-
      nam, 1959. Ill. by Ronald Wing. King Arthur
      reappears in the twentieth century, fully armed and
      driving a Rolls Royce. (A)
98.   Williams, Jay. The Sword of King Arthur. Thomas
      Y. Crowell, 1968. Twelve of the best known leg-
      ends simply told. (I)

NINTH CENTURY
(Vikings, Danes, and King Alfred the Great, 849-900)

99.   Adams, Doris Sutcliffe. The Price of Blood. Scrib-
      ner, 1962. A novel of violence and barbarity about
      the Danish invasions of Wessex at the time of Al-
      fred the Great, the main character a Norse trader
      with the difficult choice to make between loyalty to
      his heathen Norse kin and his own Christian faith.
      (A)
100. Bowers, Gwendolyn. The Lost Dragon of Wessex.
      Oxford, 1957. Ill. by Charles Geer. An adventure
      story involving the legendary King Arthur and the
      historical King Alfred. (I)
101. Crossley-Holland, Kevin. King Horn. E. P. Dutton,
      1966. Ill. by Charles Keeping. Novel about some
      boys cast adrift and made pages of the King of
      Westerness where the hero, Horn, falls in love
      with the princess. (YA)

102. DuBois, Theodora. The High King's Daughter. Farrar,
     Straus and Giroux, 1965. Novel set in the time
     before Alfred became King Alfred when the Vikings,
     under Turgesius, invaded Ireland. (YA)
103. Fitt, Mary (Freeman, Kathleen). Alfred the Great.
     Nelson, 1958. A pictorial biography. (I and YA)
104. Hodges, C. Walter. The Marsh King. Coward Mc-
     Cann, 1967. Ill. by the author. A sequel to The
     Namesake (see below) about the dangerous winter
     when Guthorm, the Danish leader, was out for King
     Alfred's head. (YA)
105. _____. The Namesake. Coward McCann, 1964.
     Ill. by the author. Novel about King Alfred and
     the birth of England. Map. (YA)
106. Ketchum, Philip. The Great Axe Bretwalda. Little,
     Brown, 1955 (first published in 1920). Exciting
     novel about an Englishman and his "Lost Brother-
     hood" enslaved by the Danes, and their perilous
     adventures in support of King Alfred. (YA)
107. Leighton, Margaret. Journey for a Princess. Farrar,
     Straus and Cudahy, 1960. Novel about the daughter
     of Alfred the Great and her travels from Wessex
     to Rome and back to Louvain where a famous bat-
     tle against the Vikings was fought, with a map of
     her journey and a note on sources. (YA)
108. Mitchison, Naomi. The Young Alfred the Great. Roy,
     n.d. Ill. by Shirley Farrow. A short biography
     of Alfred's first 16 years (849-865). (I)
109. Parker, Richard. The Sword of Ganelon. McKay,
     1958. Ill. by William Ferguson. Story of three
     young Jutes on the Isle of Thanet in the days of
     Alfred the Great and the Danish invasions, with an
     appendix showing the Tree Alphabet, a version of
     Jutish runes, and an historical note. (YA)
110. Trease, Geoffrey. Escape to King Alfred. Vanguard,
     1958. A good adventure story only slightly involv-
     ing King Alfred. (I)

ELEVENTH CENTURY

     Mainly dealing with the Norman Conquest, its prelude
and aftermath, including a bit of the tenth century.

111. Baker, George. Hawk of Normandy. Roy, 1959. A
     fictional biography of William the Conqueror with
     a chronology of his life. (YA)

112. Brady, Charles A. The Sword of Clontarf. Double-
      day, 1960. Ill. by Herman B. Vestal. A novel
      of blood feuds, the struggle between Norse and
      Christian religions, and the training of bards in
      Ireland in the time of Brian Boru, High King of
      Tara, climaxed by the Battle of Clontarf in 1014.
      Contains a map and glossary. (YA)
113. Bulwer-Lytton, Edward George. Harold the Last of
      the Saxon Kings. A novel about Harold, the rival
      of William the Conqueror, who was killed at the
      battle of Hastings. (A)
114. Costain, Thomas B. William the Conqueror. Random,
      1959 (Landmark). Ill. by Jack Coggins. A biog-
      raphy. (I)
115. deAngeli, Marguerite. Black Fox of Lorne. Double-
      day, 1956. Ill. by the author. A story for quite
      young readers about Vikings and Picts and Scots
      on the Isle of Skye at the time of Malcolm Can-
      more, King of Scotland from 1054 to 1093. (I)
116. Denny, Norman and Filmore-Sankey, Josephine. The
      Bayeux Tapestry. Atheneum, 1966. Ill. by the
      reproduction of the entire tapestry which was em-
      broidered in England shortly after the Norman Con-
      quest, in its proper sequence, with the text ex-
      plaining each scene and describing the background.
      (All ages)
117. Duggan, Alfred. Growing Up With the Norman Con-
      quest. Pantheon, 1965. Ill. by C. Walter Hodges.
      Entertainingly written, this book describes the lives
      of the children of such different parents as a Nor-
      man baron, a Saxon landowner, peasants, and a
      London family, and of boy novices in a cloister in
      1087. (I)
118. Greenleaf, Margery. Banner Over Me. Follett, 1968.
      Ill. by Charles Mikolaycak. "A Tale of the Nor-
      man Conquest," this novel, whose leading charac-
      ters are fictional twins--one serving Saxon Harold
      and the older, Norman William--enlists the read-
      er's sympathy with both heroes. The author's
      note at the end might well be read first. (YA)
119. Hamilton, Franklin. 1066. Dial, 1964. Ill. by Judith
      Ann Lawrence. A story of the Conquest with all
      the dialogue taken from near-contemporary sources
      and the majority of the illustrations from the
      Bayeux Tapestry, woven in 1086. (YA)
120. Heyer, Georgette. The Conqueror. Heinemann, 1931,
      and Pan Books, 1962. A novel mainly concerned

with William's life and conquests before 1066.   (A)

121. Kingsley, Charles. Hereward the Wake, Last of the
      English. 1866. A novel about the half-Dane who
      refused to fight under West Saxon Harold.   (A)

122. Liljencrantz, Ottilie A. The Ward of King Canute. A
      Romance of the Danish Conquest, 1903. This old
      fashioned book is about England in the early elev-
      enth century. Worth a search if only to see what
      kind of historical fiction was written for young peo-
      ple in the early twentieth century. (I)

123. Luckock, Elizabeth. William the Conqueror. G. P.
      Putnam's Sons, 1966 (first American edition). Ill.
      with photographs of the Bayeux Tapestry; jacket by
      Andy Lessin. A concise story of the Norman con-
      queror, his parentage, his life in Normandy and
      marriage, and his invasion of England, conquest
      and coronation. (I)

124. Malvern, Gladys. Heart's Conquest. Macrae Smith,
      1962. A novel whose plot is based on the English
      insurrections after the Norman conquest, although
      the story actually begins several months before the
      Battle of Hastings. (YA)

124a. Meyler, Eileen. The Story of Elswyth. Roy, 1959.
      Ill. by Monica Walker. A novel about Edward the
      Martyr who ruled from 975-979, and Ethelred the
      Unready, 179-1016. Unusual material and good
      plot. (YA)

125. Muntz, Hope. The Golden Warrior. Scribner's,
      1949. A modern classic of the Norman conquest
      with a foreword by G. M. Trevelyan and lists of
      the chief characters and geneological tables. The
      plot builds up from the times of Alfred the Great,
      Edgar the Peaceful, etc. The author says, "Where
      legend and tradition enrich the story and do not
      conflict with the known facts, I have made use of
      them." (A)

126. Oliver, Jane. Faraway Princess. St. Martin's,
      1962. Ill. by Jane Paton. The romance of Mal-
      colm III (Canmore) of Scotland (1054-93) and his
      Queen Margaret who came over to England from
      Hungary with her brother, a claimant to the Eng-
      lish throne, shortly before the Norman conquest.
      (I and YA)

127. Polland, Madeleine. The Queen's Blessing. Winston,
      1964. Ill. by Betty Fraser. We suggest that you
      read the afterword first in order to understand the
      historical setting. Merca, aged eleven, and her

little brother, orphaned by King Malcolm's soldiers
in rebellion against Norman William, are finally
taken under Queen Margaret's wing, but Merca still
seeks revenge against the King for her parents'
death. (YA)

128. _____. To Kill a King. Holt, Rinehart and Winston, 1971. Jacket by Arvis Stewart. A sequel to
"The Queen's Blessing" in which Merca, now sixteen, is haunted by her past hatred for King Malcolm and yearns to withdraw from life into a nun-
nery, refusing to take any pleasure in beauty or
happiness. At Queen Margaret's insistence she
goes to London where she meets a young man who
brings her to life, but after losing him (or thinking
so) she reverts to her retreat from life until....
(YA)

129. Shakespeare, William. Macbeth. Probably written
about 1606 and based on Holinshed's Chronicle.
Macbeth was an actual king of Scotland who actually
did murder Duncan and died himself in 1058. (A)

130. Sprague, Rosemary. Red Lion and Gold Dragon.
Chilton Books, 1965. Jacket by Jo Ann Randel.
An outstanding novel of the Conquest and its pre-
liminaries, from the English, or Saxon, viewpoint,
but fair to both Harold and William. (YA and A)

131. Sutcliffe, Rosemary. Knight's Fee. Walck, 1960.
Ill. by Charles Keeping. A suspenseful novel set
in the time of William the Conqueror's Sons, William Rufus, Duke Robert, and Henry I, with two
pages of historical notes and glossary. (YA)

132. _____. The Shield Ring. Oxford, 1956. Ill. by
C. Walter Hodges. A novel about the Viking de-
fenses against the Norman conquerors in the Lake
Country of England. (YA)

133. Treece, Henry. Man With a Sword. Pantheon, 1964.
Ill. by William Stobbs. A novel about Hereward
the Wake, Harold Hardrada, and Godwinsons and
others, and of course William the Conqueror, with
enough historical background to clarify the plot.
(YA)

134. _____. Splintered Sword. Duell, Sloane and Pearce,
1966. Ill. by Charles Keeping. A grimly realistic
novel set in the Orkney Islands thirty years after
the battle of Stamford Bridge where Harold Hardrada was defeated in 1066, with maps of the last
Viking aggressions in that area. (YA)

TWELFTH AND THIRTEENTH CENTURIES
(Medieval England under the Early Angevin Kings)

135. Cooke, Donald E. Men of Sherwood. Holt, Rinehart
      and Winston, 1961. Ill. by Peter Burchard. "New
      Tales of Robin Hood's Merry Band." A sequel to
      the Robin Hood legends about his band after his
      death. (I)
136. _____. The Silver Horn of Robin Hood. Winston,
      1956. Ill. by the author. Tales of the Merry Men
      written in contemporary style. It is believed that
      there was a real character, an English outlaw born
      about 1160 in Nottinghamshire, around whom these
      legends have been woven. (I)
137. Crossley-Holland, Kevin. The Callow Pit Coffer.
      Seabury Press, 1968. Ill. by Margaret Gordon.
      The legend of an iron ring hanging on the door of
      an old church in Limpenhoe and the story of how
      it came there, amusingly retold, with a short
      glossary. (E and I)
138. Duggan, Alfred. The Falcon and the Dove. Pantheon,
      1966. Ill. by Anne Marie Jauss, "A Life of Thom-
      as Becket of Canterbury," published after the au-
      thor's death in 1964, is a revision of an earlier
      biography. With his usual humor and story-telling
      talent, the author points out the inevitable conflict
      between hot-headed King Henry II and stubborn
      Thomas. (YA and A)
139. _____. Growing Up in 13th Century England.
      Pantheon, 1962. Ill. by C. Walter Hodges. What
      it was like to be an adolescent in England in 1270.
      (I)
140. Glubok, Shirley. Knights in Armor. Harper and Row,
      1969. Designed by Gerard Nook, photographs of
      museum pieces by Alfred H. Tomasin. An art
      book giving visualization to readers of medieval
      fiction and legends throughout the medieval world.
      (I and YA)
141. Gray, Elizabeth Janet. Adam of the Road. Viking,
      1957. Ill. by Robert Lawson. A story of an 11-
      year-old boy's search for his father and his dog,
      with a map of his travels from St. Alban's Abbey
      in June, 1294, to Oxford in April, 1295, by way
      of London and Winchester. (I)
142. Haycraft, Molly Costain. My Lord Brother the Lion
      Heart. Lippincott, 1970. The twelfth century
      Kings' Crusade is the background for this novel

about Joan, daughter of Henry II of England and
Eleanor of Aquitaine, and favorite sister of Richard, the Lion Heart.   (A)

143. Hodges, C. Walter. Magna Carta. Coward McCann,
1966. Ill. by the author. A short story of Henry
II, Becket, King John, Stephen Langton and Simon
de Montfort, reproduced from the Britannica Films
Inc. and beautifully illustrated.   (I)

144. Jewett, Eleanor M. Big John's Secret. Viking, 1962.
Ill. by Frederick T. Chapman. Big John's search
for his father leads him finally to Jerusalem on the
5th crusade with the Earl of Warenne in the years
1215-18. His experiences inspire him to become
a physician. A historical note at the end explains
the appearance of Francis of Assisi in the story.
(I)

145. _____. The Hidden Treasure of Glaston. Viking,
1946. Ill. by Frederick T. Chapman. A mystery
concerning Hugh de Morville, one of Becket's mur-
derers, about Glastonbury, Joseph of Arimathea
and the Holy Grail. Based on ancient records
from the time of Henry II.   (YA)

146. Lofts, Norah. Eleanor the Queen: The Story of the
Most Famous Woman of the Middle Ages. Doubleday, 1955. A sympathetic biography of the one-
time queen of Louis VII of France who, after di-
vorcing him, married Henry II of England.   (YA)

147. Lovett, Margaret. The Great and Terrible Quest.
Holt, Rinehart and Winston, 1967. Jacket by
Herschel Levit. A suspenseful fantasy of chivalry
set in an imaginary country in the middle ages.
(I)

148. Malcolmson, Anne. Song of Robin Hood. Houghton
Mifflin, 1947. Ill. by Virginia Lee Burton. Music
arranged by Grace Castagnetta. A unique book.
The pictures will appeal to even the youngest while
the author's selection and editing of the ballads
will interest grown-ups.   (All Ages)

149. McGovern, Ann. Robin Hood of Sherwood Forest.
Thomas Y. Crowell, 1968. Ill. by Arnold Spilka.
Enjoyable retelling.   (I)

150. McSpadden, J. Walker. Robin Hood. World, 1923
and 1946. Ill. by Louis Slobodkin and with an introduction by May Lamberton Becker which is informative about the real Robin Hood and the few
facts around which the legends grew.   (I)

151. Melnikoff, Pamela. The Star and the Sword. Crown,

1965. Ill. by Hans Schwarz. A novel about two
Jewish orphans, an English crusader collecting
money for the ransom of Richard the Lion Heart,
and even Robin Hood, in the period at the end of
the twelfth century after the persecution of the
Jews at York. (I and YA)

152. Oliver, Jane. Alexander the Glorious. G. P. Putnam's Sons, 1965. A novel about Alexander III of
Scotland who ruled from 1249 to 1285, a period
just before the great border wars between Scotland
under Robert Bruce and England under Edward I.
(A)

153. _____. The Young Robert Bruce. Roy, 1962.
Ill. by William Randell. Printed in Great Britain.
The story of young Bruce as page, esquire and
knight with informative details of royal Scotch lin-
eage (especially in relation to his mother, Lady
Marjorie, Countess of Carrick) and of heraldic
display. The story ends with the submission of
Scotland to Edward I of England near the end of
the century. [See also 189.] (YA)

154. Peart, Hendry. Red Falcons of Tremoine. Knopf,
1956. Ill. by Maurice Brevannes. A novel of the
conflict between a 15-year-old boy and his uncle,
in the days of chivalry in "New Normandy" as
England was called during the reign of Richard I.
(I)

155. Picard, Barbara Leonie. Lost John, A Young Outlaw
in the Forest of Arden. Criterion, 1962. Ill. by
Charles Keeping. A sensitive story of a lad trying
to avenge the death of his father. (I)

156. Pittenger, W. Norman. Richard the Lion-Hearted,
the Crusader King. Franklin Watts, 1970. A
good readable, factual biography of this romantic
son of Henry II, with due recognition of the legends about him and the possibility of some truth
in them. Excellent material on the Age of Chivalry. (I and YA)

157. Polland, Madeleine. Children of the Red King. Holt,
1959. Ill. by Annette Macarthur-Onslow. An exciting story about the King of Connacht's children,
Grania and Fergus, in the time of King John and
the Norman settlements in Ireland. (YA)

158. Power-Waters, Alma. The Crusader. Hawthorne
(Credo Books), 1964. Ill. by Craig Pineo. A
romantic novel of Richard the Lion Heart and his
brothers, Blondel, his page, and Thomas à Becket.
(I and YA)

159. Pugh, Ellen. Brave His Soul, The Story of Prince
          Madog of Wales. Dodd, Mead, 1970. Ill. with
          photographs and maps; jacket by Ragna Tischler
          Goddard. A little-known story of Madog's possible
          discovery of America in 1170. A masterly piece
          of historical detective work, beginning with an old
          Welsh song and legend, and still going on in Amer-
          ica with a search for the "Welsh Indians." (YA
          and A)

160. Pyle, Howard. The Merry Adventures of Robin Hood.
          1883. Scribner reprint, 1946. (I)

161. _____. Some Merry Adventures of Robin Hood of
          Great Renown in Nottinghamshire. Franklin Watts,
          n.d. Ill. by the author with a cover illustration
          by N. C. Wyeth. A large type edition, complete
          and unabridged. (I)

162. Rush, Philip. The Castle and the Harp. McGraw-
          Hill, 1963. Ill. by Charles Keeping. A novel of
          romance and high adventure showing the contrast
          between the lives of lords and harpists in 1224.
          (YA)

163. _____. The Minstrel Knight. Bobbs-Merrill, 1955.
          Ill. by Joe Krush. "A sort of Robin Hood story"
          explains the author, based on a manuscript found
          in the British Museum, translated into prose from
          a poem of 1320, about a knight who ignores God's
          voice calling him to the priesthood in order to re-
          gain the family right to a castle in Wales. (I and
          YA)

164. Scott, Sir Walter. Ivanhoe. 1819. A novel about the
          struggle between the Saxons, Danes and Normans
          in the Age of Chivalry, with two heroines, Jewish
          Rebecca and Saxon Rowena. (A)

165. Serraillier, Ian. Robin in the Greenwood. Ballads of
          Robin Hood. Henry Z. Walck, 1967. Ill. by Victor
          G. Ambrus. Some of the merry tales retold in
          ballad form, about Little John, Friar Tuck, and
          the Sheriff of Nottingham. (I)

166. _____. Robin and His Merry Men. Ballads of
          Robin Hood. Walck, 1969? Ill. by Victor Ambrus.
          A companion volume to "Robin in the Greenwood"
          at the end of which Robin, loyal to King Edward,
          is invited to Westminster. (I)

167. Sobol, Donald. The Double Quest. Watts, 1957. Ill.
          by Lili Réthi. A medieval whodunit and spy story
          with, admittedly, little basis in fact. (YA)

168. Sutcliffe, Rosemary. The Witch's Brat. Henry Z.

Walck, 1970. Ill. by Richard Lebenson. A gentle
novel about a crippled boy who has the gift of healing others, and about Rahere, once jongleur to
King Henry I, and the founding of Saint Bartholomew's Hospital in Smithfield, London.   (I and YA)

169.   Trease, Geoffrey. Bows Against the Barons. Meredith Press, First U.S. edition, 1966. Ill. by C.
Walter Hodges. A fresh interpretation of the Robin
Hood legend, dealing mainly with his last day, this
is a lively exciting story of a lad who joins the
Greenwood band in their rebellion against the barons.   (I)

170.   Weir, Rosemary. High Courage. Farrar, Straus and
Giroux, 1967. Ill. by Ian Robbins. The story of
a young prisoner of war who escapes from his
captor, a baron on the side of Simon de Montfort
against Henry III, and goes in search of his father,
a king's man. Diagrammatic drawing of a medieval castle and good description of castle life at
that time.   (I)

171.   Willard, Barbara. If All the Swords in England.
Doubleday, 1961. Ill. by Robert M. Sax. The
story of twin brothers who serve respectively Henry II and Thomas à Becket.   (YA)

172.   Williams, Ursula Moray. The Earl's Falconer. Morrow, 1961. Ill. by Charles Geer. Published in
England under the title "The Noble Hawks" this is
a novel focussing on the art of falconry in all its
aspects and the training of young squires in it,
with a glossary of falconry terms.   (YA)

FOURTEENTH CENTURY
(Border Wars with Scotland, Beginning of Hundred-Year War)

173.   Alderman, Clifford Lindsay. Flame of Freedom, the
Peasants' Revolt of 1381. Julian Messner, 1969.
With maps and illustrations. Several novels set
in the fourteenth century bring in the subject of
this revolt, in which peasants were betrayed by
King Richard II (whether by his own intention or
bad advice) but none goes into the details of this
exciting story which brings to life--and, alas,
death--its heroic leaders, John Ball, Wat Tyler,
Thomas Baker and others, as well as those who
rebelled for their own benefit and turned against
the rebellion when their own necks were in danger.
(YA)

174. Anderson, Poul. The High Crusade. Doubleday,
      1960. Science fiction set in the fourteenth century.
      Plans for going on a crusade to the Holy Land have
      to be changed when a spaceship comes to Lincoln-
      shire. (YA)
175. Arthur, Ruth. The Saracen Lamp. Atheneum, 1970.
      Ill. by Margery Gill. An enthralling "now and
      then" fantasy, beginning about 1300 when a young
      French girl marries an English knight and takes
      with her to Littleperry Manor a lamp brought back
      from the crusades by her father. The lamp is
      stolen from the house in the sixteenth century by
      a girl named Alys who haunts the twentieth century
      occupant of the Manor who, in turn, haunts her.
      (YA)
176. Church, Richard. The Bells of Rye. Day, 1960. A
      story of the French raids on England and spying
      activities in the Cinque Ports of France toward the
      end of the century. (I)
177. Chute, Marchette. The Innocent Wayfaring. Dutton,
      1943. Ill. by the author. A charming humorous
      romance set in the time of Chaucer but with twen-
      tieth century dialogue. (YA)
178. DeAngeli, Marguerite. The Door in the Wall. Double-
      day, 1949. Ill. by the author. An inspiring little
      story with excellent detail of contemporary London
      and the Welsh border. (I)
179. Doyle, Sir Arthur Conan. The White Company. 1891.
      A novel of humor and adventure about two members
      of a company of Saxon bowmen, led by Sir Nigel
      Loring under the Black Prince in 1366. (A)
180. Farjeon, Eleanor. Tales From Chaucer. Branford,
      1959. Ill. by Marjorie Walters. A translation of
      the Canterbury Tales into modern prose. (I and
      YA)
181. Faulkner, Nancy. The Yellow Hat. Doubleday, 1958.
      A novel about a young maidservant in the Chaucer
      household, and the peasant uprising. (YA)
182. Gibson, Katherine. To See the Queen. Longmans
      Green, 1954. Ill. by Clotilde Embree Funk. A
      fantasy for very young readers about the little
      seven-year-old queen of Richard II. (E)
183. Haycraft, Molly Costain. The Lady Royal. Lippin-
      cott, 1964. A novel set in mid-century England
      and France about Isobel (eldest daughter of Edward
      III and Queen Philippa) her brother, the Black
      Prince, and other brothers and sisters and the

Battles of Crecy and Poitiers and the siege of
Calais. (A)

184. Hill, Pamela. Marjorie of Scotland. Putnam, 1956.
A novel of violence and suspense about the daughter
of Robert Bruce who, in marrying Walter the Stew-
ard, founded the royal Stuart line. (A)

185. Hyman, Freda. Who's For the North? Roy, n.d.
Ill. by David Walsh. A novel about Harry Hotspur
(1366-1403). (YA)

186. Ipcar, Dahlov. The Warlock of Night. Viking, 1969.
A fantastic novel whose theme is the madness of
war, set in an imaginary country in medieval
times. It is based on a game of chess played in
1949, and, for readers who understand the game,
the moves are given at the end of the book and also listed under each chapter heading. The author's
note suggests that a knowledge of the game is not
necessary in order to enjoy the story, but I con-
fess that I felt the lack. (YA and A)

187. Lewis, Hilda. The Gentle Falcon. Criterion, 1957.
A novel about little Queen Isabella, second wife of
Richard II and what befell her after his death. (A)

188. Meyler, Eileen. The Gloriet Tower. Roy, n.d. Ill.
by Monica Walker. A romance set in Corfe Castle
after the death of Edward II. (YA)

189. Oliver, Jane. Young Man With a Sword. Macmillan,
1955. Ill. by William McClaren. A novel about
Robert the Bruce and the liberation of Scotland.
(YA)

190. Picard, Barbara Leonie. Ransom for a Knight. Oxford, 1936. Ill. by C. Walter Hodges. A novel
about a daring young girl who travels the entire
length of England and Scotland to ransom her father
and brother from the Scotch. (YA)

191. _____. One Is One. Holt, Rinehart and Winston,
1966. A sensitive novel about a lad who is torn
between knighthood and the Church. (YA)

192. Porter, Jane. Scottish Chiefs, 1809. Edited by Kate
Douglas Wiggins and Norah A. Smith. Charles
Scribner, 1956. Ill. by N. C. Wyeth. A novel
primarily about William Wallace (1272-1306) and
the border wars in general. (A)

193. Serraillier, Ian. Chaucer and His World. Henry Z.
Walck, 1967. Ill. with over 70 photographs. A
brief biography of Chaucer and description of his
period. (YA)

194. Treece, Henry. Ride into Danger. Criterion, 1959.

Ill. by Christine Price.   An adventure novel about
the Black Prince and the Battle of Crecy (1346).
(YA)
195.   Welch, Ronald.   Bowmen of Crecy.   Criterion, 1966.
Ill. by Ian Robbins.   A novel about the leader of a
band of outlaws skilled in the use of the long bow,
who proved their value in the Battle of Crecy (1346)
with a note about that weapon.   (YA)

FIFTEENTH CENTURY
(The Hundred-Year War ending and the Wars of the Roses)

196.   Aiken, Joan.   The Cuckoo Tree.   Doubleday, 1971.
Ill. by Susan Obrant.   This book doesn't any more
belong in the 15th century than I do, but I defy the
reader to place the story in time, with imaginary
King James IV and Richard IV and a plot to put
rollers under St. Paul's Cathedral just before the
coronation of one or the other.   It's all delightful
nonsense.   (I and YA)
197.   Alderman, Clifford Lindsay.   Blood-Red the Roses,
The Story of the Wars of the Roses.   Messner,
1971.   Ill. with maps and photographs; jacket by
Don Lambo.   What a tour de force this is!   To
make a clear readable story out of this most com-
plex civil strife, when there were two kings in
England at one time: Edward IV and Henry VI and
a tigress of a queen, Margaret of Anjou, wife of
Henry VI.   Charts of: chief characters of the
period and 21 principal battles, and Lancastrian
and Yorkist commanders; also, dates of battles and
the winners.   (YA)
198.   Beers, Lorna.   The Book of Hugh Flower.   Harper,
1952.   Ill. by Eleanor Mill.   A good story about
the craft of masonry and the guilds in the early
fifteenth century with a light romance.   (YA)
199.   Brown, Marcia.   Dick Whittington and His Cat.
Scribner, 1950.   Linoleum cuts by the author.
About the poor little urchin who finally became
Lord Mayor of London.   (E and I)
200.   Bulwer-Lytton, Edward George.   The Last of the
Barons, 1843.   A long Victorian novel about the
Kingmaker, Richard Neville, Earl of Warwick and
the Wars of the Roses.   (A)
201.   Daniell, David Scott.   The Boy They Made King.
Duell, Sloane Pearce, 1959.   Ill. by William

Stobbs. The story of Lambert Simnel who was
taken from his home in Oxford and trained to im-
personate the young Earl of Warwick, a possible
heir to the throne at the end of the fifteenth century. (I)

202. Eyre, Katherine Wigmore. The Song of the Thrush.
Oxford, 1952. Ill. by Stephani and Edward God-
win. A pathetic novel about Margaret Plantagenet
and Richard III. (YA)

203. Harnett, Cynthia. Caxton's Challenge. World, 1959.
Ill. by the author. A novel about Caxton (1421-91)
and early printing, difficulties in obtaining paper
supplies, smuggling, and the life and death of Sir
Thomas Malory. Drawings of presses etc. (YA)

204. _____. The Drawbridge Gate. Putnam, 1953.
Ill. by the author. A spy story involving Lollard
conspirators against Henry V in the early years of
the fifteenth century. Map of London of the period.
(YA)

205. _____. Nicholas and the Wool-Pack. Putnam,
1951. Ill. by the author. A good plot set mainly
in Burford, with a good amount of information
about the wool-producing and weaving industries at
the beginning of the reign of Henry VII (1485-1509).
Carnegie Medal Book. (YA)

206. Hill, Kay. And Tomorrow the Stars: The Story of
John Cabot. Dodd Mead, 1968. Ill. by Laszlo
Kubinyi. A fictional biography of John Cabot
whose real name was Giovanni Caboto, but who
made his voyage of discovery (of what he called
Asia but which was probably Nova Scotia) in 1497,
sailing for the English. (I)

207. Lewis, Hilda. Here Comes Harry. Criterion, 1960.
Ill. by William Stobbs. A novel about the widow
of Henry V, Catherine of Valois, who secretly
married Owen Tudor (the beginning of the Tudor
line), and about the childhood of Henry VI, their
son. (YA)

208. Lines, Kathleen. Dick Whittington. Walck, 1970.
Ill. by Edward Ardizzone. The background notes
will interest intermediate readers and their parents
and teachers who read the familiar story to younger
ones. (E and I)

209. Maiden, Cecil. The Borrowed Crown. Viking, 1960.
Ill. by L. F. Cary. A well-constructed novel
about Lambert Simnel, pretending to be the son of
the Earl of Warwick and York heir to the English
throne. (YA)

210. Malvern, Gladys. The Queen's Lady. Macrae Smith,
     1963. A novel about the Wars of the Roses, Rich-
     ard III and his courtship of Anne of Warwick. (YA)
211. Manning, Rosemary. Arripay. Ariel, 1963. Ill. by
     Victor Ambrus. A tale of piracy on the south
     coast of England. (I)
212. Maughan, A. M. Harry of Monmouth. Sloane, 1956.
     A novel in two parts (though not separated). The
     first deals largely with the Welsh Marches--Owen
     Glendower, Richard II and Henry IV, Hotspur and
     young Prince Hal. The second is about the Hun-
     dred-Year War, especially the Battle of Agincourt
     (1415) and Henry V's marriage with Catherine of
     Valois. (A)
213. Pyle, Howard. Men of Iron, 1891. Ill. by the au-
     thor. A novel of a young squire training to be-
     come a knight, showing teen-age gang warfare in
     the early fifteenth century. (YA)
214. Seibert, Elizabeth. White Rose and Ragged Staff.
     Bobbs-Merrill, 1968. Ill. by Ray Cruz. A highly
     romantic novel about a young lady companion to
     Anne, daughter of the Earl of Warwick, the king-
     maker in the period of the Wars of the Roses.
     (YA)
215. Stephens, Peter John. Battle for Destiny. Atheneum,
     1967. Ill. by Richard Lebenson. A rousing story
     about a young Welsh lad who aids the Earl of Rich-
     mond (later King Henry VII) in landing at Milford
     Haven and finally defeating Richard III at Bosworth
     Field. (YA)
216. Stevenson, Robert Louis. The Black Arrow. 1888.
     In language based on the Paston Letters, a story
     of the Wars of the Roses and the terribly confused
     period when Yorkists and Lancastrians frequently
     changed sides. (YA)
217. Tey, Josephine (Elizabeth MacKintosh). The Daughter
     of Time. Macmillan, 1952. A great book for
     those who like historical detective work. The
     geneological tables will keep you from getting com-
     pletely lost in fifteenth century relationships, and
     you may become as absorbed in the mystery of
     the two little princes in the Tower as Grant of
     Scotland Yard did, doing research from his hospi-
     tal bed on Richard III and his reputed murder of
     the princes. (A)
218. Trease, Geoffrey. Snared Nightingale. Vanguard,
     1958. A romance of chivalry on the Welsh
     Marches. (YA)

219. Vance, Marguerite. Song For a Lute. Dutton, 1958.
      Ill. by J. Luis Pellicer. A novel about Anne Ne-
      ville who married Richard III, and the mysterious
      death of the two young princes, his nephews, in
      the Tower. (YA)
220. Wibberley, Leonard. Beware of the Mouse. Putnam,
      1958. Ill. by Ronald Wing. A combination of
      whimsey, satire and common sense about the Hun-
      dred-Year War after the invention of the cannon.
      (A)
221. Willard, Barbara. The Lark and the Laurel. Har-
      court, Brace and World, 1970. Jacket by Gareth
      Floyd. Set just at the end of the Wars of the
      Roses, this neatly plotted novel is about two young
      people whose lives are mysteriously complicated
      by old family enmities during those wars. Mount-
      ing suspense to the last page. (YA)
222. Williamson, Joanne S. To Dream Upon a Crown. Al-
      fred A. Knopf, 1967. Ill. by Jacob Landau. A
      book based on the sequence of events as told by
      Shakespeare in his trilogy of King Henry VI, using
      dialogue from the plays. It requires considerable
      familiarity with the period and the Wars of the
      Roses. (YA and A)

SIXTEENTH CENTURY

A. Tudor England Before Elizabeth

223. Arthur, Ruth M. Requiem For a Princess. Atheneum,
      1967. Ill. by Margery Gill. A past-and-present
      novel about a 15-year-old girl convalescing from
      overwork and flu in an old house in Cornwall, and
      even more, suffering from an emotional shock
      caused by her identification of herself with a Span-
      ish princess in a portrait which she finds there.
      (YA)
224. Barnes, Margaret Campbell. King's Fool. Macrae
      Smith, 1959. A novel about Henry VIII (reigned:
      1509-47), his six wives and three children as told
      by the court fool, Will Summers. (A)
225. Buchan, John. The Blanket of the Dark. Houghton
      Mifflin, 1931. A novel set in England and the
      Welsh Marches during the reign of Henry VIII and
      the destruction of the monasteries. (A)

226. Drewery, Mary. Devil in Print. McKay, 1966. Ill.
      by William Stobbs. A novel about Tyndale's trans-
      lation of the Bible, the printing of it in Cologne,
      Germany, and the smuggling of it into England dur-
      ing the reign of Henry VIII. (YA)

227. Eyre, Katherine Wigmore. Another Spring. Oxford,
      1949. Ill. by Stephani and Edward Godwin. The
      sad story of Lady Jane Grey. (YA)

228. Fecher, Constance. Heir to Pendarrow. Farrar,
      Straus and Giroux, 1969. Jacket by Enrico Arno.
      A first-rate adventure story with enough basis of
      events during the last days of Mary Tudor's reign
      to give it plausibility. A 12-year-old boy sets out
      to rescue his father from the Tower where he is
      in imminent danger of execution for being part of
      a conspiracy against the Queen (a false accusation)
      and on his perilous way meets up with outcast beg-
      gars, Sir Robert Dudley, Sir William Cecil, the
      dying Queen Mary Tudor, and the Princess Eliza-
      beth. (I and YA)

228a. Feuerlicht, Roberta Straus. The Life and World of
      Henry VIII. Crowell-Collier, 1970. Ill. with a
      map and portraits. The story of England's king
      from 1509-1547, his six wives, his children, Mary,
      Elizabeth and Edward, and his court. (YA)

229. Gibson, Katherine. Oak Tree House. McKay, 1936.
      Ill. by Vera Bock. A story for very young readers
      about some people who built a house in a tree and
      how young King Edward VI came to visit them there.
      (E)

230. Harnett, Cynthia. Stars of Fortune. Putnam, 1956.
      Ill. by the author. An exciting novel about a plot
      to rescue the "Lady Elizabeth" (later Queen), in
      which the main characters are young Washingtons,
      ancestors of the first American president, with a
      Washington family tree and postscript giving the
      factual basis for the story. (YA)

231. Ince, Elizabeth M. St. Thomas More of London.
      Farrar, Straus and Cudahy, 1957. Ill. by Lili
      Réthi. A biographical novel of the courageous,
      honest, loveable "man of all seasons" who lost his
      head because he would not admit Henry VIII to be
      the supreme head of the Church in England. (I and
      YA)

231a. Lobdell, Helen. The King's Snare. Houghton Mifflin,
      1955. Ill. by C. Walter Hodges. The story of
      Wat, son of Sir Walter Raleigh, and his adventures

with his father in search of gold, after King James
I's treacherous reprieve of Sir Walter's prison sen-
tence. (YA)

232. Malvern, Gladys. The World of Lady Jane Grey.
Vanguard, 1964. Ill. with portraits. A story of
Jane Grey and her friends and enemies, about the
period between the death of Henry VIII and the coronation of Queen Elizabeth. (YA)

233. Moss, Hilda. Wild Rose of King's Chase. Warne,
1960. Ill. by Jennetta Vise. A novel, based on
local legend, about the founding of a great national
park in Sutton Coldfield, in which the heroine is a
female Robin Hood. (YA)

234. Newell, Virginia. His Own Good Daughter. Longmans
Green, 1961. Ill. by Vera Bock. A short biographical novel about Sir Thomas More and his
beloved daughter, Margaret. (YA)

235. Oliver, Jane. Watch for the Morning. St. Martin's,
1964. Ill. by Victor Ambrus. A novel about Master William Tynedale who, in 1536, was burned at
the stake because of his translation of all of the
New Testament and much of the Old. (YA)

236. Picard, Barbara Leonie. The Tower and the Traitors.
G. P. Putnam's Sons, 1961. Ill. by William
Stobbs. A collection of short biographies of some
outstanding characters who suffered imprisonment,
and usually death, in the sixteenth to eighteenth
centuries and stories of their guilt or innocence
and the unfortunate persons implicated in their ill
fates. The victims of Henry VIII considered in
this book are Sir Thomas More, Anne Boleyn, Henry's second wife, and Katheryn Howard, his fifth
queen. (YA)

237. Plaidy, Jean (Hibbert). Meg Roper. Roy, 1961. An
appealing biographical novel about the oldest daughter of Sir Thomas More, with a warm, human portrayal of the martyr himself as he appeared to his
family, especially to Meg. (YA)

238. _____. St. Thomas's Eve. Putnam, 1970. A
longer biographical novel of Sir Thomas More (1478-
1535) than "Meg Roper" (see above) though Meg
plays almost as important a role in this as in the
other. In this book, however, there is more about
King Henry's court and courtiers (especially Wolsey)
and about his divorce from Katherine of Aragon.
(A)

239. _____. The Young Elizabeth. Roy, 1961. Ill. by

William Randell. A lively story of the life of
Elizabeth I from babyhood to her accession to the
throne in 1558, telling about the dangers that beset
her in her youth, and how skillfully she evaded
them. (I and YA)

240. Roll, Winifred. The Pomegranate and the Rose: The
Story of Katherine of Aragon. Prentice-Hall, 1970.
Ill. with portraits. A scrupulously researched biography of the first wife of Henry VIII and history
of the period in which she lived (1485-1536), with
chapter notes, genealogical charts and suggested
further reading. (YA and A)

241. Twain, Mark (Samuel Clemens). The Prince and the
Pauper. 1881. An imaginary story of young
Prince Edward, later King Edward VI, changing
clothes and "way of life" with a poor little boy.
(I and YA)

242. Vance, Marguerite. Lady Jane Grey, Reluctant Queen.
Dutton, 1952. Ill. by Nedda Walker. A biography
of a short and tragic life (1537-54). (YA)

B.   Elizabethan England

243. Bill, Alfred H. The Ring of Danger. Knopf, 1959.
Ill. by Frederick T. Chapman. A good rousing
tale of derring-do in the time of the rival queens,
Elizabeth of England and Mary of Scotland. (YA)

244. Calhoun, Mary. White Witch of Kynance. Harper and
Row, 1970. Frontispiece by John Gundelfinger. A
young girl of Cornwall learns to be a white witch,
with spells, healing powers and other mysteries,
and also learns about human love and that "God is
laughter." (YA)

245. Faulkner, Nancy. Sword in the Wind. Doubleday,
1957. Ill. by C. Walter Hodges. A fantasy of a
shepherd boy, at the time of the Spanish Armada
threat, who imagines himself back in the time of
King Arthur. (I)

246. Gordon, Patricia (Howard). Romany Luck. Viking,
1946. Ill. by Rafaello Busoni. A rollicking adventure story about a gypsy boy and the old Queen
Elizabeth, with a list of Romany words translated
into English. (I)

247. Hall, Rosalys. Miranda's Dragon. McGraw-Hill,
1968. Ill. by Kurt Werth. A romantic story of
a troupe of strolling players in the time of good

Queen Bess. (YA)

248. Irwin, Margaret. Young Bess. Harcourt, Brace,
1948. A novel about the childhood of Elizabeth I.
(YA)

249. _____. Elizabeth the Captive Princess. Harcourt,
Brace, 1945. A novel of Elizabeth during the time
that her older sister Mary ruled England (1553-58).
(YA)

250. Kent, Louise Andrews. He Went With Drake. Houghton Mifflin, 1961. Ill. by Robert MacLean. A
story of piracy, espionage, and the Spanish Armada.
(YA)

251. Kingsley, Charles. Westward Ho! 1850. "The Voyages and Adventures of Sir Amayas Leigh, Knight
of Burrough in the County of Devon, in the Reign
of Her Most Glorious Majesty, Queen Elizabeth."
A sea story. (A)

252. Latham, Jean Lee. Drake, the Man They Called Pirate. Harper, 1960. Ill. by Frederick T. Chapman. A fictionalized biography of Sir Francis
Drake, 1540-96. (I)

253. Major, Charles. Dorothy Vernon of Haddon Hall.
1902. An amusing light romance about a mischievous girl and two queens. (A)

254. Malkus, Alida Sims. The Story of Good Queen Bess.
Grosset, 1953. A short biography. (I)

255. Manning-Sanders, Ruth. The Spaniards are Coming.
Franklin Watts, 1970. Ill. by Jacqueline Rivzi.
Two English children are left to fend for themselves after their father is pressed into the Queen's
service to fight the Spanish Armada. (E and I)

256. Scott, Sir Walter. Kenilworth. 1831. A novel about
the mysterious death of Amy Robsart, wife of Robert Dudley, Earl of Leicester, who was suspected
of contriving her death. (A)

257. Sutcliffe, Rosemary. The Armourer's House. Oxford, 1951. Ill. by C. Walter Hodges. A story
about a boy and girl in Tudor England and their
yearning for ships and seafaring. (I)

258. Syme, Ronald. Francis Drake, Sailor of the Unknown
Seas. Morrow, 1961. Ill. by William Stobbs. A
short biography. (I)

259. Uttley, Alison. A Traveler in Time. Viking, 1964.
Copr. 1939. A romantic novel about a young girl
of the twentieth century who feels a sense of iden-
tity with the sixteenth century through the atmos-
phere of an old house once belonging to the Babing-

tons who were involved in a plot to rescue Mary,
Queen of Scots. (YA)

260. Vance, Marguerite. Elizabeth Tudor, Sovereign Lady.
Dutton, 1954. Ill. by Nedda Walker. The major
portion of this biography concerns Elizabeth before
she became queen. (YA)

261. Watson, Sally. Linnet. Dutton, 1971. A headstrong
girl is kidnapped into Elizabethan London's under-
world and becomes innocently involved in a plot to
overthrow Queen Elizabeth. (I and YA)

262. Welch, Ann. The Woolacombe Bird. William Morrow,
1968. Ill. by Joseph Acheson. A thriller about a
man who, with the help of two youngsters, at about
the time of the Spanish Armada, builds and flies a
glider, following the designs of Leonardo da Vinci.
Purely fiction but one feels it could have happened.
(YA)

263. Welch, Ronald. The Hawk. Criterion, 1969. Ill. by
Gareth Floyd. Another of the vigorous stories of
the Welsh Carey family but preceding all the others
in time. Here young Harry, a lieutenant in his father's fleet of galleons, proves his worth at sea
and at home where Walsingham, Queen Elizabeth's
chief of espionage, calls on Harry for support. Genealogical chart included. (YA)

264. Wibberley, Leonard. The King's Beard. Ariel, 1952.
Ill. by Christine Price. A splendid novel of adventure, full of vivid characterizations of such people as Queen Elizabeth, Raleigh, Drake, and others,
and climaxed by the English raid on Cadiz in 1587.
(YA)

265. Winwar, Frances. Queen Elizabeth and the Spanish
Armada. Random, 1954 (Landmark). A biography
in which the author has effectively condensed the
whole exciting century. (I)

266. Wood, James Playsted. The Queen's Most Honorable
Pirate. Harper, 1961. Ill. by Leonard Everett
Fisher. An absorbing story of English and Irish
pirates, especially Sir Francis Drake, during the
reign of Queen Elizabeth I. (YA)

C. Scotland and Ireland

267. Criss, Mildred. Mary Stuart, Young Queen of Scots.
Dodd, Mead, 1939 and 1958. Ill. by Rose Cha-
vanne. The story of Mary's youth. (YA)

268. Hahn, Emily. Mary, Queen of Scots. Hale, 1953.

Ill. by Walter Buehr. A fair and restrained biography of this intensely dramatic queen (1542-1587) giving both sides of the cases of Darnley's death at Kirk O'Field and the authenticity (or not) of the Casket Letters. (YA)

269. Hunter, Mollie (McIlwraith). The Spanish Letters. Funk and Wagnalls, 1967. A novel of espionage and counter-espionage laid in Edinburgh in 1589 when there was a plot to imprison King James VI and make possible an invasion of Queen Elizabeth's England by Philip of Spain. (YA)

269a. _____. The 13th Member. Harper and Row, 1970. Jacket by Carl Mayan. A suspenseful novel based on records of a plot, in 1590, to murder King James VI of Scotland by means of witchcraft. Young Adam, a "charity boy" and Gilly, a kitchen maid, risk fiery deaths as they conspire with a "good" Alchemist to expose the plot and even the Devil himself. (YA)

270. Kiely, Mary. O'Donnell of Destiny. Oxford, 1939. Ill. by Victor Dowling. A well documented novel about Hugh Roe O'Donnell, Prince of Triconnel, his capture by the English, his hairbreadth escapes, and, at the very end of the century, the Battle of Kinsale and the "Flight of the Earls." (YA)

271. King, Marian. Young Mary Stuart. Lippincott, 1954. A biography relating only to Mary's early life in France, with all the dialogue quoted from letters. (YA)

272. Knight, Ruth Adams. Search for Galleon's Gold. McGraw-Hill, 1956. A tale of the Spanish Armada based on the search, in 1954, for a sunken vessel in Tobemory Harbour, Scotland, supposedly the "Florencia," flagship of the Spanish forces. (YA)

273. Meyer, Edith Patterson. Pirate Queen. Little, Brown, 1961. The story of Ireland's Graine O'Malley in the days of Queen Elizabeth. Map. (YA)

274. Oliver, Jane. Queen Most Fair. Macmillan, 1959. Ill. by J. S. Goodall. A novel about Mary of Scotland's imprisonment in the Castle of Loch Leven and her attempted escapes. (YA)

275. Polland, Madeleine. Queen Without Crown. Holt, Rinehart and Winston, 1966. Ill. by Herbert Danska. A swashbuckling novel about the Irish queen, Graine O'Malley and young Patrick O'Flaherty who comes to Clare Island to enlist her aid in rescuing his family from the British during the occupation of

Ireland under Queen Elizabeth. (YA)

276. _____. The Town Across the Water. Holt, Rinehart and Winston, 1961. Ill. by Esta Nesbitt. A
novel about the conflict between an English occupied
town in Ireland and an Irish village at the time of
the Spanish Armada threat. (YA)

277. Vance, Marguerite. Scotland's Queen. Dutton, 1962.
Ill. by J. Luis Pellicer. A biographical story of
Mary Stuart. (YA)

278. Walsh, Maurice. Blackcock's Feather. Stokes, 1932.
A novel of high adventure in Ireland, the peaceful
pursuits of hunting and fishing, and a romance between a young Scot and an English loyalist. (A)

D.   Shakespearian England

279. Barker, Shirley. Liza Bowe. Random, 1956. A
novel about the Mermaid Tavern in Elizabethan
times (about 1588) when it was frequented by young
poets and dramatists such as Kit Marlow, Tom
Nashe and Will Shakespeare. (YA)

280. Bennet, John. Master Skylark. 1896. (later ed. by
Grosset, ill. by Reginald Birch). A charming little
classic about the Shakespearian period, along the
banks of the Avon, in Tudor London, and behind
the scenes of the theaters. (I)

281. Bowers, Gwendolyn. At the Sign of the Globe. Walck,
1966. The story of an orphan of 14 who goes to
Stratford to work for a glovemaker, and there
meets the playwright, William Shakespeare who of-
fers him an opportunity to work in the London theater. (I)

282. Brown, Ivor. Shakespeare in His Time. Nelson,
1960. Ill. by old prints, maps and interesting
photographs. A good short biography (1564-1616).
(YA)

283. Buckmaster, Henrietta. Walter Raleigh, Man of Two
Worlds. Random, 1964 (Landmark). Ill. by H.
B. Vestal. A biography of the man who lived most
of his life in the sixteenth century but who spent
many years in prison and had many adventures,
ending with his death under James I. (I)

284. Chute, Marchette. The Wonderful Winter. Dutton,
1954. Ill. by Grace Golden. A charming, gently
humorous story of Shakespeare's London and the
theater. (I)

285. Faulkner, Nancy. Great Reckoning. Dutton, 1970.
      Jacket by Herbert Danska. A 15-year-old boy is
      entrusted by his dying brother with the mission of
      warning Christopher Marlowe of a plot against his
      life. (YA)
286. Gray, Elizabeth Janet. I Will Adventure. Viking,
      1962. Ill. by Corydon Bell. A story of a boy
      growing up in England in 1596, with good period
      detail and glimpses of Burbage and Shakespeare.
      (I)
287. Hill, Frank Ernest. King's Company. Dodd Meade,
      1950. Ill. by Addison Burbank. A novel about the
      Globe Theater in the early years of the seventeenth
      century--Shakespeare, Burbage, Inigo Jones and
      others. (YA)
287a. Hodges, C. Walter. Shakespeare and the Players.
      Coward McCann, 2nd edition, 1970. Ill. by the
      author. First published in 1949, this is a lively
      story of the bard and his associates in the theater
      which is illustrated in detail. (I and YA)
288. Household, Geoffrey. Prisoner of the Indies, The
      Adventures of Miles Philips. Atlantic-Little,
      Brown, 1967. Maps and decorations by Warren
      Chappell. Based on Hakluyt (1589), these are the
      adventures of a real person, related in fictional
      form. (I and YA)
289. Jowett, Margaret. A Cry of Players. Roy, 1961.
      Ill. by Asgeir Scott. A novel about the Elizabethan
      theater and a "player's boy, " showing the growing
      Puritan antagonism toward the theater and play-
      acting. (YA)
290. Lawrence, Isabelle. Two for the Show. Bobbs Mer-
      rill, 1949. A story about some young theater-
      goers around the turn of the century. (I)
291. Noble, Iris. William Shakespeare. Messner, 1961.
      A good brief biography (1564-1616). (YA)
292. Sutcliffe, Rosemary. Brother Dusty-Feet. Oxford,
      1952. Ill. by C. Walter Hodges. The story of a
      band of strolling players in the southern counties
      of Elizabethan England. Nice nature detail. (I)
293. Trease, Geoffrey. Sir Walter Raleigh, Captain and
      Adventurer. Vanguard, 1950. A biography in ex-
      citing narrative form (1552-1618). (YA)
294. _____. Cue for Treason. Vanguard Press, n.d.
      Starting out simply with a boy throwing a stone at
      a Lord who was fencing in Cumberland freeholds,
      the boy's adventures take him into the Shakes-

pearian theater in the countryside, in London, and
even at Court and finally involve him in a plot
against the life of the aging Queen Elizabeth. Great
reading! (YA)
295. Watson, Sally. Mistress Malapert. Holt, 1955. Ill.
by Genia [Wennerstrom]. A quite unlikely but
thoroughly entertaining story of a young girl mas-
querading as a boy in order to be taken on as a
player at the Globe Theater, when all female parts
were taken by boys whose voices hadn't changed.
(I)
296. White, Anne Terry. Will Shakespeare and the Globe
Theater. Random, 1955. Ill. by C. Walter Hodges.
A biography of the poet-playwright beginning when,
at the age of 22, he rode to London to seek his fortune on the stage. (I)
297. Wood, James Playsted. The Man With Two Countries.
Seabury, 1967. Ill. by W. T. Mars. A young man
of Irish-English descent must choose sides when
violence erupts between the two groups during the
last years of the sixteenth century. (YA)

SEVENTEENTH CENTURY

A.   The Stuart Kings, Cromwell, Civil War

298. Aldis, Dorothy. Ride the Wild Waves. Putnam, 1957.
Ill. by Robert Henneberger. A story about the
motivations and plans, in England, for the emi-
gration to the American colonies by the founders
of the Massachusetts Bay Colony in 1628; the harrowing ocean voyage and presence in their midst
of a suspected witch (later hanged in Salem, Massachusetts). A list of historical figures with notes
on their further lives. (I)
299. Barker, Shirley. Rivers Parting. Crown, 1950. A
novel about the difficult transference of loyalty
from England to the new colonies in America, with
much of the action set in Nottingham and London.
(A)
300. Barnes, Margaret Campbell. Mary of Carisbrooke.
Macrae Smith, 1956. A novel about Charles I's
imprisonment on the Isle of Wight, and how a
young laundress tried to aid his escape. (A)
301. Barr, Gladys. The Pilgrim Prince. Holt, Rinehart

and Winston, 1963. A biographical novel of John
Bunyan (1628-88), author of "Pilgrim's Progress."
(A)

302. Beatty, John and Patricia. Campion Towers. Macmillan, 1965. A suspense story about the English
Civil War, Cromwell and Charles II, with an author's note about the English spoken in that period.
(YA)

303. _____. Pirate Royal. Macmillan, 1969. The
main character of this novel becomes a young ac-
countant and scrivener for the famous buccaneer,
Henry Morgan, after having been falsely accused
of theft and deported to the American colonies as
an indentured servant. (YA)

304. _____. The Queen's Wizard. Macmillan, 1967.
Jacket by Bernard Bratt. A novel based on thor-
ough research, documented in the author's note,
about an astrologer for Queen Elizabeth who takes
into his care two homeless boys; one is "moon-
struck" with extrasensory perception and the elder
becomes an apprentice to the "Wizard of Montlake."
The story begins in the last years of Queen Elizabeth's reign but reaches its climax during that of
King James' with the discovery of the gunpowder
plot in 1605. (YA)

305. _____. King's Knight's Pawn. Morrow, 1971.
Jacket by Franz Altschuler. A story of suspense
and treachery in which an English boy joins the
Cavalier army in Ireland, fighting against Cromwell's forces. The novel is climaxed by the
Roundhead massacre of Irish and English Royalists
at Drogheda. An historical note gives the long
buildup of Catholic-Protestant and Irish-English
conflicts. (YA)

306. _____. Witch Dog. Morrow, 1968. Jacket, endpapers and map by Frank Altschuler. Prince
Rupert's big white poodle is the most important
character in this unusual novel about the English
Civil War. Copious notes on the Stuarts, Prince
Rupert's mother and her family and other historical characters, with a genealogical chart. (YA)

307. Buchan, John. Witch Wood. 1927. A novel about a
young Scotch minister in the time of Montrose,
who is caught between the old heathen witchcraft
customs and an inhuman bigoted Kirk. (A)

308. Burton, Hester. Beyond the Weir Bridge. Crowell,
1970. Ill. by Victor Ambrus. A serious novel of

the period 1651 to 1667, with a love theme against
the grim background of persecution of the Quakers
and the Great Plague of 1665. A genealogical
chart and note on the Civil War. (YA)

309. Cawley, Winifred. Down the Long Stairs. Holt, Rinehart and Winston, 1964. A starkly realistic novel
set in the mining country near Newcastle during the
1648 part of the Civil War. Prologue, postscript
and glossary. (YA)

310. _____. Feast of the Serpent. Holt, Rinehart and
Winston, 1970. A young orphan girl, half-Gypsy
and half-English, is accused of witchcraft during
Cromwell's rule, 1653-58. Glossary. (YA)

311. Clarke, Mary Stetson. Piper To the Clan. Viking,
1970. Jacket by Joshua Telford. A novel about a
lad whose father has been killed at Dunbar by Cromwell's army and who, himself, is taken prisoner by
the English and deported to America as an indentured worker in the Saugus Iron Works. (YA)

311a. Cooper, Lettice. Gunpowder, Treason and Plot. Abe-
lard-Schumann, 1970. Ill. by Elizabeth Grant.
The fifth of November, 1605: the Houses of Par-
liament in imminent danger of being blown up, with
King James I and the Prince of Wales in it! Read
all about it: the plot, the plotters, (Guy Fawkes
and others) and the outcome. Based on historical
records. (I and YA)

312. Dunham, Montrew. Anne Bradstreet, Young Puritan
Poet. Bobbs-Merrill, 1969. Childhood of Famous
Americans Series. Ill. by Paul and Patty Karch.
Though Anne became famous as America's first
woman poet, her childhood and youth, the subjects
of this book, were spent in Northampton, England,
where her father, Thomas Dudley, was business
manager for the Earl of Lincoln. (E and I)

313. Farrington, Benjamin. Francis Bacon, Pioneer of
Planned Science. Praeger, 1969. Ill. with photographs. A scholarly presentation of the life (1561-
1626), thought and political activity of a man ahead
of his time (and perhaps our's) who believed in
man's moral obligation to study both Nature and the
Bible in order to use his scientific studies for the
benefit of all mankind. (YA and A)

314. Fecher, Constance. The Link Boys. Farrar, Straus
and Giroux, 1971. Ill. by Richard Cuffari. A
sparkling, cleverly plotted novel of seventeenth
century England in the reign of the Merry King

Charles II, in which a vagrant boy joins a band of "link boys" (torchbearers to guide theater-goers home through the dark, dangerous streets of London) who aid him in rescuing his falsely accused uncle from the gallows. (I and YA)

315.   Finkel, George. The Loyal Virginian. Viking, 1968. Beginning and ending in the Virginia colony, the main part of this novel is about the English Civil War. (YA)

316.   Fuller, Edmund. John Milton. Seabury Press, 1944 and 1967. A vivid biography, using some of the techniques of the novel, of the author of "Paradise Lost" (1608-74) who was, besides being a great poet, courageously active in the causes of freedom of the press and religion, and even divorce (for husbands, that is). (YA and A)

317.   Garnett, Henry. Gamble for a Throne. Barnes, 1958. Ill. by Peter Jackson. A novel about the Royalist underground movement in the 1650s, with a documentary note. (YA)

318.   Goudge, Elizabeth. The Child From the Sea. Coward McCann, 1970. Jacket by Biro. A long, old-fashioned historical romance about Lucy Walters, mistress (and, as she claimed, wife) of Prince Charles before he became King Charles II, and mother of his son, later known as the Duke of Monmouth. (A)

319.   Gould, Heywood. Sir Christopher Wren, Renaissance Architect, Philosopher and Scientist. Franklin Watts, 1970. After reading this biography, those who associate the name mainly with the rebuilding of St. Paul's in London, will appreciate Sir Christopher's (1632-1723) many other accomplishments-- his scientific inventions, anatomical and astronomical studies, etc. (YA and A)

320.   Harrison, William C. Dr. William Harvey and the Discovery of Circulation. Macmillan, 1967. Ill. by Laszlo Kubinyi. The story of Dr. Harvey's life (1578-1657) with emphasis on his great discovery and his adventures in trying to obtain recognition. (YA)

321.   Hawes, Charles Boardman. The Dark Frigate. Atlantic, 1923. Ill. by Anton Otto Fischer (1971 ed. ill. by Warren Chappell). "Wherein is told the story of Philip Marsham who lived in the time of King Charles and was bred a sailor but came home again to England after many hazards by sea and

land and fought for the King at Newbury and lost
a great inheritance and departed for Barbados in
the same ship, by chance in which he had long before ventured with the pirates." (YA)

322. Haycraft, Molly Costain. Too Near the Throne. Lippincott, 1959. A novel about Lady Arabella Stuart,
a niece of Mary Queen of Scots and cousin to King
James I of England. (YA)

323. Heyer, Georgette. Royal Escape. Doubleday, 1938.
A novel about young Prince Charles (much later
King Charles II) who was crowned King of Scots in
Scotland but had a price on his head in England;
how he was abandoned by his Scotch troops after
the Battle of Worcester, and how he made his escape to the coast in 1651. (A)

324. Holm, Anne. Peter. Harcourt, Brace and World,
1968. Translated from the Danish by L. W. Kingsland. Jacket by W. T. Mars. This past and present novel carries Peter first back into ancient
Greece, than to Norman England, and finally to
Cromwell's time when he helps to save Charles II
from the Roundheads. (YA)

325. Hope-Simpson, Jacynth. The Great Fire. E. P.
Dutton, 1961. Ill. by Pat Marriott. A story of
two youngsters trying to escape from the great
fire of 1666 in London, one because he has been
accused of starting the fire in Pudding Lane, and
his girl companion because she wants to go to sea
anyway. How quickly people find a scapegoat in a
panic. (I)

326. Knight, Frank. The Last of Lallows. Macmillan,
1961. Ill. by William Stobbs. A novel about a
young girl whose father and brother are fighting
on opposite sides in the Civil War. (YA)

327. Knipe, Emilie Benson and Arthur Alden. A Cavalier
Maid. Macmillan, 1928. The story of a wealthy
young English miss who is kidnapped and sent to
the American colonies during the English civil war.
(I)

328. Latham, Jean Lee. The Frightened Hero. Chilton
Books, 1965. Ill. by Barbara Latham. At last
an historical story for very young readers, and an
exciting one of the siege of Latham Castle by the
Roundheads in 1644 in which a young boy learns
the meaning of courage. (E)

329. MacGibbon, Jean. A Special Providence. Coward
McCann, 1964. Ill. by William Stobbs. The first

two-thirds of the story take place in England with
the preparations for going to America on the "May-
flower," the rescue of William Brewster, details
about the construction and provisioning of the "May-
flower," and waiting for the Puritans at Leyden.
The last third is about the voyage itself, and all
told from the viewpoint of young Giles Hopkinson
and based on an eye-witness account by William
Bradford. (I)

330.   Malvern, Gladys. So Great a Love. Macrae, Smith,
1962. A novel about Henrietta Marie of France,
courageous queen of Charles I, and the first part
of the Civil War. (YA)

331.   Marcus, Rebecca B. William Harvey, Trailblazer of
Scientific Medicine. Watts, 1962. Ill. by Richard
Mayhew. A biography of the discoverer of circulation of the blood, with a chronology of his life
(1578-1657) and a glossary of medical terms used
in the book. (YA)

332.   Norman, Charles. The Flight and Adventures of
Charles II. Random, 1958 (Landmark). Ill. by
C. Walter Hodges. (I)

333.   Peart, Hendry. The Loyal Grenvilles. Knopf, 1958.
Ill. by Richard M. Powers. A novel about the daring resistance to Puritan control of two Royalist
boys in Cromwell's Commonwealth, a year after
the beheading of Charles I. (YA)

334.   Picard, Barbara Leonie. The Tower and the Traitors.
G. P. Putnam's Sons, 1961. Ill. by William Stobbs
[See notes to no. 236]. Those who met their fates
in the Tower in the seventeenth century were Sir
Walter Raleigh, Thomas Overbury, Thomas Blood
(who tried to steal the crown jewels), James Scot,
Duke of Monmouth, and his judge, George Baron
Jeffreys. (YA)

335.   "Q" [Quiller-Couch, A. T.] The Splendid Spur. 1889.
"Adventures of Mr. John Marvel, a servant of his
Late Majesty King Charles I in the years 1642-43.
Written by Himself. Edited in Modern English."
An incredible historical romance but good fun. (A)

336.   Ross, Sutherland. The English Civil War. Putnam,
1962. Ill. by Salem Tamer. A good, short readable history of the war making all the exciting fiction about it more understandable. (I)

337.   Scott, Sir Walter. The Legend of Montrose. A novel
of the Royalists under Montrose in the war in the
Scottish highlands (1644-45). (A)

338. Softly, Barbara. <u>Plain Jane</u>. Macmillan, 1963. Ill.
by Shirley Hughes. An exciting story of a young
girl's attempts to outwit Roundhead troops in 1643
and, at the same time, to evade a marriage her
father is insistent upon. (YA)

339. _____. <u>Place Mill</u>. St. Martin's, 1963. Ill. by
Shirley Hughes. A suspense story set on the
Hampshire coast near the Isle of Wight during
Charles II's get-away. Map. (YA)

340. _____. <u>A Stone in the Pool</u>. Macmillan, 1964.
Ill. by Shirley Hughes. A novel about a young
girl's attempts to rescue Charles I from Carisbrooke Castle on the Isle of Wight, resulting in
her being accused of witchcraft. (YA)

341. Sutcliffe, Rosemary. <u>Rider on a White Horse</u>. Coward
McCann, 1959. A novel about Lady Anne Fairfax
whose husband, Sir Thomas, fought on the Parlia-
ment side of the Civil War but opposed the execution of Charles I. (A)

342. _____. <u>Simon</u>. Oxford, 1953. Ill. by Richard
Kennedy. A story of young friends on opposite
sides in the Civil War and about the Battle of Tor-
rington, with an author's note and map. (I)

343. Syme, Ronald. <u>Walter Raleigh</u>. William Morrow,
1962. Ill. by William Stobbs. A biography of one
of the great Elizabethans, who, however, lived on
and died in the seventeenth century (1552-1618). (I)

344. Varble, Rachel M. <u>Pepys' Boy</u>. Doubleday, 1955.
Ill. by Kurt Werth. A story of the main events of
the Restoration Period, the reign of Charles II,
1660-85, as told by a young page boy of Pepys,
the diarist. (I)

345. _____. <u>Three Against London</u>. Doubleday, 1962.
Ill. by C. Walter Hodges. The story of a serving
girl in the Pepys household and of the London fires.
(YA)

346. Walsh, Maurice. <u>The Dark Rose</u>. Stokes, 1938. "A
Story of the Wars of Montrose as seen by Martin
Somers, Adjutant of Women in O'Cahan's Regiment."
A Gaelic tale of clan warfare and the Scotch against
the "Sassenachs" (the English) and the Covenanters.
(A)

347. Watson, Sally. <u>Witch of the Glens</u>. Viking, 1962.
Ill. by Barbara Werner. A novel about a young
would-be witch and the conflict between Covenanters
and Royalists in Scotland, with Argyle and Montrose
as their respective leaders. Includes an historical

note, a map of the relevant section of Scotland,
and a glossary of Gaelic terms with suggestions
as to their pronounciation. (YA)

348.   _____. Lark. Holt, Rinehart and Winston, 1964.
A romance set in the time of the Battle of Worcester (1651) concerning Gypsies, Royalists, Roundheads, and a remarkable pair of grandparents and
Charles II. (YA)

349. Weir, Rosemary. The Star and the Flame. Ariel,
1964. Ill. by William Stobbs. The adventures of
a London boy during the Great Plague and the
Great Fire of 1666. (I)

350.   _____. The Lion and the Rose. Farrar, Straus,
and Giroux, 1970. Ill. by Richard Cuffari. About
a boy yearning to be a stonecutter who stows away
to London, then rebuilding after the Great Fire.
(YA)

351. Welch, Ronald. For the King. Criterion, 1962. An
historical note at the beginning sets the stage for
this Civil War novel in which the hero is a member
of a wealthy Welsh-English family named Carey.
Other generations of this same fictional family appear in other books and all play exciting roles in
history. (YA)

352. Willard, Barbara. Flight to the Forest. Doubleday,
1967. Ill. by Gareth Floyd. A strong novel about
the generation gap in the time of Cromwell when
the theaters are closed down. An old actor tries
to imbue his grandson with the tradition of the
Shakespearean stage, but the boy has other ideas.
(YA)

B. The Latter Part of the Century
(James II, William and Mary, William alone, and Queen Anne)

353. Alderman, Clifford Lindsay. Stormy Knight, The Life
of Sir William Phips. Chilton Books, 1964. Jacket by George L. Connelly. When Willie Phips was
born in the American colony of Maine in 1651,
there was a superstition that because he was the
21st son of his parents he would "stand before
kings." How this came to pass makes quite a
story. (YA)

354. Blackmore, R. D. Lorna Doone. 1869. If you can
really "get into it" and understand the dialect, this
is an exciting romance set in Exmoor after the

Monmouth Rebellion of 1685.   (A)

355.   Dolson, Hildegarde.   William Penn, Quaker Hero.
Random, 1961 (Landmark).   Ill. by Lenard Everett
Fisher.   Biography (1644-1718).   (I)

356.   Grierson, Edward.   Dark Torrent of Glencoe.   Doubleday, 1960.   A novel about the infamous massacre
of the McDonalds by the Campbells, in 1692, upon
secret orders from King William, with an excellent
map of the Glencoe region and an outline map of
the entire British Isles.   (YA)

357.   Harnett, Cynthia.   The Great House.   World, 1949.
Ill. by the author.   Drawings, text, and plot together weave an exceptionally vivid picture of the
time.   (I and YA)

358.   Haviland, Virginia.   William Penn, Founder and Friend.
Abingdon, 1952.   Ill. by Peter Burchard.   A biography largely devoted to Penn's life in England and
Ireland, his conversion to the Quaker faith and the
persecution resulting from it,   but also a book
about his establishment of Pennsylvania.   (E and
I)

359.   Hodges, Margaret.   Lady Queen Anne.   Farrar, Straus
and Giroux, 1969.   Ill. with photographs of paintings.   An absorbingly readable story of the queen
and her period (she ruled from 1702 until her death
in 1714) and of many of the important characters of
her time--the Marlboroughs, Godolphin, Sir Christopher Wren, Alexander Pope, Laurence Sterne and
others.   (YA and A)

360.   Hunt, Mabel Leigh.   Beggar's Daughter.   Lippincott,
1963.   A novel about a girl who, abandoned as a
baby on the doorstep of a Quaker home at the time
of great persecution of the Quakers, must, as a
young woman, decide whether to stay a Quaker or
not.   (YA)

361.   Hunter, Mollie.   The Ghosts of Glencoe.   Funk and
Wagnalls, 1969.   Ill. with scenic photographs.   The
terrible story of the massacre of Glencoe in 1692
when the Campbells took advantage of the McDonald's hospitality, claiming to come there in peace
and then putting all to the sword who could not
manage to escape.   The character of Robert Stewart who refused to obey orders to kill and who
aided the escaping McDonalds is based on a story
told by one of the survivors.   Map.   (YA and A)

362.   Knight, David C.   Isaac Newton, Mastermind of Modern Science.   Franklin Watts, 1961.   Ill. by John

Griffin. Biography (1642-1727). (YA)
363. Kyle, Elizabeth. The Story of Grizel. Nelson, 1963.
A short novel about a young Scottish girl exiled
with her family to Holland until the flight of James
II from England and the beginning of the reign of
William and Mary when she is able to return to
Scotland. (YA)
364. Land, Barbara and Myrick. The Quest of Isaac Newton. Garden City, 1960. A short simple biography. (I)
365. Moore, Patrick. Isaac Newton. Putnam, 1958. Ill.
by Patricia Cullen. This biography of the discoverer of the law of gravitation contains a list
of important dates in his life. (YA)
366. Peare, Catherine Owens. William Penn. Holt, 1958.
Ill. by Henry C. Pitz. An adaptation of the author's definitive adult biography (1644-1718) published by Lippincott in 1957. (YA)
367. Polland, Madeleine. Shattered Summer. Doubleday,
1969. Jacket by Lou Sadella. A novel of the Monmouth Rebellion of 1685 and a young lady's 19th
summer shattered by dissension in the country and
in her own heart. Map of the route of Monmouth's
army. (YA)
368. Sabatini, Rafael. Captain Blood. Houghton Mifflin,
1924. A rattling good novel, with illustrations,
about Peter Blood, soldier, country doctor, slave,
pirate and, finally governor of Jamaica. (A)
369. Sootin, Harry. Isaac Newton. Messner, 1955. Biography with a good bibliography of those who want
to know still more about this much-written-about
scientist (1642-1727). (YA)
370. Tannenbaum, Beulah and Stillman, Myra. Isaac Newton, Pioneer of Space Mathematics. McGraw-Hill,
1959. Ill. by Gustav Schrotter. Biography relating Newton to the Space Age. (YA)
371. Wilkie, Katherine. William Penn, Friend to All. Garrard, 1964. Ill. by J. L. Pellicer. A short biography with emphasis on the founding of Pennsylvania.
(I)

EIGHTEENTH CENTURY

A. England, Ireland, and Wales
(The Hanover Kings; French and American Revolutions)

372. Ballard, Martin. The Monarch of Juan Fernando.
      Scribner, 1967. Ill. by A. R. Whitear. The
      stranger-than-fiction story of the model for Defoe's
      "Robinson Crusoe," Alexander Selkirk, a Scotch
      sailing master who lived alone on the uninhabited
      island of Juan Fernando, in the South Pacific, for
      four years and four months. (YA)
373. Beatty, John and Patricia. At the Seven Stars. Mac-
      millan, 1963. Ill. by Douglas Gorsline and re-
      productions of Hogarth prints. A spy story about
      a plot to unseat King George II in 1752, involving
      such real characters as Dr. Samuel Johnson and
      David Garrick. Note on sources. (YA)
374. Bentley, Phyllis. The Adventures of Tom Leigh.
      Doubleday, 1966. Ill. by Burt Silverman. A mur-
      der mystery, set in the West Riding in Yorkshire,
      about a weaver's apprentice and the weaving trade
      in the early eighteenth century and the administra-
      tion of justice at that time. (YA)
375. _____. Forgery. Doubleday, 1968. Another mur-
      der mystery also set in the West Riding of York-
      shire in which a 14-year-old weaver's son and an
      old English sheepdog play the major roles. (I and
      YA)
376. Berry, Erik (Best, Allena). The Four Londons of William
      Hogarth. David McKay, 1964. With illustrations
      from Hogarth's work. A biography of the artist
      (1697-1764) interestingly framed by changing London
      scenes: 1) the city of William's father, 2) that of
      young Billy's youth, his apprenticeship and mar-
      riage, 3) the London of Hogarth in his prime, and
      4) the scene of his unhappy conflicts with other
      artists and his unwise foray into the realm of pol-
      itics. (YA and A)
377. Blackstock, Josephine. Songs for a Sixpence. Follet,
      1955. Ill. by Maurice Bower. A biography of
      John Newbery (1713-67), English publisher of
      newspapers and childrens' books, in whose name
      the Newbery medal, founded in 1921, is awarded
      annually for the best children's book of the year
      written by an American. (I)
378. Brown, Ivor. Dr. Johnson and His World. Walck,
      1966. Ill. with over 60 photographs. The story
      of the great dictionary maker (1709-84) and his
      times. (YA)
379. Bulla, Clyde Robert. Pirate's Promise. Crowell,
      1958. Ill. by Peter Burchard. The story of an

English boy sold by his uncle to a sea captain who planned to re-sell him in America as a bond servant, but whose plans are foiled by the boy's capture by pirates. (E and I)

380. Clarke, Clorinda. The American Revolution, A British View. McGraw-Hill, 1967. Ill. with maps, drawings and contemporary prints. A book first written to tell British boys and girls about the American Revolution, it sheds a fresh light for American readers on the causes and results of the Revolution and the most decisive battles. Written vividly, excitingly and fairly. (YA)

381. Cordell, Alexander. The White Cockade. Viking, 1970. Jacket by Paul Nonnast. A mighty and exciting novel, the first of a trilogy based on the 1798 rebellion in which the "United Irishmen" led by Lord Edward Fitzgerald, counted on the support of the French under Napoleon against the English. A young Irishman tried to get a message from Napoleon to Lord Fitzgerald. A list of historical characters, notes on the parts they played in the rebellion and their fates. (YA)

382. _____. Witches' Sabbath. Viking, 1970. Jacket by Paul Nonnast. The second in the trilogy of which the first is "The White Cockade." Based on the 1798 rebellion of United Irishmen against Irish loyalists and British. John Regan is embroiled in espionage and counterespionage. (YA)

383. _____. The Healing Blade. Viking, 1971. Jacket by Paul Nonnast. The tension-filled last of the 1798 Rebellion trilogy, in which the audacious young patriot performs his last mission for his Ireland. (YA)

384. Crane, William D. The Discoverer of Oxygen: Joseph Priestley. Messner, 1962. Biography of an English theologian and scientist (1733-1804) whose independent and radical ideas forced him to emigrate to America in 1794. (YA)

385. Crawford, Deborah. The King's Astronomer, William Herschel, with an introduction by Willy Ley. Julian Messner, 1968. In the light of current space work this narrative biography is especially valuable for giving readers an understanding of the early research and discoveries by men like Herschel (1738-1832) and women like his sister Caroline, an honored astronomer in her own right. The discoverer of the planet Uranus began life as a musician but

ended it as one of the great figures of astronomical research. (YA)

386. Daringer, Helen Fern. Pilgrim Kate. Harcourt,
Brace and World, 1949. Ill. by Kate Seredy. A
family story in which a 15-year-old girl, though
living comfortably in England, feels compelled to
leave her country in order to worship in freedom
[for sequel, see entry 769b]. (I and YA)

387. Delderfield, R. F. The Adventures of Ben Gunn.
Hodder and Stoughton, England, 1956. Ill. by
William Stobbs. Written as a sequel to Stevenson's
"Treasure Island." (YA)

388. de la Torre, Lillian. The Actress, Being the Story
of Sarah Siddons. Harper and Row, 1957. "Showing How she began as a Strolling Player; how her
stage Lover won her Heart and Hand; how she
struggled for Fame and Fortune; and how she became Queen of the London Stage" (in the last half
of the eighteenth century). (YA)

389. DeWitt, James. In Pursuit of the Spanish Galleon.
Criterion, 1961. A true story based on Commodore
Anson's famous voyage around the world, 1740 to
1744, with a chart of the route of the Centurion.
(YA)

390. Dickens, Charles. Barnaby Rudge. 1841. Dodd,
Mead, 1931. Ill. in color by Rowland Wheelwright.
A novel about the terrible anti-Catholic Gordon
riots of 1780 and their cause, a government heed-
less of the needs of the poor. (A)

391. _____. A Tale of Two Cities. 1859. One of
Dickens' few historical novels, about London and
Paris during the French Revolution. As a Dickens
enthusiast, I don't rate this book as highly as most
of his works, but I know those whose favorite this
is. (A)

392. Dolan, Edward F. Jenner and the Miracle of Vaccine.
Dodd, Mead, 1960. A biography. (1749-1823)
(YA)

393. Falkner, J. Meade. Moonfleet. Little, Brown, 1951.
Ill. by Fritz Kredel. A novel about smuggling on
the Dorset coast in mid-century and the search for
a diamond supposedly hidden by Blackbeard a century before in Carisbrooke Castle on the Isle of
Wight. (YA)

394. Freeman, Barbara. A Book by Georgina. W. W.
Norton, 1962. Ill. by the author. A light-hearted
"now and then" story in which an old house is the

focal point. Georgina "likes to feel time going back and back and back and everything tying on to everything else." (I)

395. Garfield, Leon. Devil in the Fog. Pantheon, 1966. Ill. by Anthony Maitland. A mystery novel about an inheritance and an attempted murder. (YA)

396. _____. The Drummer Boy. Pantheon, 1969. Ill. by Anthony Maitland. An impressionistic novel about a drummer boy who is one of few to survive a witless battle between the English and French and manages somehow, in spite of his weird raffish companions to regain his ideals. Somber and grimly humorous. (YA)

397. _____. Jack Holborne. Pantheon, 1964. Ill. by Anthony Maitland. A violent novel of pirates, slave traders, adventures and mystery. (YA)

398. _____. Mister Corbett's Ghost. Pantheon, 1968. Ill. by Alan E. Cober. A spookily narrated and illustrated ghost story. (YA)

399. _____. The Restless Ghost. Pantheon, 1969. Ill. by Saul Lambert. Three stories, only one of which is actually a "ghost story" all have the same qualities of macabre humor and compassion for the dregs of society to be expected from this author. (YA)

400. _____. Smith. Pantheon, 1967. Ill. by Anthony Maitland. A mystery about a young pickpocket's adventures after stealing a document from an old man who is murdered immediately after the theft. Humor, suspense and a Dickens flavor. (YA)

401. _____. The Strange Affair of Adelaide Harris. Pantheon, 1971. Ill. by Fritz Wegner. A colorful tale of intrigue and hilarious humor. (YA and A)

402. Glendinning, Sally. Thomas Gainsborough, Artist of England. Garrard, 1969. Ill. by Cary and with 12 Gainsborough paintings in color. A short biography of the artist (1727-88) with interesting material on how he worked. (I)

403. Hall, Aylmer. Beware of Moonlight. Nelson (1st U.S.) 1970. Jacket by Graham Humphreys. Larry O'Driscoll, a cousin of the young English owner of Corcalee Castle in Ireland, is torn between his family loyalty and the violent defense of the starving tenant peasants carried on by Captain Moonlight and the "Whiteboys," and tries to steer a course between them, to his own peril. (YA)

404. Hunter, Mollie (McIlwraith). The Fairlie. Funk and
     Wagnalls, 1968. Ill. by Joseph Cellini. A fantasy
     about a young herdsman who was to make a difficult
     choice between fairyland and the real world. (I)
405. Knight, Frank. Clemency Draper. St. Martin's, 1963.
     Ill. by William Stobbs. A Dickens-like story about
     an orphan girl and the characters she meets after
     leaving the orphanage in Sussex in the 1790s. (I)
406. _____. The Slaver's Apprentice. St. Martin's
     Press, 1961. Ill. by Patrick Jobson. A novel set
     in the last years of the century, about a boy's part
     in the voyage of a slave-carrying ship bound for the
     West Indies, with an introduction about the African
     slave trade at that time and how much worse it be-
     came after emancipation in the U.S.A. (I and YA)
407. Latham, Jean Lee. The Voyager; The Story of James
     Cook. Harper and Row, 1970. Maps by Karl
     Stuecklen. A fictional biography of Captain Cook
     (1728-79), with many interesting nautical details of
     his youthful days at sea. (I)
408. Levine, I. E. Conqueror of Smallpox, Dr. Edward Jen-
     ner. Messner, 1960. Biography (1749-1823). (YA)
409. McNeer, May. John Wesley. Abingdon Press, 1951.
     Ill. by Lynd Ward. The story of the long, full,
     adventurous life of the founder of Methodism (1703-
     91) toward the end of which John Wesley said, "I
     look upon all the world as my parish." (I)
410. Marcus, Rebecca B. Joseph Priestley, Pioneer Chem-
     ist. Franklin Watts, 1961. Ill. by Peter Constan-
     za. (I)
411. Melville, Herman. Billy Budd, Foretopman. 1891.
     A short novel (usually found in a collection) about
     the famous mutiny at Spithead in 1797. (A)
412. Myers, Elizabeth P. Singer of Six Thousand Songs.
     Nelson, 1965. Ill. by Leonard Vosburgh. A biog-
     raphy of the great hymn writer, Charles Wesley
     (1707-88). (YA)
413. Orczy, Baroness. The Scarlet Pimpernel. Putnam,
     1905. (New ill. Macmillan Classic, 1964.) A
     highly entertaining novel about a band of young Eng-
     lishmen devoting themselves to the rescue of French
     aristocrats from the guillotine. (A)
414. _____. The Elusive Pimpernel. 1908. A sequel
     to "The Scarlet Pimpernel." (A)
415. Parks, Aileen Wells. James Oglethorpe, Young De-
     fender. Bobbs-Merrill, 1958. Ill. by Maurice
     Rawson. The story of the childhood and youth in

England of the man who later founded the American colony of Georgia in 1733 and served with Prince Eugene in the war against the Turks, defender of the poor and especially those imprisoned for debts. (E)

416. Picard, Barbara Leonie. The Tower and the Traitors. Putnam, 1961. Ill. by William Stobbs. The so-called traitor in this book (listed also under the sixteenth and seventeenth centuries) is most importantly William Maxwell, The Earl of Nithsdale, who imprudently took part in the Scottish rebellion of 1715, supporting the claim of the "Old Pretender," son of James II. His associates were more unfortunate than he in the end, and the real heroine of the story is his wife, Lady Nithsdale. (YA)

417. _____. The Young Pretenders. Criterion, 1966. Ill. by Victor Ambrus. A finely perceptive novel about two English children who find themselves alone in their family and village in their loyalty to Prince Charles of Scotland (when he, after the Battle of Culloden, 1746, is being sought by the English), and their problem of hiding a supposed follower of the Prince. (YA)

418. Polling, James. The Man Who Saved Robinson Crusoe. Norton, 1967. Ill. by Fermin Rocker. "The Strange, Surprising Adventures of the Original Robinson Crusoe and His Most Remarkable Rescue" and a great tale of British privateering in the Pacific under the leadership of the intrepid Captain Woodes-Rogers who came to the rescue of Alexander Selkirk. (YA and A)

419. Rush, Philip. Frost Fair. Roy, 1965. Ill. by Philip Gough. A story of two orphans kidnapped to be sold as indentured servants in the American colonies, and how a natural phenomenon and a young girl's courage brought about their rescue. Factual material with fictional characters. (I)

420. Savery, Constance. The Reb and the Redcoats. Longmans Green, 1961. Ill. by Vera Bock. An American Revolutionary officer, captured by the British, is imprisoned in an English home and develops a warm friendship with the children of the house. (YA)

421. Selsam, Millicent. The Quest of Captain Cook. Doubleday, 1962. Ill. by Lee J. Ames. A well organized story of Cook's three voyages (1768, 1772-75, 1776-8) each with a two-page map. (I and YA)

422. Spencer, Cornelia. More Hands for Men. John Day,
          1960. The story of the industrial revolution, 1760-
          1850, in fictional form. (YA)
423. Spier, Peter. London Bridge is Falling Down. Double-
          day, 1967. Ill. by the author. A charmingly il-
          lustrated nursery song with a history of London
          Bridge at the end. A picture book. (E)
424. Syme, Ronald. Captain Cook, Pacific Explorer. Mor-
          row Junior Books, 1960. Ill. by William Stobbs.
          A biography of the good, peace-loving explorer
          (1728-1799) who charted the New Zealand coastline
          and the east coast of Australia and explored some
          of the Arctic Ocean before being killed by Hawaiian
          natives. (I)
425. Tarkington, Booth. Monsieur Beaucaire. 1901. A
          little drama of intrigue laid in Bath during the
          Beau Nash regime, at the time of the French Rev-
          olution. (A)
426. Trease, Geoffrey. The Silken Secret. Vanguard,
          1954. A mystery story set early in the century.
          (YA)
427. Welch, Ronald. Captain of Dragoons. Oxford, 1957.
          A spy story about the Duke of Marlborough's cam-
          paign against the French in the early part of the
          century. (YA)

B. Scotland

428. Barker, Shirley. Swear By Apollo. Random, 1958.
          A novel about a young American doctor on a Scot-
          tish isle at the time of the American revolution
          and the struggle there between science and magic
          and old and new world attitudes. (A)
429. Beatty, John and Patricia. The Royal Dirk. Morrow,
          1966. All stories of Bonnie Prince Charlie's es-
          capes after the uprising of 1745 are exciting, and
          this is no exception, with an author's note at the
          end giving the history of the period. (YA)
430. Buchan, John. Midwinter. Doran, 1923. A novel of
          the "troubles" in 1745, involving Prince Charles
          and Dr. Johnson. Full of adventure, romance and
          intrigue. (A)
431. Cormack, Maribelle and Alexander, William P. Last
          Clash of Claymores. Appleton-Century, 1940. A
          story of Scotland in the time of Prince Charlie,
          full of suspense, with a genealogical chart, list of

principal characters, and a glossary of Gaelic
words. (YA)

432. de la Torre, Lillian. The White Rose of Stuart. Nelson, 1954. A novel about hardy Flora McDonald
who came to Prince Charlie's aid in 1745 and later
emigrated to America. (YA)

433. Gray, Elizabeth Janet. Young Walter Scott. Viking,
1953. Jacket and endpapers by Kate Seredy. A
biographical novel about the boyhood and youth of
Sir Walter (1771-1832) who, in spite of lameness
and several illnesses and devotion to books (especially about Scotch history and deeds of daring),
was a "regular boy." A vivid picture of the Edinburgh of his youth and its environs and a list of
people he knew in his early life and their names
when they appeared in his novels. (I and YA)

434. Hunter, Mollie (McIlwraith). The Lothian Run. Funk
and Wagnalls, 1970. Jacket by Charles Buchanan.
A novel of detection, based on the Porteus Riot in
Edinburgh in 1736 in which a 16-year-old law clerk
becomes dangerously involved by going in pursuit of
a smuggler on the route called the Lothian Run.
There is more serious matter than smuggling, however, in the resultant riot. (YA)

435. Knight, Peter. Shadow on Skjarling. Coward McCann,
1964. Ill. by Walter Stobbs. A novel of adventure
on a bleak, wild island off the coast of Scotland
just before the uprising of 1745. (YA)

436. Linklater, Eric. The Prince in the Heather. Harcourt, Brace and World, 1965. Ill. by scenic
photographs by Don Kelly. A day-to-day account
of Prince Charlie's escape from the English in
August of 1746, based on journals and other contemporary sources, with a map. (A)

437. Noble, Iris. Master Surgeon, John Hunter. Julian
Messner, 1971. Jacket by Don Lambo. A biography of the Scottish surgeon, (1728-93) who rose
from obscurity to become one of Britain's most
distinguished physicians and scientists. Of particular interest today, almost 200 years after his
death, is the account of his demonstrations of the
relationship between all creatures and their de-
pendence on environment--what we now call ecology.
(YA)

438. Scott, Sir Walter. Waverley. 1814. This first of
Scott's historical novels is about the return of
Prince Charles Edward in 1745 and the effect it

had on various classes of Englishmen and Scots.
(A)

439. Stevenson, Robert Louis. Kidnapped. 1886. The
story of orphaned David Balfour whose own uncle
had him "trepanned" on a brig bound for Carolina
to be sold as a laborer on the plantations. (YA)

440. _____. David Balfour. 1892. A sequel to "Kidnapped." (YA)

441. Vinton, Iris. The Story of John Paul Jones. Grosset,
1953. Ill. by Edward A. Wilson. A brief biography of the young Scot who became an American
hero, ending with the British surrender at York-
town. (I)

442. Watson, Sally. The Hornet's Nest. Holt, Rinehart
and Winston, 1968. The first chapters of the book
deal with events on the Isle of Skye where the Scots
were being very harshly treated by the British after the 1745 uprising. The last half takes place
in Williamsburg, Virginia, in 1775. (I and YA)

443. _____. Highland Rebel. Holt, 1954. Ill. by Scott
Maclean. A story of clan warfare in Scotland between the Camerons and the Campbells and of
Prince Charlie's escape in 1745. With a review
of Stuart history and a note identifying historical
characters. (I)

444. Whitney, Phyllis A. Mystery on the Isle of Skye.
Westminster Press, 1955. Ill. by Ezra Jack
Keats. An ingenious grandmother sets a series
of mysteries for her 12-year-old granddaughter to
solve when she visits the homeland of her MacLeod
ancestors. (I)

NINETEENTH CENTURY

A. Pre-Victoria

This section covers the events of the century before
Victoria became queen in 1837. There were threats of an
invasion by the French under Napoleon and the Napoleonic
Wars with their sea battles, and the Regency of George III's
son (later George IV) during the King's periods of madness.

445. Barker, Shirley. Corner of the Moon. Crown, 1961.
A novel of witchcraft and invasion threats on the
Romney Marshes in 1804. (A)

446. Bentley, Phyllis. <u>Oath of Silence</u>. Doubleday, 1967.
      Ill. by Burt Silverman. A novel about the Luddite
      uprising in 1812 against the use of machinery in the
      Yorkshire mills. The beginning of labor resistance.
      (YA)
447. Beyer, Audrey White. <u>The Sapphire Pendant</u>. Knopf,
      1961. Ill. by Robin Jacques. A novel of espionage
      and romance during the period of the Napoleonic
      wars. (YA)
448. Brink, Carol Pyrie. <u>Lad With a Whistle</u>. Macmillan,
      1941. Ill. by Robert Ball. A delightful mystery
      novel, set in Edinburgh in 1810 and slightly involv-
      ing Sir Walter Scott. (YA)
449. Burton, Hester. <u>Castors Away</u>. World, 1962. Ill.
      by Victor C. Ambrus. A story of medical and
      naval history, based on an actual event in 1805
      when a sailor was apparently restored to life 13
      hours after his death. (YA)
449a. Cookson, Catherine. <u>The Nipper</u>. Bobbs-Merrill,
      1970. Ill. by Tessa Jordan. The time: 1830;
      the place: Northumberland, where 16-year-old
      Sandy, his widowed mother, and his beloved pony,
      Nipper, are turned off their small farm, compell-
      ing both Sandy and Nipper into darkness and back-
      breaking labor of pitmining at a time when there
      is labor trouble. Some workers are for negotia-
      tion, but some are for violence. As Sandy makes
      a desperate effort to prevent an explosion, Nipper
      comes to the fore. (I and YA)
450. Cross, John Keir. <u>Blackadder</u>. Dutton, 1951. Ill.
      by Robin Jacques. An adventure story about smug-
      glers, spies and naval engagements in the days of
      Nelson and Trafalgar. (YA)
451. Delderfield, R. F. <u>Too Few for Drums</u>. Simon and
      Schuster, 1971. Jacket by Brian Fraud. A novel
      of blood and brutalities of men at war during
      the Napoleonic period, in which a 19-year-old Eng-
      lish ensign must lead his eight men to safety from
      behind the French lines. (YA)
452. Forester, C. S. <u>The Hornblower Series</u>. Little,
to   Brown. Listed in approximately the proper se-
461. quence: [452] Mr. <u>Midshipman Hornblower</u> (1950);
      [453] <u>Lieutenant Hornblower</u> (1952); [454] <u>Horn-</u>
      <u>blower and the Atropos</u> (1953); [455] <u>Captain Horn-</u>
      <u>blower (Beat to Quarters)</u> (1937); [456] <u>Flying Col-</u>
      <u>ours</u> (1939); [457] <u>Ship of the Line</u> (1942); [458]
      <u>Commodore Hornblower</u> (1945); [459] <u>Lord Horn-</u>

blower (1946); [460] Admiral Hornblower (1958);
[461] Hornblower and the Hotspur (1962). Naval
adventures during the Napoleonic era. See "The
Life and Times of Horatio Hornblower" by Parkinson, no. 478. (A)

462. Grice, Frederick. Aidan and the Strolling Players.
Duell, Sloan and Pearce, 1960. Ill. by William
Stobbs. A novel about a runaway boy who joins
up with a company of players and travels with them
through rural England in the early part of the century. Good nature descriptions and theater stuff.
(I and YA)

463. Griggs, G. P. Little, Brown. Selections from the
to   Hornblower novels in the Cadet edition. Vol. I
466.   [463] Hornblower Goes to Sea; Vol. II [464] Hornblower Takes Command; Vol. III [465] Hornblower
in Captivity; Vol. IV [466] Hornblower's Triumph.
All ill. by Geoffrey Whittam. (I and YA)

467. Heyer, Georgette. An Infamous Army. Dutton, 1937
and 1965. A novel set in Brussels before and at
the time of the Battle of Waterloo (1815) in which
the author has allowed the Duke of Wellington to
speak for himself "borrowing freely from the
twelve volumes of his dispatches." (A)

468. _____. A Civil Contract. Putnam, 1961. A period piece whose slight plot hangs on the Battle of
Waterloo. (A)

469. _____. Cousin Kate. Dutton, 1968 (Bantam paperback 1970). A typical Heyer Regency period piece
about a young woman threatened with marriage to
the insane son of a dominating mother. Either you
"go for" Georgette Heyer novels or you don't but
if you do, there are plenty of them and all good,
and many in paperback. (A)

470. Hyde, Lawrence. Captain Deadlock. Houghton Mifflin,
1968. Ill. by Charles Geer. A swashbuckling tale
of a young man who becomes embroiled with pirates,
highwaymen and smugglers and is finally captured
as a spy. From frying pans to fires. (YA)

471. Komroff, Manuel. The Battle of Waterloo, One Hundred Days of Destiny. Macmillan, 1964. Ill. by
photographs of paintings and engravings and special
maps by Harry Rosenbaum. An hour-by-hour account of the battle. (YA)

472. Laski, Marghanita. Jane Austen and Her World.
Viking, 1969. With 137 illustrations. For devotees
of Jane Austen's works, this book is almost as good

as a pilgrimage to those places in England which
provide the settings for her novels of the Regency
Period. (YA and A)

473.   Llewellyn, Richard. The Witch of Merthyn. Doubleday, 1954. A tale of smuggling in the time of
scarlet cape and red tricorne on the Welsh coast
during the Napoleonic period. (YA)

474.   Lobdell, Helen. Thread of Victory. McKay, 1963.
A story of conditions in England's cotton mills,
the reformers Robert Owen and Henry Hunt, and
the Peterloo Massacre in 1819. (YA)

475.   McKown, Robin. The Ordeal of Anne Devlin. Julian
Messner, 1963. A novel about a true heroine of
the Irish uprising in 1803 led by Robert Emmet,
and her long, dreadful imprisonment because she
would not betray him or others. (YA)

476.   Nelson, C. M. With Nelson at Trafalgar. Reilly and
Lee, 1961. Ill. by Douglas Relf and with four diagrams of the "Victory," the Battle of Trafalgar,
a ship's sail and mast structure. This good historical novel is mistitled for the big battle takes
up only the last chapter, and much more attention
is given to the Battle of the Nile and the rescue of
the King and Queen of Naples--all from the stand-
point of a young midshipman under Nelson. (YA)

477.   O'Connor, Patrick (Leonard Wibberley). The Society
of Foxes. Ives Washburn, 1954. Ill. by Clifford
N. Geary. A humorous spy story set in England
and France in the first year of the century. (YA)

478.   Parkinson, C. Northcote. The Life and Times of
Horatio Hornblower. Little, Brown, 1970. A
complete, full-length biography of the famous fictional military hero of the Hornblower series with
many gaps filled in. (A)

479.   Pope, Dudley. Ramage. Lippincott, 1965. This
great sea yarn and its sequel should properly go
into the eighteenth century but somehow they seem
to fit much better in the beginning of the nineteenth.
In this novel there is a naval trial brought about by
the rescue of some prominent Italians from the
French by an Englishman, aided by an American,
and some contact with Commodore Nelson. Map.
(A)

480.   _____. Drumbeat. Doubleday, 1968 (Pocket Books,
1970). A sequel to "Ramage" in which Ramage, as
captain of the smallest cutter of the British fleet,
does his bit to defeat the Spanish at the Battle of

Cape Vincent in 1796. (A)

481.   Southey, Robert. Life of Nelson. Houghton-Mifflin
       illus. ed., 1915. A good nautical biography (au-
       thor's dates: 1774-1843). (YA)

482.   Thackeray, William Makepeace. Vanity Fair, 1848.
       The main character, Becky Sharpe was the Scar-
       lett O'Hara of her day. Of historical interest par-
       ticularly because of the Battle of Waterloo. (A)

483.   Villiers, Alan. The Battle of Trafalgar. Macmillan,
       1965. Ill. with drawings, photographs, and dia-
       grams. The story of the one-day battle in 1805,
       written by a naval captain. (YA)

484.   Warner, Oliver. Nelson and the Age of Fighting Sail.
       American Heritage, 1963. A Horizon Caravel Book
       illustrated with paintings, drawings, letters and
       maps. (I and YA)

485.   Whipple, A. B. C. Hero of Trafalgar. Random,
       1963. Ill. by William Hoffmann. The story of
       Lord Nelson's life (1758-1805). (I)

                    B.   Victorian England

486.   Aiken, Joan. The Wolves of Willoughby Chase.
       Doubleday, 1962. Ill. by Pat Marriott and jacket
       by Edward Corey. A humorous Victorian melo-
       drama in which two small girls encounter human
       wolves as well as animals. (I and YA)

487.   Almedingen, E. M. Ellen. Straus, and Giroux, 1969.
       Jacket by Richard Cuffari. The fictionalized story
       of the author's grandmother, Ellen Southee, of her
       childhood and youth in a Jane Austen-ish setting in
       Kent near Canterbury, her wanderings about Europe
       with her charming but reckless father, and finally
       her marriage to one of the richest men in Russia.
       (YA)

488.   Avery, Gillian. Call of the Valley. Holt, Rinehart
       and Winston, 1966. Jacket by David K. Stone. A
       boy seeks his fortune in England only to find con-
       tentment in his own Welsh valley. (YA)

488a. _____. The Elephant War. Holt, Rinehart and
       Winston, 1971. Ill. by John Verney. The delight-
       fully humorous story of a purely fictitious reaction
       on the part of the people of Oxford to the sale of
       an elephant named Jumbo to Barnum's circus in
       America. Eleven-year-old Harriet takes up the
       cause of saving Jumbo for England. (I)

489. Bonnet, Theodore. The Mudlark. Doubleday, 1949.
A charming novel about a small waif who creates
a great commotion when he gets into Windsor Castle during the period of Queen Victoria's retire-
ment after her husband's death. The climax is a
speech by Disraeli which brought about some social
changes in England. (A)

490. Booth, Arthur. The True Story of Queen Victoria,
British Monarch. Childrens' Press (Chicago), 1964.
Ill. by Parviz Sadighian. A short biography. (I)

491. Brown, Roy. The Viaduct. Macmillan, 1967. Jacket
by Roger Hans. A past and present story in which
a boy of ten comes to identify himself with a lad
in his ancestry, who died at eleven, as he seeks
to find a treasure supposedly hidden away by that
lad's father, a pioneer engineer in railroading.
The plot revolves about an old viaduct in the dis-
trict of Deptford in southeast London and the first
engines that went across it. (I and YA)

492. Bull, Angela. The Friend With a Secret. Holt, Rinehart and Winston, 1965. Jacket by Ellen Raskin.
A 13-year-old girl still having her meals in the
nursery (1870) becomes involved in a dangerous
adventure through her "friend with a secret." (I
and YA)

493. _____ . Wayland's Keep. Holt, Rinehart and Winston, 1966. Jacket by Emily McCully. Some present day children try to unravel a mystery of the
1870s--how did Wayland get the money to purchase
the Keep? An old diary and some old letters help
in the solution. Good research and detective work
on the part of the children. (I and YA)

494. Burton, Hester. Time of Trial. World, 1963. Ill.
by Victor C. Ambrus. A novel about the earliest
beginning of socialism in England, brought about
because of the unspeakable slum conditions in London. (YA)

495. _____ . No Beat of Drums. World, 1966. Ill. by
Victor C. Ambrus. A novel about the effects of
the industrial revolution on farming folk, and about
how a young girl and her two brothers were deported to Van Dieman's Land after a slight mis-
demeanor in one case, a non-violent protest in
another, and rebellion in the third. (YA)

496. Crane, William D. The Man Who Transformed the
World, James Watt. Julian Messner, 1963. Jacket by Don Lambo. A lively inspiring story of the

inventor (1736-1819) of the steam engine which (for
better or for worse) introduced the industrial revolution. (YA)

497. Curtis, Rosemary A. Jennie, the Young Lady Churchill. Chilton, 1963. Ill. with photographs and
with a foreword by Sir Shane Leslie. The story
of Jennie Jerome Churchill, American born, concluding with the birth of her son, Winston, in 1874.
(YA)

498. Farmer, Lawrence. Master Surgeon: A Biography of
Joseph Lister. Harper, 1962. The story of the
founder of antiseptic surgery (1827-1912). (YA)

499. Fecher, Constance. Bright Star, A Portrait of Ellen
Terry. Farrar, Straus and Giroux, 1970. Ill.
with 23 photographs. An entrancing biography of
an entrancing woman (1847-1928) whose greatest
stage years were those associated with Sir Henry
Irving, and who was one of a theatrical family
still prominent in the theater world of today. (YA
and A)

500. Freeman, Barbara. Lucinda. Norton, 1965. Ill. by
the author. A 13-year-old girl, living with her
widowed mother in the manor house of a tightwad
and cruel uncle, breaks loose in a most surprising
and exciting way. (YA)

501. _____. The Name on the Glass. Norton, 1964.
Ill. by the author. A 12-year-old girl runs away
from a cruel cousin and finds new friends in the
London slums. (I)

502. Garfield, Leon. Black Jack. Pantheon, 1968. Ill.
by Anthony M. Maitland. A grim picaresque novel
about a gigantic ruffian who manages to survive
hanging, a gentle draper's apprentice, and a "poor
thing, " a young girl considered mad--and how their
relationship to each other changes each life. (YA)

503. Garnett, Emmeline. Tormented Angel: A Life of
John Henry Newman. Ariel, 1966. Biography of
the English churchman and author whose conversion
from Anglicanism to Roman Catholicism in 1845
caused a tremendous stir in England. (YA and A)

504. Glendinning, Sally. Queen Victoria, English Empress.
Garrard, 1970. Ill. with portraits. The life of
the British queen who ruled over the Empire at its
time of greatest extent and power, and whose name
describes an age of great industrial and social
change. (I and YA)

504a. Grant, Neil. Victoria, Queen and Empress. Watts,

1970. Ill. with prints, portraits, and genealogical chart. The story of Victoria and England during her reign, 1837-1901. (YA)

505. Greene, Carla. Charles Darwin (1809-82). Dial Press, 1968. Ill. by David Hodges. A biography of the author of "Origin of the Species" (which caused repercussions way into the twentieth century) and especially the story of his voyage on the "Beagle." (I)

506. Goudge, Elizabeth. The Dean's Watch. Coward Mc-Cann, 1960. Ill. by A. R. Whitear. A gentle novel about gentle people in the fen country of England in 1870, with some historical review. (A)

507. _____. The Little White Horse. Coward McCann, 1946. Ill. by C. Walter Hodges. A fantasy set in the west country of England, recommended for nature-poetry lovers. (I)

508. Gregor, Arthur S. Charles Darwin. Dutton, 1966. Ill. with photographs and drawings. A well organized biography in three parts: 1) voyage (of the "Beagle"), 2) discovery (of the origin of the species and theory of evolution) and 3) homecoming. A glossary of scientific terms, a Darwin calendar, and bibliography. (YA)

509. Hadfield, Alice Mary. Williver's Quest. Bobbs-Merrill, 1965. A story of violence, with relieving touches of humor, about the industrial revolution in 1818 and a young man's perilous investigations at a Welsh ironworks. (YA)

510. Hardy, Thomas. The Mayor of Casterbridge. 1886. Washington Square Press paperback, 1956, with an introduction by Albert J. Guerard. A typically (for Hardy) sorrowful novel about a man who sold his wife and suffered great retribution even after his efforts to atone for his sin. (A)

511. Haugaard, Erik Christian. Orphans of the Wind. Houghton-Mifflin, 1966. Ill. by Milton Johnson. The hazardous adventures of a 12-year-old English deckhand on a ship carrying guns to the Confederacy during the Civil War in America. (YA)

512. Haycraft, Molly Costain. Queen Victoria. Messner, 1956. A short biography (1819-1901) with a genealogical chart. (I)

513. Hodges, C. Walter. The Overland Launch. Coward, 1969. Ill. by the author. A true story of a terrible storm in the Bristol Channel and on the Dev-

onshire Coast, January 12, 1899, in which a life-
boat had to be hauled over hill and dale and through
a narrow street in Porlock, for 13 miles. The
names of real people are altered and there are one
or two wholly fictional ones, but there is humor as
well as wild struggle in the story. (YA)

514.   Horne, Richard Henry. Memoirs of a London Doll,
1846. Macmillan, 1967, with an introduction and
notes by Margery Fisher. Ill. by Margaret Gillies
and Richard Shirley Smith. To be read by little
girls as a delightful doll story and by their mothers
as a Victorian antique. The children may skip the
introduction. (I)

515.   Hume, Ruth Fox. Florence Nightingale. Random,
1960. Ill. by Robert Frankenberg. A Landmark
biography of "the lady with lamp, " (1820-1910). (I)

516.   Hunter, Mollie (McIlwraith). A Pistol in Greenyards.
Funk and Wagnalls, 1965. A realistic, grim and
skilfully plotted novel about the eviction of tenants
on small farms in a Highland glen, and the threat
of hanging for a 15-year-old boy. (YA)

517.   Karp, Walter [and the editors of Horizon Magazine]
Charles Darwin and the Origin of the Species (consultant, Dr. J. W. Burrow). Harper and Row,
1968. Ill. with drawings, scientific diagrams,
photographs, paintings, etc. A biography of Darwin (1809-82). (YA)

517a. Komroff, Manuel. Disraeli. Messner, 1963. A biography of one of Queen Victoria's most illustrious
prime ministers in 1868 and again from 1874 to
1880. (YA)

518.   Larson, Jean Russell. Jack Tar. Macrae-Smith,
1970. Ill. by Mercer Mayor. A tall tale about
the adventures of a sailor in Queen Victoria's navy
who is discharged for serving salt in the captain's
tea. (I)

519.   Leighton, Margaret. The Story of Florence Nightingale.
Grosset, 1962. Ill. by Corinne Boyd Dillon. A
biography of interest to boys as well as girls because of its story of the Crimean War (1853-56).
(I)

520.   McLean, Allan Campbell. Ribbon of Fire. Harcourt,
1962. A tense novel about the fight of the "crofters" on the Isle of Skye, in the late nineteenth
century, against the encroachments of their ab-
sentee landlords. (YA)

520a.   _____. A Sound of Trumpets. Harcourt, 1966.

A sequel to "Ribbon of Fire" about the crofters on
the Isle of Skye. (YA)

521. Malone, Mary. Actor in Exile: The Life of Ira Aldridge. Crowell-Collier, 1969. Ill. by Eros
Keith. Often called, "the greatest Othello of them
all, " Aldridge, born a free Negro in New York in
1807, felt it necessary to go to England at the age
of 17 to study for the stage. There, and on the
Continent, he became a famous actor of white as
well as black roles and died there in 1867, never
having been recognized in the country of his birth.
(YA and A)

522. Manton, Jo. Elizabeth Garrett, M.D. Abelard Schu-
man, 1960. Inspired by the American Dr. Black-
well, Elizabeth Garrett became the first woman
medical student in England's history and succeeded
in opening the medical profession to women there.
(YA)

523. Meynell, Lawrence [Tring, Stephen A.]. Bridge Under
the Water. Roy, n.d. Ill. by J. S. Goodall.
About the Thames Tunnel.   (I)

524. Miller, Mabel. Michael Faraday and the Dynamo.
Thomas Nelson, 1968. Jacket by Harry Eaby.
Inspiring, instructive and exceedingly readable biography of the great physicist and chemist (1791-
1867) who, though poor and with little education,
rose, through his dedication to the science of elec-
tricity, to become a Fellow of the Royal Society.
(YA)

525. Moorehead, Alan. Darwin and the Beagle. Harper
and Row, 1969. Richly illustrated. The story of
Darwin's five-year voyage as the naturalist on
board H. M. S. Beagle, during which he made ob-
servations resulting in his book, "The Origin of
the Species" (1859). Entertainingly written and
richly illustrated, it is a book for all ages but usually placed in the adult section. (All Ages)

526. Noble, Iris. The Courage of Dr. Lister. Messner,
1960. Biography of the founder of antiseptic surgery (1827-1912). (YA)

527. Olivant, Alfred. Bob, Son of Battle. Doubleday, 1898.
A murder mystery in Scottish dialect (but reason-
ably understandable) set in the northernmost corner
of England and involving sheep and dogs. (YA)

528. Peyton, K. M. The Maplin Bird. World, 1965. Ill.
by Victor C. Ambrus. Smuggling on the Essex
coast, with good nautical detail and a most unusual
ending. (YA)

529. Riedman, Sarah R.   Charles Darwin.   Holt, 1959.
      Maps. Biography (1809-82). (YA)
530. Rolt, L. T. C.   The Story of Brunel.   Abelard-Schu-
      man, 1968. Ill. by Paul Sharp. A good story for
      young people of either sex interested in an engineer-
      ing career, of a young man who at nineteen was in
      charge under his father of the building of the Thames
      Tunnel (twice flooded while he was in it) and who
      later was noted for the building of railroads,
      bridges and steamships and the designing of a pre-
      fabricated hospital during the Crimean War (1806-
      59). (I and YA)
531. Streatfield, Noel.   Queen Victoria.   Random Landmark,
      1958. Ill. by Robert Frankenberg. A biography of
      the woman who was crowned Queen of England at
      age eighteen (1837) and ruled until her death in
      1901. (I)
531a. Tennyson, Alfred.   The Charge of the Light Brigade.
      Golden Press, 1964. Ill. by Alice and Martin
      Provensen. A picture book of the famous poem
      about the "death charge of the 600" at Balaclava
      in the Crimea, September 20, 1854. (E and I)
532. Thirkell, Angela.   Coronation Summer.   Knopf, 1953.
      A novel about the coronation of Queen Victoria, in
      the form of reminiscences of a young lady who at-
      tended the ceremony. (A)
533. Webb, Robert N.   We Were There with Florence
      Nightingale in the Crimea.   Grosset and Dunlap,
      1958. Ill. by Evelyn Copelman. A story largely
      about the Crimean War, 1853-56, between Great
      Britain, Turkey, France and Sardinia on one side,
      and Russia on the other. (I)
534. Wibberley, Leonard.   Kevin O'Connor and the Light
      Brigade.   Farrar, Straus and Cudahy, 1957. A
      humorous blend of fact and fiction about the Cri-
      mean War (1853-56). Part of the title recalls
      Tennyson's famous poem, "The Charge of the Light
      Brigade." (YA)
535. Willard, Barbara.   Hetty.   Harcourt, Brace and World,
      1962. Ill. by Michael Hampshire. The story of
      the young daughter of a merchant in the late nine-
      teenth century when it was not "the thing" to be
      "in trade." (I)
536. _____.   The Richleighs of Tantamount.   Harcourt,
      Brace and World, 1966. Ill. by C. Walter Hodges.
      A mystery, with rising suspense, about four chil-
      dren finding themselves left alone in a spooky, tur-

reted castle in Cornwall. (I)
537. Wise, Winifred. Fanny Kemble, Actress, Author and
     Abolitionist. G. P. Putnam's Sons, 1966. Ill.
     with a portrait by Sully. A biography of a many-
     sided woman (1809-93) who gave up a successful
     stage career and acceptance by London society to
     marry a rich American plantation owner, Pierce
     Butler, and go to live under distressing conditions
     on his Georgia Island plantations. Her "Journal of
     a Residence on a Georgia Plantation" was a strong
     influence against England's supporting the Confeder-
     acy in the American Civil War. (YA)
538. Woodham-Smith, Cecil. Lonely Crusader: The Life
     of Florence Nightingale. McGraw, 1951. An
     abridged edition of the same author's definitive bi-
     ography of the woman (1820-1910) who revolution-
     ized the nursing profession, based on private papers
     made public shortly before the original book was
     written. (YA)

NINETEENTH AND TWENTIETH CENTURY WRITERS

539. Aldis, Dorothy. Nothing is Impossible: The Story of
     Beatrix Potter. Atheneum, 1969. Ill. by Richard
     Cuffari. The story of the secluded but productive
     life of the author and illustrator (1866-1943) of
     "Peter Rabbit" and 31 other such little books which
     have delighted children for so many years. In-
     cludes a list of those books valuable for collectors.
     (I)
540. Becker, May Lamberton. Presenting Miss Jane Austen.
     Dodd, Mead, 1952. Jane Austen's world was really
     that of the eighteenth century, but her novels be-
     came classics in the nineteenth and continue to be.
     This biography (1775-1817) is based on those nov-
     els. (YA)
541. Benet, Laura. The Boy Shelley. Dodd, Mead, 1937
     and 1961. Ill. by James MacDonald. What a boy
     he was! If he'd lived in the 1970s he'd surely
     have been taken into custody for his dangerous ex-
     periments and pranks (a bullfrog inside the teach-
     er's desk was a fairly minor one) and given psy-
     chiatric care. This biographical novel of the young
     rebel (1792-1822) takes him from his early child-
     hood through his first schooldays and even up to the
     time when he was 18, as he was starting at Oxford.
     (YA)

542.   Bentley, Phyllis. The Brontës and Their World.
       Viking, 1969. A Studio Book with 140 illustrations.
       Fond readers of "Jane Eyre" and "Wuthering
       Heights" will be conducted by this book into the
       Yorkshire country and visit the Brontë's Parsonage
       and the Haworth Moor. (YA and A)

542a. _____. The Young Brontës. Roy, 1960. Ill. by
       Marie Nartley. About the childhood of all the
       Brontës with a last sad chapter about their later
       years. (I)

543.   Brown, Ivor. Jane Austen and Her World. Walck,
       1966. Ill. by photographs which bring to life the
       scenes of her novels. (YA)

544.   Burnett, Constance Buel. The Silver Answer: A
       Romantic Biography of Elizabeth Barrett Browning
       [1806-1861]. Knopf, 1955. Ill. by Susan Foster.
       (YA)

545.   Coolidge, Olivia. George Bernard Shaw. Houghton-
       Mifflin, 1968. Ill. with photographs. A biography
       of the brilliant, eccentric, long-lived playwright
       (1856-1950) who only found his true line in middle
       age, with a list of his plays and three recordings.
       Also the story of socialism in England and the Fa-
       bian Society. (YA)

546.   Daugherty, James. William Blake [1757-1827]. Viking,
       1960. Ill. with drawings by Blake. A special book
       for special readers who enjoy a sense of the super-
       natural and mystic in art and poetry. At the end
       are 21 drawings for the Book of Job with interpre-
       tations by Mr. Daugherty. (YA and A)

547.   Gerin, Winifred. The Young Fanny Burney. Nelson,
       1961. A biographical novel of a writer more eigh-
       teenth century than nineteenth in many ways (1752-
       1840), especially in being a member of Dr. John-
       son's circle. (YA)

548.   Gould, Jean. Young Thack. Houghton-Mifflin, 1949.
       Ill. with Thackeray's original sketches. Most of
       us probably have not been aware of William Make-
       peace Thackeray as an artist, or caricaturist, but
       this biography, with its illustrations, shows his tal-
       ents in that direction. The emphasis is on his
       schooldays and college life and unenthusiastic study of
       law, but the book does not cover his whole life (1811-
       63). (A)

549.   Graham, Eleanor. The Story of Charles Dickens [1812-
       70]. Abelard-Schuman, 1954. Ill. with plates from
       the original editions of his works and additional

drawings by Norman Meredith. (YA)

550. Hoehling, Mary. The Real Sherlock Holmes. Messner, 1965. A biography of A. Conan Doyle (1859-1930) with lists of books by and about him. (YA)

551. Howard, Joan (Patricia Gordon). The Story of Robert Louis Stevenson. Grosset, 1958. Ill. by Jo Polseno. A biography stressing his youthful years with a pictorial chronology of the great events in his life. He was born in Edinburgh in 1850 and died in Samoa, 1894. (I)

552. Kyle, Elizabeth (Agnes Mary Robertson Dunlop). Girl With a Pen: Charlotte Brontë. Holt, Rinehart and Winston, 1964. The story of her life (1816-55) from the age of 17 to 32, with an afterword about the later years. (YA)

553. _____. Great Ambitions: A Story of the Early Years of Charles Dickens. Holt, Rinehart and Winston, 1966. Jacket by Fritz Kredel. A biographical novel showing many of the sources from which Dickens drew his characters and plots inspiring one to read or reread his novels. (I and YA)

554. Manley, Seon. Rudyard Kipling, Creative Adventurer. Vanguard, 1965. The story of a life (1865-1936) almost equally divided between two centuries and spent in many countries--England, India, the U.S.A., and the South Sea Island where he died. (YA)

555. Newcomb, Covelle. The Secret Door, The Story of Kate Greenaway. Dodd, Mead, 1946. Ill. with drawings after Kate Greenaway by Addison Burbank. Although she was an illustrator rather than a writer, she belongs in the company of writers because of her reciprocated devotion to Ruskin. (YA and A)

556. Peare, Catherine Owens. Charles Dickens, His Life. Henry Holt, 1959. Ill. by Douglas Gorsline. A simply told biography with especial attention to his works. (I)

557. Schultz, Pearle Henriksen. Sir Walter Scott: Wizard of the North. Vanguard, 1967. A biography full of the color of Scotland, Scott's sense of adventure, his high courage and love of his native land. (YA)

558. Sprague, Rosemary. Forever in Joy: The Life of Robert Browning. Chilton Books, 1965. In this biography of the poet (1812-89) and a study of his (often difficult) poetry and his period, there is also the story of the development of the Italian states

into a united nation, for Browning and his wife
(Elizabeth Barrett) lived most of their married life
in Italy during the tempestuous times of Mazzini,
Garibaldi and Cavour. (YA and A)

559.   Trease, Geoffrey. Byron, A Poet Dangerous to Know.
Holt, Rinehart and Winston, 1969. Jacket by Riki
Levinson and photographs of paintings. A comprehensive biography of the romantic poet who "woke
one morning to find himself famous," based on his
letters and journals and emphasizing the relationship between his poetry and his life. (YA)

560.   Vipont, Elfrida. Towards a High Attic: The Early
Life of George Eliot, 1819-1880. Holt, Rinehart
and Winston, 1970. Ill. with contemporary drawings and an eight-page photo insert. Jacket by
Tom Upshur. A biography of Mary Anne Evans
Cross, the brilliant novelist, who lived at a time
when women took masculine names in order to get
published. (YA and A)

561.   Waite, Helen E. How Do I Love Thee? The Story of
Elizabeth Barrett Browning, for Teen-Age Girls.
A true love story. Macrae-Smith, 1953.

562.   White, Hilda. Wild Decembers, A Biographical Portrait of the Brontë Family. Dutton, 1957. A novel
based largely on Mrs. Gaskell's "Life of Charlotte
Brontë." (A)

563.   Wilkie, Katherine. Charles Dickens, The Inimitable
Boz. Abelard, 1970. (YA)

564.   Wood, James Playsted. The Snark Was a Boojum: A
Life of Lewis Carroll. Pantheon, 1966. Ill. by
David Levine. A biography of the author of "Alice
in Wonderland," "Through the Looking Glass," etc.
whose real name was Charles Lutwidge Dodgson
(1832-98). (YA and A)

565.   _____. The Man Who Hated Sherlock Holmes, A
Life of Sir Arthur Conan Doyle. Pantheon, 1965.
Ill. by Richard M. Powers. The story of an eye
doctor, writer, athlete, war correspondent and
spiritualist (1859-1930). (YA)

566.   _____. The Lantern Bearer, A Life of Robert
Louis Stevenson. Pantheon, 1965. Ill. by Saul
Lambert. A biography with chronology of the main
events of his life (1850-94). (YA)

567.   _____. I Told You So: A Life of H. G. Wells.
Pantheon, 1969. Ill. with photographs. A lively
biography (1866-1946) of an extremely lively author,
historian, prophet and originator of science fiction

in English (Jules Verne being French), with reviews of his books. (YA and A)

TWENTIETH CENTURY

A. Through World War I and Its Aftermath

568. Blassingame, Wyatt. Baden-Powell, Chief Scout of
      the World. Garrard, 1966. Ill. by Gray Morrow.
      His full name was Robert Stephenson Smyth Baden-
      Powell (1857-1941), but he was usually and under-
      standably called B-P. A military hero in the Boer
      War, in 1908 he founded the Boy Scouts. (E and I)
569. Church, Richard. The White Doe. John Day, 1968.
      Ill. by John Ward. A somewhat mystical story of
      a woodsman son's feeling for the world of nature
      and particularly for a white doe which he only rare-
      ly glimpses, in contrast with his feelings for the
      "people" world where the caste system in the early
      twentieth century threatens his friendship with the
      son of a squire and where he encounters human
      cruelty. Growing suspense and vivid nature detail.
      (I and YA)
570. Dillon, Eilis. The Seals. Funk and Wagnalls, 1968.
      Ill. by Richard Kennedy. Three boys sail from
      their island to the mainland near Galway to rescue
      the uncle of one who has been caught by the Black
      and Tans in the "troubles" in 1920. Suspenseful
      plot, excellent characterizations and fine Irish fla-
      vor. (I and YA)
571. _____. The Sea Wall. Farrar, Straus and Giroux,
      1965. Ill. by W. T. Mars. A short novel about
      the reluctance of Irish islanders to let a Galway
      engineer strengthen their sea wall even when they
      have experienced two disasters from deluging
      waves, and about a young boy's difficult act of
      diplomacy. (I and YA)
572. Elkon, Juliette. Edith Cavell, Heroic Nurse. Mess-
      ner, 1966. Biography of the English nurse (1865-
      1915) executed as a spy by the Germans in Bel-
      gium. (YA)
573. Fairfax-Lucy, Brian, and Philippa Pearce. The Chil-
      dren of the House. Lippincott, 1968. Ill. by
      John Sergeant. A sensitive story of a family of
      children living in penury in a great Edwardian

house until World War I saved them from their
isolation.   (I)

574. Grey, Elizabeth. Friend Within the Gates, The Story
of Nurse Edith Cavell. Houghton-Mifflin, 1961.
Dell Yearling Paperback. A biographical novel
about the English nurse (1865-1915) executed in
Belgium by the Germans during World War I.   (YA)

575. _____ . Winged Victory, The Story of Amy Johnson.
Houghton-Mifflin, 1960. A biography of the English
counterpart of American Amelia Earhart and a
thrilling story about the early days of record-
breaking flights and the hazards of flying in the
late twenties and early thirties.   (YA)

576. Kamm, Josephine. Emmeline Pankhurst. Meredith
Press, 1961. Ill. with photographs. The story of
the militant leader of the womens' suffrage movement in England, who stopped at nothing in the way
of violence and suffering on her own part and that
of her followers in her crusade for votes for wom-
en.   (YA)

577. Lavine, Sigmund A. Evangeline Booth, Daughter of
Salvation. Dodd, Mead, 1970. Ill. with photographs and jacket by Thomas Upshur. Most of
this remarkable woman's life was spent in America, but she was born and brought up in England,
the daughter of General William Booth who established the Salvation Army in 1878. This book is
an interesting story of that organization as inspired, fostered and led by three members of the
Booth family: the father, William, and the brother
and sister, Bramwell and Evangeline (1865-1950).
(YA)

578. McLean, Allan Campbell. Storm Over Skye. Harcourt, Brace, 1956. Ill. by Shirley Hughes. A
good Scottish whodunit--sheep stealing and murder--
with a glossary of Gaelic words, a list of characters, and a chart of the scene.   (YA)

579. Peyton, K. M. Flambards. World, 1967. Ill. by
Victor Ambrus. A novel of Edwardian times with
strong characterizations and plot, and interesting
material about fox hunting, very early flying, and
the conflict between the old and the new. In the
main, rather dour.   (YA)

580. _____ . The Edge of the Cloud. World, 1969. Ill.
by Victor G. Ambrus. The core of this sequel to
"Flambards" is Will's single-minded and success-
ful drive to design and fly planes, Christina's de-

votion to Will and fear of flying, and the hazards and tragedies of stunt flying. The time is shortly before World War I. (YA)

581. _____. Flambards in Summer. World, 1969. Ill. by Victor G. Ambrus. The third in a trilogy about the Russells, following "The Edge of the Cloud" in which Christina Russell, now a 21-year-old widow, tries to rebuild Flambards with very little help as most able-bodied men are away at war in 1916. (YA)

582. _____. Thunder in the Sky. World, 1966. Ill. by Victor G. Ambrus. A strong tense novel of World War I about three brothers, told from the viewpoint of the youngest who, still under the age for enlistment, becomes mate on a barge carrying ammunition to Calais, and is torn by conflicting fraternal and patriotic loyalties. (YA)

583. Pumphrey, George. Grenfell of Labrador. Dodd, Mead, 1959. Ill. with photographs. The exciting story of the brave medical missionary (1865-1940) to the Eskimos of Labrador. (YA)

584. Robbins, Ian. Tuesday 4 August, 1914. David White, 1970. Ill. by the author. The story of what took place on the first day of World War I, based on material from memoirs, letters, newspapers, Admiralty and War Office records. (I and YA)

585. Rowland, John. The Rolls-Royce Men. Roy, 1970. Ill. with drawings. A dual biography of two men with entirely different backgrounds, who pooled their talents to produce one of the world's greatest test cars. Also included is the story of early automobile races and the company's production of airplane engines during World War II. (YA)

586. Streatfield, Noel. Thursday's Child. Random, 1971. Ill. by Peggy Fortnum. A light novel of the turn of the century, about a spirited orphan who "was found ... in a basket on the church steps with three of everything of the very best quality." A drab orphanage and a cruel matron drive her to devise an escape plan with two boys, and they have adventure aplenty in eluding pursuit. (I and YA)

587. Vaughan-Jackson, Genevieve. Carramore. Hastings House, 1968. Ill. by the author. A story of 11-year-old twins on a farm in Ireland during the "troubles" of 1922. (I)

B.   World War II--Before, During, and After

588.   Armstrong, Richard.   Ship Afire.   John Day, 1959.
       A gripping sea story of World War II, about U-
       boats and escape from a burning ship.   (YA)
589.   Burton, Hester.   In Spite of All Terror.   World, 1969.
       Ill. by Victor G. Ambrus.   A novel about a 15-
       year-old girl, an orphan unhappily evacuated to a
       small village in Oxfordshire at the beginning of
       World War II where she is lodged with a family
       who had expressly asked for a boy rather than a
       girl.   However, her experiences in connection with
       the Miracle of Dunkirk and the Battle of Britain,
       when she is 16, convince her that "it is a good
       time to live in spite of all terror."   (YA)
589a. Cooper, Susan.   Dawn of Fear.   Harcourt, 1971.   Ill.
       by Margery Gill.   Young schoolboys, living in a
       London suburb during the early 1940s, at first find
       the war more exciting than frightening until the
       bombs come too close.   (I)
590.   Crawford, Marian.   The Little Princesses.   Curtis,
       1950.   Ill. with photographs.   The story of Queen
       Elizabeth II's childhood (born 1926) and that of her
       younger sister, Margaret Rose, as told by their
       childhood governess.   (I and YA)
591.   Hamilton, Ian R.   No Stone Unturned.   Funk and Wag-
       nalls, 1952.   The true story of the theft of the
       Stone of Scone from Westminster Abbey in 1950
       as related by one of the thieves.   (A)
592.   MacLean, Alistair.   H. M. S. Ulysses.   Doubleday,
       1956.   A novel about the Murmansk Run in 1942,
       with a map and detailed drawings of the light cruis-
       er.   (A)
593.   Prince, Alison.   The House on the Common.   Farrar,
       Straus and Giroux, 1970.   Ill. by W. T. Mars.   A
       charming little story of two small English children
       believing they have discovered some German spies
       in a house on the common, and endeavoring to
       prove that they are right, during the Blitz of Sep-
       tember, 1943.   A story of suspicion and courage.
       (I)
594.   Reynolds, Quentin.   The Battle of Britain.   Random
       Landmark, 1953.   Ill. with photographs.   The sto-
       ry of "England's Finest Hour."   (I)
595.   _____.   Winston Churchill.   Random Landmark,
       1963.   Ill. with photographs.   A biography of the
       man (1874-1964) who is certain to live in history

for his deeds, his writings, (including his speeches),
and especially for his leadership when England
stood alone.   (I)

596.   Walsh, Jill Paton.   The Dolphin Crossing.   Macmillan,
1967.   Jacket by Gareth Floyd.   A story of the
Dunkirk evacuation and the part played by two teen-
agers in the rescue operations.   (YA)

597.   _____.   Fireweed.   Ariel, Farrar, Straus and
Giroux, 1971.   Jacket by Ron Bowen.   A haunting,
impressive novel about two teen-age wanderers in
London, both escaping from "evacuation" to the
country, and about what it was like to be homeless
and 15 in the thick of the London blitz of 1940.
(YA)

598.   Wibberley, Leonard.   The Life of Winston Churchill.
Ariel, 1956.   Ill. with photographs.   Winston
Churchill (1874-1965) still had almost another decade of life after this book was published, but his
most active years were over and he took to painting as a hobby.   (I)

599.   _____.   The Hands of Cormack Joyce.   Putnam,
1960.   Ill. by Richard Bennet.   A short novel
about a great storm on the islands of the County
Galway coast, and how the people there withstood
it.   (I)

C.   "Now and Then"--Adventures in Time

600.   Andrews, J. S.   The Green Hill of Nendrum.   Hawthorne Books, 1970.   Jacket by Charles Water-
house.   This wierd, wild story of a 15-year-old
modern-day lad who sails his 12-foot dinghy out
through the islands of Strangford Lough in northern
Ireland to the monastery of Aendrum (as it was
called in the tenth century) is based on archaeological digs.   A map makes his adventures great to
follow, and the ruins of Nendrum as it is now
called) are still there and some of the artifacts in
the story still to be seen in the museum of Belfast.
(YA)

601.   Clewes, Dorothy.   Mystery of the Lost Tower Treasure.   Coward-McCann, 1960.   Ill. by Marianne J.
Moll.   We have sneaked this good detective story,
set in the mid-twentieth century, into our historical
fiction lists because anything connected with the
Tower of London can't avoid historical references,

and particularly because of the diagrams of the
many towers within the historic walls. (I and YA)

602.   Farmer, Penelope. Charlotte Sometimes. Harcourt,
       Brace and World, 1969. Ill. by Chris Connor. A
       fantasy about a schoolgirl who suddenly finds her-
       self changing places with a schoolgirl of 50 years
       earlier. She alternates from 1968 to 1918, day in,
       day out, for a while but finally feels trapped in the
       world of the first World War and determines to es-
       cape back to 1968. Good suspense. (YA)

603.   Hall, Aylmer. The Search for Lancelot's Sword.
       Criterion, 1962. Jacket by Simon Jeruchim. An
       excellent mystery novel, set in contemporary Wales,
       about some teen-agers and their endeavor to find a
       treasure which they believe to be concealed some-
       where in the crumbling towers on the grounds of
       the castle in which they live. They find clues in
       old books, legends and gravestone carvings and
       meet with many dangers before their mystery is
       solved. (YA)

604.   Hunter, Mollie (McIlwraith). The Walking Stones.
       Harper and Row, 1970. Ill. by Trina Schart Hy-
       man. A suspense story about a prehistoric ring
       of stones (like Stonehenge but not so large) and a
       boy who inherits "second sight" from an aged man
       who reveals to him the secret of the walking stones.
       Old Celtic lore in the modern setting of the build-
       ing of a dam. (YA)

605.   Lively, Penelope. Astercote. Dutton, 1970. Jacket
       by Emily McCully. A combination of suspense,
       adventure and fantasy involving a brother and sis-
       ter and the superstition of villagers nearby who
       believe that because of the disappearance of their
       talisman, the chalice from the church in Astercote,
       their village will be visited by the Black Death as
       it was in the fourteenth century. (YA)

606.   Mayne, William. Earthfasts. Dutton, 1966. So fan-
       tastic a mixture of past and present, the real and
       the imaginary that it is hard to place, but for
       those who enjoy poetic fantasy it is certainly the
       ticket. (YA)

607.   Turner, Philip. Colonel Sheperton's Clock. World,
       1964. Ill. by Philip Gough. The mystery of
       Colonel Sheperton's death is finally solved by
       three young choir boys in a small town church-
       yard 50 years later. Very very English. (I)

608.   _____ . The Grange at High Force. World, 1965.

Ill. by W. T. Mars.   Another mystery to be
solved by the three boys of "Colonel Sheperton's
Clock" involving a statue hidden away in the eighteenth century.   (I)

609.   _____. Steam on the Line.   World, 1968.   Ill. by
Gareth Floyd.   Again the main characters are three
modern-day boys, but the story is of early rail-
road building in England and the bitter opposition
to it in the time of the boys' grandfather and the
Industrial Revolution.   (I and YA)

PART II: CENTRAL EUROPE
(Germany, Austria, Hungary, Czechoslovakia)

MYTHS, LEGENDS AND FOLKLORE

610. Almedingen, E. M. The Treasure of Siegfried. Lippincott, 1964. Ill. by Charles Keeping. A story
based on the Niebelungenlied, now best known
through Richard Wagner's operas of the Ring cycle.
(YA)

611. Baldwin, James. The Story of Siegfried. Scribner,
1931. Ill. by Peter Hurd. A medley of northern
myths and sagas, woven into a consecutive story.
(YA)

612. Clarke, Mollie. The Three Feathers. Follett, 1963.
Ill. by Graham Oakley. Not much of a story but
such colorful illustrations that it is a joy to read.
(E)

613. Domjan, Joseph. Hungarian Heroes and Legends.
Van Nostrand, 1963. A book with exceptionally
interesting art work. (All Ages)

614. Orgel, Doris. Baron Munchhausen, His Truly Tall
Tales. Addison-Wesley, 1971. Selected and illustrated by Willi Baum. The first version of
these extravagant lies by Raspe and others, was
published in England in 1785 when Raspe sought
refuge there from imprisonment in Hanover, Germany for gambling debts and thievery. Though he
defies you to call him a liar, his tales are truly
tall and so are the illustrations in this delightful
book. (E and I)

615. Picard, Barbara Leonie. German Hero-Sagas and
Folk Tales. Walck, 1958. Ill. by Joan Kiddell-
Monroe. (I and YA)

616. Sawyer, Ruth and Molles, Emmy. Dietrich of Berne
and the Dwarf King, Laurin. Hero Tales of the
Austrian Tyrol Retold. Viking, 1963. Ill. by
Frederick T. Chapman. Legends about the historic figure of Theodoric the Great (474-526). (I)

617. Seredy, Kate. The White Stag. Viking, 1937. Ill.
by the author. A combination of legend and his-

86

tory leading up to the establishment of Attila the
Hun. (I)

618. Siskin, Stephen. The Stone in the Road. Van Nostrand, 1968. Ill. by Ursula Arndt. A short story
of a poor town and a good baron. (E)

FIFTH CENTURY A.D.

619. Gardonyi, Geza. Slave of the Huns. Bobbs-Merrill,
1969. First published in Hungary in 1901, translated by Andrew Feldmar. Foreword and illustrations by Victor G. Ambrus. An historical romance
of Attila's sweeping drive from Eastern Europe to
Gaul in the middle of the fifth century, and of a
young slave attached to Attila's army by his own
choice in order to be near the daughter of one of
his noblemen. (YA and A)

620. Johnstone, Paul. Escape from Attila. Criterion,
1969. Ill. by Joseph Phelan. Two Frankish hostages make a perilous escape from the Huns in an
attempt to warn their people of Attila's planned invasion. (YA)

621. Webb, Robert N. Attila, King of the Huns. Franklin
Watts, 1965. A biography of the Hunnish king
called the Scourge of God (ca. 233-453) who ex-
torted tribute from Rome but was finally defeated
by the Roman General, Aetius, at Châlons in 451.
(YA)

EIGHTH THROUGH TENTH CENTURIES

622. Andrews, F. Emerson. For Charlemagne. Harper,
1949. Frontispiece by Joseph Karov. The story
of a 14-year-old student at the Palace School of
Aachen in 789 at the court of Charles, King of
the Franks (Charlemagne). The plot centers on
his part in protecting the King against Pepin the
Hunchback, one of Charlemagne's illegitimate sons.
(I)

623. Maiden, Cecil. A Song for Young King Wenceslas.
Addisonian, 1969. Ill. by Cary. A novel, set in
tenth century Bohemia and based on fact, in which
14-year-old Wenceslas must overcome the pagan
powers of his own mother and brother in order to
save his country. (I and YA)

624. Tybor, Sister M. Martina. <u>Sts. Cyril and Methodius.</u>
      Bruce, 1963. Ill. by Joseph G. Crucik. The
      story of the saints who brought Christianity to
      eastern Europe and led the church in Slovakia to
      the western Roman establishment in the ninth cen-
      tury. (YA)

THIRTEENTH AND FOURTEENTH CENTURIES

625. Best, Herbert. <u>Bright Hunter of the Skies.</u> Mac-
      millan, 1961. Ill. by Bernarda Bryson. A story
      of falconry and the great falconer, Frederick II,
      ruler of the Holy Roman Empire from 1220 to 1250.
      (I)
626. Freeman, Godfrey. <u>The Owl and the Mirror.</u> Duell,
      Sloane and Pearce, 1961. Ill. by Joan Kiddell-
      Monroe. Although this is almost completely leg-
      endary, that mischievous character Till Eulenspie-
      gel was probably as real as Robin Hood in England,
      and is thought to have lived in the first half of the
      fourteenth century. (I)
627. Gombrich, Lisbeth and Hemsted, Clara. <u>Master Till's</u>
      <u>Amazing Pranks.</u> The story of Till Eulenspiegel
      retold. Chanticleer Press, n.d. Ill. by Elias
      Katzer's drawings and 16 scenes photographed in
      full color. (I)
628. Pyle, Howard. <u>Otto of the Silver Hand,</u> 1888. Scrib-
      ner, 1940. Ill. by the author. A story of the
      robber barons of Germany in the thirteenth century
      during the reign of the first Habsburg emperor,
      Rudolf I. (YA)

FIFTEENTH CENTURY

629. Almedingen, E. M. <u>Stephen's Light,</u> 1956. Holt,
      Rinehart and Winston, 1969. Jacket by Herbert
      Danska. A novel for older teens and up, about a
      Hanseatic merchant's daughter who, when jilted by
      her betrothed, pursuades her father to let her enter
      his business instead of a convent. The setting is
      an imaginary cathedral city possibly in northern
      Germany, during the period of the Wars of the
      Roses in England and the Renaissance in Italy.
      (A and YA)
630. _____. <u>The Scarlet Goose,</u> 1957. Holt, Rinehart

and Winston, 1970. Jacket painting by Jacob Landau. The dominant theme of this novel with many different threads in its texture, is that of the sensitive younger brother of two Hanseatic merchants in a city state in Germany at the end of the century and of his finding expression for his talents in toy-making for which he is rejected by his brothers. He finally seeks his own way of life, with a devoted young wife in a suburb of outcasts. (YA and A)

631. McMurtrie, Douglas, with Don Farran. Wings for Words. Rand McNally, 1940. Ill. by Edward A. Wilson. A biography of Gutenberg (1397-1468) and the story of his great contribution to the world, with pages on the mechanics of early printing, diagrams of his press, and a page of the Donatus, the Latin grammar printed in numerous editions by Gutenberg. (YA)

632. Steck, Max. Dürer and His World. Viking Studio Book, 1964. Translated from the German by J. Maxwell Brownjohn. 148 illustrations. A beautifully written and pictured sketch of the life and activities of the artist Albrecht Dürer (1471-1528) with a chronology and notes on the pictures. (YA and A)

633. Yonge, Charlotte. Dove in the Eagle's Nest. 1870. This rather heavy novel is set in the Holy Roman Empire of Maximilian I toward the end of the century in southern Germany near Ulm. It is included here as an example of nineteenth century "juvenile" writing and also because there is a dearth of historical fiction about fifteenth century Germany. (YA)

SIXTEENTH CENTURY

634. Fosdick, Harry Emerson. Martin Luther. Random Landmark, 1956. Ill. by Steel Savage. A biography (1483-1546) with a brief chronology of his life. (YA)

635. Ish-Kishor, Sulamith. A Boy of Old Prague. Pantheon, 1963. Ill. by Ben Shahn. Thought to be found in the childrens' room in libraries, this story of the Jewish Ghetto in sixteenth century Czechoslovakia requires mature understanding. The endpapers are reproduced from a century map of the

city of Prague. (YA)

635a. _____. The Master of Miracle: A New Novel of
The Golem. Harper and Row, 1971. Ill. by
Arnold Lobel. A clay figure is brought to life by
the High Rabbi of Prague, to save his people from
destruction, but Gideon, an orphan boy, the ghostly
narrator of the story, makes a fatal mistake for
which he is punished by not being allowed to die
until Jerusalem is restored to the Jews. (YA)

636. McNeer, May and Lynd Ward. Martin Luther. Abing-
don-Cokesbury, 1953. Ill. by Lynd Ward. A biography of the Father of the Reformation (1483-1546).
(I)

637. Rinkoff, Barbara. The Pretzel Hero. Parents' Maga-
zine Press, 1970. Ill. by Charles Mikolaycak.
How the pretzel maker's apprentice helped save
Vienna from the Turks in 1529. (I)

638. Rosen, Sidney. The Harmonious World of Johann Kepler. Little, Brown, 1962. Ill. by Rafaello Bri-
soni. The story of the difficult but highly produc-
tive life of the German Protestant astronomer at a
time when even the Protestants struggled among
themselves theologically. The time of the terrible
religious war (the 30-year-war) between Catholics
and Protestants, the Peasants' Revolt, and witch
hunting in which Kepler's own mother was accused
of being a witch. Kepler's discoveries and theories
are clearly described and illustrated, the main one
being that there is a mathematical harmony in the
universe. (YA)

SEVENTEENTH AND EIGHTEENTH CENTURIES

639. Gass, Irene. Mozart: Child Wonder, Great Composer.
Lothrop, Lee and Shepard, 1970. Ill. by J. C. B.
Knight. A moving and informative story of the
Austrian composer's all-too-short life (1756-91)
with charming illustrations of musical instruments
of his time, events in his life, lines from his music, and scenes from his operas. (I)

640. Habeck, Fritz. Days of Danger. Harcourt, Brace
and World, 1963. Ill. by a map of Vienna in 1683.
An adventure story about the siege of Vienna by the
Turks, a story of war, pillage, and violence of all
sorts, but also of humor and courage. (YA)

641. Holst, Imogen. Bach: A Study. Crowell, 1965. Ill.

with reproductions of contemporary engravings.
Mainly about Bach's musical career, with 23 easy
examples of his compositions. (YA)

642. Manton, Jo. A Portrait of Bach. Abelard-Schuman,
1957. Ill. by Faith Jacques. A brief concise biography. (YA)

643. Mirsky, Reba Paeff. Johann Sebastian Bach. Follett,
1965. Ill. by Steele Savage. The story of his life
and times (1685-1750). (YA)

644. _____. Mozart. Follett, 1960. Ill. by W. T.
Mars. A short biography of a short life (1756-
1791). (YA)

645. Pauli, Hertha. The Two Trumpeters of Vienna.
Doubleday, 1961. Ill. by Emil Weiss. An exciting tale of the Turkish invasion of Austria and
the siege of Vienna in 1683, with a map on the inside covers. (I and YA)

646. Reingold, Carmel Berman. Johann Sebastian Bach,
Revolutionary in Music. Franklin Watts, 1970.
Ill. with photographs of portraits, engravings, etc.
Have you ever considered Bach the real founder of
jazz? This biography shows how this might indeed
be so. A glossary of musical terms and chronology.
(YA)

647. Seroff, Victor. Wolfgang Amadeus Mozart. Macmillan, 1965. Ill. with paintings and prints. A
biography (1756-1791) with a selected discography.
(YA)

648. Singmaster, Elsie. I Heard of a River. Holt, Rinehart and Winston, 1948. Ill. by Henry C. Pitz.
The greater part of this novel is set in the New
World, but the first four chapters so vividly de-
scribe the desperate conditions in the Palitinate of
Germany (between France and Holland) as an aftermath of the Thirty-Year War and a later war between France and Holland that it seems appropriate
to list it here. (YA)

649. Snyder, Louis L. and Brown, Ida Mae. Frederick
the Great: Prussian Warrior and Statesman.
Franklin Watts, 1968. Map by Dyno Lowenstein.
An exceptionally lively and absorbing story of a
lonely man (1712-86), son of a brutal father and
neglectful mother, who made a small young kingdom into a powerful state. (YA)

650. Wheeler, Opal. Handel at the Court of Kings. Dutton, 1943. Ill. by Mary Greenwalt. A biography
(1732-1809) for very young readers and pianists

with 14 pieces of music. (E and I)

651. Wheeler, Opal and Deucher, Sybil. Sebastian Bach,
     the Boy from Thuringia. Dutton, 1937 and 1964.
     Ill. by Mary Greenwalt. Biography (1685-1750)
     with 14 pieces of music. (E and I)

652. _____. Mozart the Wonder Boy. Dutton, 1934,
     1941 and 1955. Ill. by Mary Greenwalt. For the
     youngest readers of words and music, a biography
     (1756-91) with 35 pieces. (E and I)

653. Woodford, Peggy. Mozart. Walck, 1966. Ill. by
     David Knight. From the series, "Composers and
     Their Times," a biography (1756-91) without music.
     (YA)

653a. Young, Percy M. Haydn. David White, 1969. Ill.
     by Richard Shirley-Smith. This story of the life
     of Franz Joseph (Papa) Haydn (1732-1809) focusses
     on the role of the artist in the eighteenth century
     and Haydn's supremacy as a symphonist and also
     the disposition and personality which led him to be
     called "Papa." (YA)

NINETEENTH CENTURY

654. Ambrus, Victor. Brave Soldier Janosh. Harcourt,
     Brace and World, 1967. Ill. by the author. A
     Hungarian legend of a soldier who conquered Na-
     poleon and his army. (E Picture Book)

655. Apsler, Alfred. Iron Chancellor, Otto von Bismarck.
     Messner, 1968. The story of a genius in diplo-
     macy, a ruthless manipulator of rulers and foreign
     affairs, a paradoxical figure in many ways, de-
     signing a peace that lasted for 40 years and yet,
     basing his policy on "blood and iron," laying the
     foundation for nationalism and militarism that led
     to two world wars and the barbarity of Hitlerism.
     (YA and A)

656. Baker, Rachel. Sigmund Freud. Messner, 1952. A
     clear, simple narration of the psychiatrist's life
     (1856-1939) and exposition of his theories with a
     glossary of terms and a reading list. (YA and A)

657. Benary-Isbert, Margot. Under a Changing Moon.
     Harcourt, Brace and World, 1964. Translated
     from the German by Rosaleen Ockenden and the
     author. A charming novel of young love set in the
     old Rhineland. (YA)

658. Gendron, Val. The Dragon Tree, A Life of Alexander

von Humboldt. Longmans Green, 1961. Ill. with
photogravures from von Humboldt's works. A
scholarly biography of a man (1769-1859) who was
an explorer, writer, statesman and scientist, and
who made original contributions in such areas as
zoology, physiology, botany, astronomy, geology,
and anthropology, and for whom the Humboldt Current was named. (YA and A)

659. Goss, Madeleine B. Beethoven, Master Musician.
Doubleday, Doran, 1936, revised 1946. Ill. by
Karl Schültheiss. A sympathetic biography of a
sad life (1770-1827) including stories of other musicians of his time, Haydn, Mozart, and, at the
very end, Schubert. A catalogue of Beethoven's
works and recordings, and a chronology of his life
and the musical events during it. (YA and A)

660. _____. Unfinished Symphony, The Story of Franz
Schubert. Holt, 1941. Ill. by Karl M. Schültheiss. A biography of the short but highly pro-
ductive life of the Song King (1797-1828) with a
list of his works, with dates, and a chronology of
"The World Schubert Lived In" showing where his
work paralleled that of Beethoven, his idol. (YA)

661. Greene, Carla. Gregor Mendel. Dial Press, 1970.
With pictures and diagrams by Richard Cuffaro.
A lively biography (1822-84) and accurate descrip-
tion of Mendel's discoveries of the laws of genetics
and later, twentieth century, advances, including
D.N.A. and the genetic code. Glossary. (I and
YA)

661a. Hurd, Michael. Mendelssohn. Crowell, 1971. Ill.
with prints, portraits, musical scores, and some
of Mendelssohn's own sketches. A biography of
the composer (1809-1847) who, born of wealthy
Jewish parents, never had to face the financial
struggles of most musicians but did suffer from
German anti-Semitism. Considered by some a
second-rate major composer, and, by others, a
first-rate minor one, he is generally acknowledged
a superb draftsman. (YA)

662. Jacobs, Robert. Wagner. Collier Books, 1947 (first
printed in 1935). A small book but packed full of
important information: a short biography of Richard Wagner (1813-83) a chronology including dates
of other composers and musicians of his period,
separate discussions of his music and his personality, a catalogue of his musical works, a selected

list of his literary works, and a synopsis of the
Niebelungenlied. (A)

663. Jacobs, David. Beethoven. American Heritage, 1970
(consultant, Elliot Forbes). Many period illustrations in color and black and white. Besides the
biography (1770-1827) there are some first-hand
accounts of his life and times by Beethoven's con-
temporaries. A basic record library. (YA)

664. Kyle, Elizabeth (Dunlop). Duet, The Story of Clara
and Robert Schumann. Holt, Rinehart and Winston,
1968. Jacket by Ellen Raskin. An engrossing biographical novel about Clara Wieck (1819-96) a
gifted and famous pianist from childhood, and the
composer, Robert Schumann (1810-56) whom she
finally married against her father's adamant opposition. (YA)

665. Mann, John. Sigmund Freud, Doctor of Secrets and
Dreams. Macmillan, 1964. Ill. by Clare Romano
and John Ross. A friendly introduction to the
great psychiatrist (1856-1939) and some of his
basic ideas, delightfully illustrated. (E and I)

666. Mirsky, Reba Paeff. Beethoven. Follett, 1957. Ill.
by W. T. Mars. A biography of the great composer who, in spite of the obstacles of poverty
and deafness (which began to come on when he
was 28) became one of music's immortals. (I)

667. _____. Brahms. Follett, 1966. Ill. by W. T.
Mars. Biography of Johannes Brahms (1833-97).
(I and YA)

668. Pahlen, Kurt. The Waltz King, Johann Strauss, Jr.
Rand McNally, 1965. Translated and adapted from
the German by Theodore McClintock and charming-
ly illustrated by an unnamed artist. A biography
of the younger Strauss (1825-99). (I and YA)

669. Panofsky, Walter. Wagner, A Pictorial Biography.
Viking Studio Book, 1964. Translated from the
German by Richard Rickett. A readable text with
notes on the many illustrations and a chronology.
(YA)

670. Purdy, Claire Lee. Antonin Dvorák, Composer from
Bohemia. John Messner, 1950. Jacket by Edgard Cirlin. Aside from musical interest this
biography (1841-1904) covers a period of great
historical importance, including the Crimean and
Franco-Prussian Wars, the establishment of Italy
as a kingdom, emancipation of the serfs in Russia,
and the collapse of the House of Habsburg. All

with little Bohemia in the thick of things. (YA)
671. Seroff, Victor. Franz Liszt. Macmillan, 1966. Ill.
with photographs and engravings. A biography of
the Hungarian pianist and composer (1811-1866)
with a discography. (YA)
672. Sootin, Harry. Gregor Mendel, Father of the Science
of Genetics. Vanguard, 1959. A biography of the
Austrian scientist and Roman Catholic priest, 1822-
84. (YA)
673. Vance, Marguerite. Ashes of Empire. Dutton, 1959.
Ill. by J. Luis Pellicer. A dual biography of Maximilian (1832-1867, brother of Austrian Emperor
Franz Joseph) and his wife, Carlotta (1840-1927)
who, for three short years, were Emperor and
Empress of Mexico, pursuaded to take the crowns
by Napoleon III of France. When Napoleon with-
drew French troops from Mexico, Maximilian was
shot by the Mexicans, but Carlotta, in Europe seeking aid, survived him by 60 years. (YA)
674. _____. Flight of the Wilding. Dutton, 1957. The
life story of the fascinating Empress of Austria and
Queen of Hungary, consort of Emperor Francis
Joseph, and Mother of Archduke Ferdinand who
died at Mayerling. (YA)
675. Webb, Robert N. Gregor Mendel and Heredity. Watts,
1963. A short easy biography, with a chronology.
(I)
676. Webster, Gary (Webb, B. Garrison). The Man Who
Found Out Why: The Story of Gregor Mendel.
Hawthorne Credo Books, 1963. Ill. by Greg and
Tim Hildebrandt. A brief biography (1822-84). (I)
677. Werstein, Irving. The Franco-Prussian War: Germany's Rise as a World Power. Messner, 1965.
Ill. with maps and drawings. A short readable objective story of the battles, the leaders on both
sides and the causes and results of the war of 1870
and 1871. (YA and A)
678. Wheeler, Opal. Adventures of Richard Wagner. Dutton, 1960. Ill. by Floyd Webb. The story of
Wagner's childhood and youth, with a bit of his
Lohengrin wedding march. (I)
679. Woodford, Peggy. Schubert. Walck ("Composers and
Their Times") 1969. A short biography of the too
short life (1797-1827) of the Austrian composer,
never duly recognized in his own time. (I and YA)

TWENTIETH CENTURY

680. Benary-Isbert, Margot. _A Time to Love._ Harcourt,
      Brace, 1962. Translated from the German by
      Joyce Emerson and the author. A novel about a young
      German girl's life from the beginning of the Hitler
      regime to the beginning of World War II, the hero-
      ine first in a private school to avoid Nazi influence
      and later at the University. (YA)

681. _____. _Dangerous Spring._ Harcourt, Brace, 1961.
      Translated from the German by James Kirkup. A
      novel about the final days of World War II in the
      medieval village of Eberstein. (YA)

682. _____. _The Arc._ Harcourt, Brace, 1953. Trans-
      lated from the German by Clara and Richard Win-
      ston. A novel about the courage and humor shown
      by a German family, destitute and fatherless in the
      aftermath of World War II. (YA)

683. _____. _Rowan Farm._ Harcourt, Brace, 1954.
      Translated from the German by Richard and Clara
      Winston. A sequel to "The Arc" about the same
      family in 1948, rebuilding on the rubble of the old
      Germany. (YA)

684. Bonham, Frank. _The Ghost Front._ Dutton, 1968.
      Map by Veit-Martin Ass. A novel about the Battle
      of the Bulge, as experienced by twin brothers who
      enlisted in the American 106th infantry division af-
      ter the invasion at Normandy. (YA)

685. Crawford, Deborah. _Lise Meitner, Atomic Pioneer._
      Crown, 1969. Jacket by W. T. Mars. A biog-
      raphy of one of the first woman physicists (1878-
      1968) who was forced to leave Germany because of
      Nazi anti-Semitism, and who became one of the
      foremost scientists responsible for the making of
      the atomic bomb. (YA)

686. Forman, James. _Horses of Anger._ Farrar, Straus
      and Giroux, 1967. A strong terrifying, realistic
      novel about a German boy living near Munich dur-
      ing the years of World War II, drafted into an anti-
      aircraft unit at fifteen, and admiring the Fuehrer
      almost until the end. (YA)

687. _____. _The Traitors._ Farrar, Straus and Giroux,
      1968. Warning! Don't start this novel unless you
      can stay with it to the suspenseful end. The main
      characters are a young Nazi, his sensitive and sol-
      itary younger brother and the latter's Jewish friend,
      the story beginning with the rise of Hitler and end-

ing with the coming of the Americans. An historical note gives the background. (YA)

688. _____. Ceremony of Innocence. Hawthorne Books,
1970. Jacket by Marilyn Hirsh. The brother and
sister in this novel of idealistic and courageous opposition to Nazi tyranny, Hans and Sophie Scholl,
are drawn from history as are most of the other
characters in the book, all victims (in one way or
another) of the barbarous atrocities and inhuman
philosophy of the Hitler regime. A good book for
older people too, to increase their understanding of
youthful idealism. (YA and A)

689. Garth, David. The Watch on the Bridge. Putnam,
1959. A novel based on the events connected with
the fighting over Remagen Bridge, near the end of
World War II. (A)

690. Goldston, Robert. The Life and Death of Nazi Germany. Bobbs-Merrill, 1967. Ill. by Donald Carrick and with photographs. A book as hard to lay
down as many works of fiction, with a gruesome
cast of characters. (YA and A)

691. Hamori, Laszlo. Dangerous Journey. Harcourt,
Brace and World, 1959. Translated from the
Swedish by Annabelle Macmillan. A story of two
Hungarian boys escaping from a Russian-run youth
labor camp in Budapest to seek freedom over the
border. (I and YA)

692. Heaps, Willard A. The Wall of Shame. Duell, Sloane
and Pearce, 1964. Ill. with photographs and a map.
A complete documented account of the building of
the infamous wall erected in August, 1961, between
East and West Berlin. (YA)

693. Henry, Marguerite. White Stallion of Lipizza. Rand
McNally, 1964. Ill. by Wesley Dennis. Along
with a good story line about a Viennese lad who as-
pires to become a riding master in the Lipizzaner
stables, early in this century, there is some history of equestrianism, going back as far as the
writing of Xenophon of Greece. (I and YA)

694. McSwigan, Marie. All Aboard for Freedom. Dutton,
1954. Ill. by E. Harper Johnson, with a foreword
by Jan Papanek. A tense, exciting story, based
on fact, of the "Freedom Train" which "ran away"
over the Czechoslovakian border into the American-
occupied zone of Germany. (I and YA)

695. Manton, Jo. Albert Schweitzer. Abelard-Schuman,
1955. Ill. by Astrid Walford. A biography "to be

read as a story," of the Alsatian musician, philosopher, missionary and medical doctor (1875-1965)
who founded a hospital in Lambarene in Africa and
received the Nobel peace Prize in 1952. It only
covers his life until he was 75, but he lived on
until the age of 90. (I and YA)

696. Noble, Iris. Physician to the Children, Dr. Béla
Schick. Julian Messner, 1963. Jacket by Dave
Dippel. The tender story of the life of the Hungarian doctor (1877-1967) who loved children so
dearly that he struggled to gain a medical education
against his father's strong opposition. From his
work and study came the Schick test for diphtheria
and the beginning of the science of pediatrics. In
1923 he went to America to become head pediatri-
cian at Mt. Sinai Hospital in New York City where
he became an American citizen and received world-
wide honors. (YA)

697. Peare, Catherine Owens. Albert Einstein, A Biography for Young People. Holt, 1949. Ill. with
photographs. Born in Germany in 1879, Einstein
was forced to leave, because he was a Jew, in
1933. He came to the United States where he became an American citizen and a life member of
the Institute for Advanced Studies in Princeton,
New Jersey. The genius who developed the theory
of relativity (which the author does not attempt to
explain) was a staunch pacifist until his death in
1955. (YA)

698. Reeman, Douglas. The Last Raider. Putnam, 1963.
A novel of naval warfare in World War II, vividly
depicting its horror but also the nobility and courage of some of its leaders, both German and Al-
lied. (A)

699. Remarque, Erich Maria. All Quiet on the Western
Front. Little, Brown, 1928. A classic of World
War I. A realistic, compassionate novel about
trench warfare. (A)

700. Richter, Hans Peter. Friedrich. Holt, Rinehart and
Winston, 1970. Jacket by Wendell Minor. Translated by Edite Kroll. A tragic, gripping, episodic
novel of the Nazi destruction of the Jews in Germany in the 1930s, told by a young Gentile boy
who witnessed the sufferings of his childhood neighbors. (I and YA)

701. Sentman, George Armor. Russky. Doubleday, 1965.
Jacket, endpapers and map by Gil Walker. The

action of this novel (based on the experiences of
the 28th U.S. infantry division, the "Bloody Buck-
et") takes place in Alsace during the fighting in the
Colmar Pocket after the Battle of the Bulge, near
the end of the war in 1945. The main character
is a Russian lad escaping from a German slave-
labor camp to the American lines, his part in the
cold, waiting, and bloody fighting and his ambition
to become an American citizen. (YA)

702. Seredy, Kate. The Singing Tree. Viking, 1939, and
1950. Ill. by the author. A story about the Hun-
garians in World War I and their high hopes kin-
dled by Woodrow Wilson. (I)

703. _____. The Chestry Oak. Viking, 1948. Ill. by
the author. A story of a young Hungarian aristocrat and his horse during the Nazi occupation in
World War II. (I)

704. Seymour, Alta Halverson. Toward Morning--A Story
of the Hungarian Freedom Fighters. Follett, 1961.
Cover painting by David Stone. About the Hungarian
revolution of 1956. (I)

705. Shirer, William L. The Sinking of the Bismarck.
Random Landmark, 1962. Ill. with photographs.
The thrilling story of the one-week chase and the
courage and endurance of both German and English
crews. (I)

706. _____. The Rise and Fall of Adolph Hitler. Random Landmark, 1961. Ill. with photographs. (I)

707. Simon, Charlie May. Martin Buber, Wisdom in Our
Time. Dutton, 1969. Ill. with photographs. More
than just a biography of the great Jewish thinker
and humanist (1878-1965) who was born in Gallicia,
lived mostly in Austria but settled in Israel in
1938, this is the story of his wisdom as expressed
to Christians as well as Jews, and of his great
faith in the spiritual values of life. (YA)

708. Stiles, Martha Bennett. Darkness Over the Land.
Dial, 1966. A grimly realistic novel about a
Polish orphan, brought up as a German in Munich
and the effects on him of Hitler's rise to power,
Naziism, the war, and the American occupation,
and the philosophic problem of "collective guilt."
A map of the Munich region on the inside covers
and a back cover map of the Nazi occupation of
Europe and an appendix listing non-fictional char-
acters. (YA)

709. Werstein, Irving. The Battle of Aachen. Crowell,

1962. Ill. with maps by Ava Morgan. The story
of the five, fearful weeks of fighting for the first
major city on German soil to be captured by the
Americans. Tense and suspenseful. (YA)
710. Williams, Eric. The Wooden Horse. Abelard-Schuman, 1958. Ill. by Martin Thomas. A true adventure story about the escape of three young English prisoners of war from a German prison camp.
Diagrams, a map and glossary. (YA)

GENERAL HISTORY

711. MacGregor, Mary. The Story of France, Told to
      Boys and Girls. Stokes, n.d. With 20 color plates
      and charts of the rulers. (I)

MYTHS, LEGENDS AND FOLKLORE

712. Baldwin, James. The Story of Roland. Scribner, 1883
      and 1930. Ill. by Peter Hurd. About Roland, the
      hero of the eleventh century epic, "La Chanson de
      Roland" and Charlemagne's defeat at Roncesvalles
      in the eighth century. (YA)
713. Collier, Virginia M. and Eaton, Jeanette. Roland the
      Warrior. Harcourt, Brace, 1934. Ill. by Frank
      Schoonover. (YA)
714. Norton, André. Huon of the Horn; "Being a Tale of
      that Duke of Bordeaux who came to sorrow at the
      hands of Charlemagne and yet won the favor of
      Oberon, the Elf King, to his lasting fame and glory."
      Harcourt, Brace, 1951. Ill. by Joe Krush. An
      adaptation from the "Boke of Duke Huon of Bur-
      deux." (YA)
715. Picard, Barbara Leonie. French Legends, Tales and
      Fairy Stories. Oxford, 1955. Ill. by Joan Kiddell-
      Monroe. A book in four parts: 1) French epic
      heroes (Roland, et al.); 2) courtly tales of the Mid-
      dle Ages (Aucassin and Nicolette, et al.); 3) pro-
      vincial legends; and 4) fairy stories. (I)
716. Price, Hilda Cumings. The Song of Roland. Warne,
      1961. Ill. by Christine Price. A new abridged
      translation in verse. (I)
717. Pyle, Katherine. Charlemagne and His Knights. Lip-
      pincott, 1932. Ill. by the author. Some stories
      sung by the troubadours in the middle ages. (I)
718. Reesink, Maryke. The Golden Treasure. Harcourt,
      1968. Ill. by Jaap Tol. A haunting legend of the
      death of a town dramatically told and pictured.
      (E and I Picture Book)

719.   Spicer, Dorothy Gladys. The Owl's Nest--Folk Tales
       from Friesland. Coward-McCann, 1968. Ill. by
       Alice Wadowski-Bak. Stories from the most north-
       erly part of the Netherlands, told with humor and
       zest. (I)
720.   Todd, Mary Fidelis. The Juggler of Notre Dame.
       Whittlesey House, 1954. Ill. in color by the author.
       No matter how often one has read or heard or even
       seen this legend, it is always a pleasure to find a
       new retelling with new pictures. (E and I)
720a. Williams, Jay. The Tournament of Lions. Walck,
       1960. Ill. by Ezra Jack Keats. Framed by a
       fifteenth century romance, this is, in fact, the
       Song of Roland, in prose form, with its underlying
       question whether it is better to run away and live
       to fight another day, or to stay on and fight to the
       death. (I and YA)

                       SIXTH CENTURY

721.   Polland, Madeleine. Fingal's Quest. Doubleday, 1961.
       Ill. by W. T. Mars. A novel about St. Columban's
       attempt to bring Christianity back to pagan France
       and the attempts of one of his scholars to join him
       there. (YA)

                EIGHTH AND NINTH CENTURIES

722.   Almedingen, E. M. A Candle at Dusk. Farrar,
       Straus and Giroux, 1969. Jacket by Judith Ann
       Lawrence. A novel about the period when the
       Franks, led by Charles Martel, met the attack of
       the Saracens at Poitiers in 732 and how a boy
       proved to his father that learning could be an im-
       portant defensive force. (YA)
723.   Boyce, Burke. The Emperor's Arrow. Lippincott,
       1967. Ill. by Paul Frame. A legend, charmingly
       told and illustrated about Charlemagne and his
       search for a cure for the plague. (I)
724.   Finkel, George. The Long Pilgrimage, 1967. Viking
       (first U.S.). A fine, comprehensive novel of the
       period between Charlemagne's advance into Spain
       in 778 and the Viking raids on the Tyne and Wear
       in 794. The protagonist is a Northumbrian, but the
       book is placed here because it largely concerns a mis-

sion undertaken for Charlemagne (plain Karl then)
which carries the narrator to far places before he
returns to England where the Viking raids may have
been the result of Charlemagne's policies. Best
read the historical note first, and then the maps
and glossary of place names will make the story
pleasantly clear. (YA)

725. Miller, Shane. The Hammer of Gaul, The Story of
Charles Martel. Hawthorne Credo Books, 1964.
Ill. by the author. The life and times of the great
Frankish Mayor of the Palace, from 714-41, who
united all the Merovingian kingdoms under his rule
and halted the Saracen invasion of Tours and Poitiers in 732. He was the grandfather of Charlemagne. Maps help somewhat to clarify the terri-
torial boundaries of the peoples of western Europe
at that period of the Dark Ages. (YA)

726. Winston, Richard [and the editors of Horizon Magazine].
Charlemagne. (consultant, Harry Baker.) American Heritage, 1968. 137 illustrations (64 in color)
of stained glass windows and manuscripts and min-
iatures from the eighth to the fourteenth centuries,
pictures of artifacts and reliquaries and a color
map of Europe in 800. (YA)

727. Leighton, Margaret. Judith of France. Houghton-
Mifflin, 1948. Ill. by Henry C. Pitz. A biographical novel about a ninth century French princess,
daughter of Louis I, the Bold, who, at 15, married
the widowed father of Prince Alfred of Britain (later King Alfred the Great). (YA)

TENTH THROUGH TWELFTH CENTURIES

728. Bishop, Claire Huchet. Bernard and His Dogs.
Houghton-Mifflin, 1952. Ill. by Maurice Brevannes. A biography of the Alpine saint, Bernard
de Menthon (ca. 923-1008). Recommended especially to skiers or mountain climbers because of
its informative material and humorous narration
about a mountaineer saint. (I and YA)

729. Hubbard, Margaret Ann. The Blue Gonfalon. Doubleday, 1960. Ill. by Shane Miller. A novel about
the stable squire of Geoffrey, Duke of Lorraine,
who seeks to win his spurs in Palestine in the
first Crusade, 1095-99. (YA)

730. Rockwell, Anne. Glass, Stones and Crown. Atheneum,

1968. Ill. by the author. A biography of the Abbé
Sugar and the building of St. Denis. (I)

THIRTEENTH AND FOURTEENTH CENTURIES
(Medieval Period)

731. Daniel, Hawthorne. Shuttle and Sword. Macmillan,
     1932. Ill. by Thomas W. Vater. The adventures
     of Diereck van der Weyden of Bruges, a weaver's
     son in old Flanders in the fourteenth century, and
     Jacob van Artevelde, burgher of Ghent, whose sta-
     tue now stands in that city. (YA)
732. DeJong, Meindert. The Tower by the Sea. Harper
     and Row, 1950. Ill. by Barbara Comfort. A leg-
     endary story of witch hunting, a cat with a blue
     eye, and a baby in a cradle floating in on the
     morning tide. (I)
733. DeLeeuw, Cateau. The Turn in the Road. Nelson,
     1961. Ill. by Lili Rethi. A story of a draper's
     apprentice in Dordrecht in 1285 and the wool trade
     with England in the time of King Edward I, with a
     glossary of terms used in the woolen industry. (YA)
734. Guillot, René. The Troubadour. McGraw-Hill, 1967.
     Ill. by Laszlo Acs. Translated by Anne Carter.
     A highly imaginative novel of medieval France when
     King Philip was trying to curb the power of the
     Knights Templar and their Grand Master. (I and
     YA)
735. Lanier, Sidney. The Boy's Froissart. Scribner, 1879.
     A history of fourteenth century Europe, translated
     and adapted from the French of Jean Froissart
     (1337?-?1410) poet and historian, by the American
     poet, Lanier. It is often biased and inaccurate
     but very close to "first hand." (YA)
736. Leekley, Thomas B. King Hurla's Quest. Vanguard,
     1956. Ill. by Johannes Troyer. Part history and
     part legend, this and other medieval stories are
     recreated from the writing of twelfth century Walter
     Map. (YA)
737. Stein, Evaleen. The Little Count of Normandy. Page,
     1911. Ill. by John Goss. An old-fashioned story
     with the fascinating setting of Mount Saint Michel,
     whose great tides provide the material for the plot.
     (I)
738. Treece, Henry. Perilous Pilgrimage. Criterion, 1958.
     Ill. by Christine Price. A frightful tale of the

Children's Crusade led by young Stephen of Cloyes.
Map and author's note. (YA)

739. Uden, Grant. Hero Tales from the Age of Chivalry.
Retold from the Froissart Chronicles. World, 1969.
Ill. by Doreen Roberts. These tales were first
translated into English about 1523 and are lots of
fun. What a jolly fellow Froissart must have been,
and how impartial he was about the 100-year struggle between France and England. Mainly the tales
are about that long war and its most famous battles; Edward III of England and his Queen Philippa,
and Philip of France and the indomitable Countess
Jeanne. (I and YA)

740. Williams, Paul. The Warrior Knights. Time-Life,
dist. by Little, Brown, 1969. Ill. by the author.
Focusing on the thirteenth century, this book follows the career of a young man from a page through
his training to be a knight. Details are given of
his armor, weapons and siege machinery. (I and
YA)

FIFTEENTH CENTURY

741. Brock, Emma L. Little Duchess Anne of Brittany.
Knopf, 1948. Ill. but no name. A biographical
novel of a little duchess who, at 16, became Queen
of France as the wife of Charles VIII, and, later,
as the wife of Louis XII, with a chronology of the
events in her life (1476-1514) and map. (YA)

742. Butler, Mildred Allen. Twice Queen of France, Anne
of Brittany. Funk and Wagnalls, 1967. Ill. by
Bette Davis. A biography with plentiful historical
detail of the Queen of Charles VIII and later his
successor, Louis XII, who led an exceedingly full
and busy life (1476-1514) and who, when she died
at age 38, was greatly mourned in both France and
Brittany. (YA)

743. deWohl, Louis. Saint Joan, the Girl Soldier. Farrar,
Straus and Cudahy, 1957. Ill. by Harry Barton.
Biography (1412-31). (I)

744. Fisher, Aileen. Jeanne D'Arc. Crowell, 1970. Ill.
by Ati Forberg. Text and illustrations in this biography of the young saint (1412-31) are equally
beautiful and sensitive. A finely made book. (I
and YA)

745. Herold, J. Christopher. Joan, Maid of France. Alad-

din Books, 1952. Ill. by Frederick T. Chapman.
A biography (1412-1431) based on contemporary
documents, with a map of northern France. (I)

746. Hugo, Victor. The Hunchback of Notre Dame. 1831.
A novel of medieval Paris and the great cathedral.
(A)

747. Johnston, Johanna. Joan of Arc. Doubleday, 1961.
Ill. by W. T. Mars. A biography (1412-31) with
all the chapter headings taken from Joan's own
words in her testimony at her trial. (I)

748. Lownsbery, Eloise. The Boy Knight of Rheims.
Houghton-Mifflin, 1955. Decorated with small
wood blocks and a map of Rheims. The story of
an apprentice, first to a goldsmith and then to a
sculptor, of special interest for its details about
the building of the great cathedral there--the stone-
work, sculpture, glass and beams. The slight plot
is climaxed by the crowning of Charles VII by Joan
of Arc in 1429. (YA)

749. Nugent, Frances Roberts. Jan Van Eyck, Master
Painter. Rand McNally, 1962. Ill. by the author
with reproductions of some of Van Eyck's most
famous paintings. A biography (1385-1441) of the
man who created a style of visual reality, and also
good historical material on fifteenth century Flanders.
(YA)

750. Paine, Albert Bigelow. The Girl in White Armor.
Macmillan, 1927. Ill. with facsimiles, plates and
maps. An abridgement of the author's earlier
book about Joan of Arc for adults, with every epi-
sode and detail from the sworn testimony taken at
her trials and other authentic contemporary sources.
(YA)

751. Reade, Charles. The Cloister and the Hearth, 1859.
A classic of historical fiction, set mainly in the
Lowlands with a dramatic plot concerning the par-
ents of Erasmus. (A)

752. Ridge, Antonia. The Royal Pawn. Appleton-Century,
1962. A novel about Katherine of Valois, the queen
for a short time of Henry V of England, mother of
his son who became the unhappy Henry VI, and,
through a secret marriage to Owen Tudor, the
grandmother of Henry VII. (A)

753. Ross, Nancy Wilson. Joan of Arc. Random Landmark, 1953. Ill. by Valenti Angelo. Biography
(1412-31). (I)

754. Scott, Sir Walter. Quentin Durward. 1823. A ro-

mantic novel about a young member of Louis XI's
Scottish guards.   (A)

755. Williams, Jay. Joan of Arc. American Heritage,
      1963. Ill. with paintings, maps, illuminations and
      drawings. A Horizon Caravel biography with many
      details of her campaigns and her martyr's death.
      (YA)

SIXTEENTH CENTURY

756. Baker, Nina Brown. William the Silent. Vanguard,
      1947. A biography of William of Orange (1533-
      84), a stadtholder of Holland from 1558 to 1584.
      (YA)

757. Coblentz, Catherine Cate. Beggar's Penny. McKay,
      1943. Ill. by Hilda Van Stockum. A story of the
      Spanish siege of Leyden, 1574 and 75.   (I)

758. Greenberg, Dorothy Rossen. Siege Hero. Reilly and
      Lee, 1965. Ill. with woodcuts by Robert Borja.
      A story of the siege of Leyden (1574-75) and a boy
      who carried a warning to William of Orange. (I)

759. Greenleaf, Margery. Dirk: A Story of the Struggle
      for Freedom in Holland, 1572-1574. Map and
      plan. Follett, 1971. Sixteen-year-old Dirk has
      two goals: to help free Holland from the Spanish
      tyrant and to find his missing sister. Through his
      struggles we learn much about the Dutch "sea beg-
      gars" (a rough lot, often as ruthless as the Span-
      iards under the Duke of Alva). The map and plan
      of the siege of Leyden help greatly to clarify the
      story of this two-year segment of a war that did
      not end until 1648. (YA)

760. Haycraft, Molly Costain. The Reluctant Queen. Lip-
      pincott, 1962. A novel about Mary Tudor, the
      vivacious sister of Henry VIII of England, who,
      though in love with Charles Brandon, was forced
      to marry Louis XII of France for political reasons.
      (A)

761. Kelly, Eric P. At the Sign of the Golden Compass.
      A Tale of the Printing House of Christopher
      Plantin in Antwerp, 1576. Macmillan, 1938.
      Ill. by Raymond Lufkin. A suspenseful novel
      about the early days of printing. (YA)

762. Koningsberger, Hans. The Golden Keys; A Dutch
      Boy Sails for the Indies. Rand McNally, 1956.
      Ill. by John Gretzer. The explorations of Barents

(sixteenth century) and Van Noort (seventeenth) are
the basis of these stories of tremendous courage
and endurance on the part of Gerrit de Veer (an
actual character, aged 17 at the beginning). A
great sea story. (I and YA)

763. Lownsbury, Eloise. Lighting the Torch. Longmans
Green, 1934. Ill. by Elizabeth Tyler Wolcott. A
novel about the Peasants' Rebellion in France, Germany and the Lowlands, and Erasmus, and the new
printing. (YA)

764. Marshall, Rosamund. None But the Brave. Houghton-
Mifflin, 1942. Ill. by Gregor Duncan. A harrowing novel about the siege and relief of Leyden (1574
and 75), showing the indomitable courage of the
Dutch against the Spanish forces. (YA)

765. Miller, Eugenia. The Sign of the Salamander. Holt,
Rinehart and Winston, 1967. A novel about a contemporary American boy attending school in France
who, while visiting the castle at Amboise and the
nearby chateau (where Leonardo da Vinci spent his
last three years, 1516-19) suddenly becomes a
would-be printer's apprentice in the sixteenth century and meets Leonardo himself. (I and YA)

766. Vance, Marguerite. Dark Eminence, Catherine de
Medici and Her Children. Dutton, 1961. Ill. by
Luis Pellicer. An exciting history of the period
in France from 1547 to 1588 as well as a biography of Henri II's guileful Queen (1519-89) and
her family, with a chart showing the connections
between the Houses of Medici, Valois, Bourbon,
Navarre, Guise, Lorraine and Habsburg. (YA)

767. Wilkinson, Burke. The Helmet of Navarre. Macmillan, 1965. Ill. by James W. Williamson. A
biographical novel about the prince who, in 1589,
became Henri IV (the Magnificent) and about the
religious wars between Catholics and Protestants,
the Huguenots, and the dreadful St. Bartholomew
Massacre, August 24, 1572. Chronology of Henri's
life and list of principal characters in the story.
(YA)

SEVENTEENTH CENTURY

768. Apsler, Alfred. The Sun King: The Story of Louis
XIV. Messner, 1965. The story of the man who
ruled France from 1643-1715, with a genealogical

chart and timetable of important events. (YA)
769.   Butler, Mildred Allen. Rapier for Revenge. Funk
       and Wagnalls, 1969. The adventures of Armand de
       Lys, seeking to avenge the murder of his father,
       and associating with Cyrano de Bergerac, the Three
       Musketeers, and other notables of the time, before
       finally coming face to face with the man he has
       sworn to kill. (YA)
769a.   _____. Ward of the Sun King. Funk and Wagnalls,
       1970. Adrienne was happy to be admitted to Saint
       Cyr, a school instituted by Mme de Maintenon, but
       before long she found the discipline too strict and
       made her escape from the frying pan into the fire.
       (YA)
769b. Daringer, Helen Fern. Debbie of the Green Gate.
       Harcourt, Brace, and World, 1950. Ill. by Edward
       and Stephani Godwin. A sequel to "Pilgrim Kate"
       [entry 386] in which the English pilgrims are now
       living in Leyden, Holland. (I and YA)
770.   Dumas, Alexander. The Three Musketeers, 1844. A
       romance of the time of Louis XIII and Anne of Aus-
       tria. D'Artagnan was modeled on a real character
       named Charles Baatz D'Artagnon. (A)
771.   Graham, Alberta Powell. LaSalle, River Explorer.
       Abingolon, 1954. Ill. by Avery Johnson. Although
       the dangerous adventures and explorations of La
       Salle took place in the New World, his youth in
       France where he found his faithful Tonti, the sup-
       port he received from Louis XIV, and his frequent
       returns to France to report his findings and, most
       importantly, his taking possession of the Louisiana
       Territory for France, makes this a bridge book be-
       tween Europe and America. (I)
772.   Guillot, René. The Fantastic Brother. Translated
       from the French by Christopher Hampton. Rand
       McNally, 1963. Ill. by Richard Kennedy. A mix-
       ture of fantasy, mystery, and adventure in which
       the 15-year-old son of an old count's master of the
       hunt goes on a long sea voyage and is cast away
       in the jungles of Africa where he becomes part of
       a legend before he returns to France. (YA)
773.   Kyle, Elizabeth (Dunlop). Princess of Orange. Holt,
       Rinehart and Winston, 1965. A novel about Mary,
       daughter of James II of England, who spent most
       of her life in the Netherlands as wife of William of
       Orange with whom she later ruled England from
       1689-1694. (YA)

774.   Ripley, Elizabeth. Rembrandt. Oxford, 1955. Ill. with
       drawings, etchings and paintings by Rembrandt. An
       art book with a short biography of the painter, 1606-
       69. (YA)
775.   Rostand, Edmond. Cyrano de Bergerac. 1897. (New
       English version by Louis Untermeyer, Heritage
       Press, 1955.) A play based on a real French play-
       wright with a very long nose. (A)
775a. Stearns, Monroe. Louis XIV of France. Watts, 1971.
       Ill. with maps and portraits. A biography of the
       Sun King whose long reign covered the years from
       1643 to 1715, with a chronology. (YA)
776.   Widdemer, Mabel Cleland. Peter Stuyvesant, Boy with
       Wooden Shoes. Bobbs-Merrill, 1950. Ill. by
       Charles V. John. A bridge book between Holland and
       America, but mainly about stubborn Peter's boyhood
       in Holland before he joined the West India Co. and lat-
       er became governor of Manhattan (1592-1672). (E)
777.   Wilkinson, Burke. Young Louis XIV, The Early Years
       of the Sun King. Macmillan, 1971. Ill. by Doreen
       Roberts. History as exciting as a Hitchcock movie,
       of the youth of the long-lived (1638-1715) and long-
       ruling (1643-1715) Sun King. (YA)

               EIGHTEENTH CENTURY

778.   Alderman, Clifford Lindsey. Liberty! Equality! Fra-
       ternity! The Story of the French Revolution.
       Messner, 1965. Ill. by Barry Martin. Obviously
       exciting history. (YA)
779.   Bishop, Claire Huchet. Lafayette, French-American
       Hero. Garrard, 1960. Ill. by Maurice Brevannes.
       Biography for very young readers (1757-1834). (E
       and I)
780.   Carter, Hodding. The Marquis de Lafayette, Bright
       Sword for Freedom. Random Landmark, 1958.
       Ill. by Mimi Korach. An exciting "bridge" book
       joining France and America. (I)
781.   Cooper, Leonard. The Young Napoleon. Roy, n.d.
       Ill. by Anne Linton. The story of the often mis-
       spent youth of this hero (or villain, as you choose)
       which accounts for the events of his later years.
       (I and YA)
782.   Dowd, David L. The French Revolution. American
       Heritage, 1965. Ill. with paintings, drawings and
       documents of the period. Written with the cooper-

ation of the editors of Horizon Magazine. (YA)

783. Eimerl, Sarel. Revolution! France, 1789-94. Little, Brown, 1967. Ill. with portraits. A vivid, chronological account as exciting (if not more so) as any work of fiction about the revolution. (YA and A)

784. Garnett, Henry. The Red Bonnet. Doubleday, 1964. A novel about a young French aristocrat disguised as a Breton corsair in order to take part in an attempted rescue of Marie Antoinette. (YA)

785. Gerson, Noel B. The Mohawk Ladder. Doubleday, 1951. A novel of high adventure, the hero an American colonial in the service of the Duke of Marlborough and caught up in the toils of French espionage during the War of the Spanish Succession, 1701-14. (YA)

786. Graham, Alberta Powell. Lafayette, Friend of America. Abingdon, 1952. Ill. by Ralph Ray. A biography for very young readers, emphasizing Lafayette's service to America. (E and I)

787. Kielty, Bernardine. Marie Antoinette. Random Landmark, 1955. Ill. by Douglas Gorsline. Biography (1755-93). (I)

788. Komroff, Manuel and Odette. Marie Antoinette. Messner, 1967. Jacket by Frank Kramer. A good concise biography of the unhappy queen (1755-93) showing clearly but also sympathetically, her faults and mistakes. (YA)

789. Kyle, Elizabeth (Dunlop). Portrait of Lisette. Nelson, 1963. A biographical novel about the painter, Mme. Vigee Le Brun, and her life in Paris just before the revolution. (YA)

790. MacOrlan, Pierre. The Anchor of Mercy. Random, 1967. Translated from the French by Frances Frenaye. Ill. by David K. Stone. A 16-year-old boy, in Brest in 1777, becomes involved in some mysterious murders and the search for a desperate piratical character. (YA)

791. Malvern, Gladys. Patriot's Daughter. Macrae, Smith, 1960. A story of Anastasia Lafayette, her famous father and her intrepid mother. (YA)

792. Miller, Eugenia. The Golden Spur. Holt, Rinehart and Winston, 1964. Ill. by Leonard Everett Fisher. A short story of a boy, a horse, and, incidentally, Louis XVI. (I)

793. Mossiker, Frances. More Than a Queen: The Story of Josephine Bonaparte. Knopf, 1971. Ill. by Michael Eagle. Born in Martinique in 1763, Jose-

phine married a French noble who was guillotined
during the terror (she herself barely saved from
the same gruesome death) and secondly Napoleon
who made her an empress but divorced her. She
died sadly alone in 1814. (YA)

794. Pratt, N. S. The French Revolution. John Day, 1971.
Ill. with drawings by Elizabeth Hammond, maps and
reproductions. An information-packed account from
the beginning development at the start of Louis
XVI's reign in 1774 to Bonaparte's announcement
in 1799 that the revolution was over. (YA)

795. Riedman, Sarah R. Antoine Lavoisier, Scientist and
Citizen. Nelson, 1957. A biography of the "father
of modern chemistry" (1743-94) who was guillotined
during the reign of terror. (YA)

796. Ritchie, Rita. Night Coach to Paris. Norton, 1970.
Jacket by Herold Berson. A highly improbable plot
but interesting for its portrayal of the terror under
Robespierre, about a young American seeking to
ransom his French cousin. (YA)

797. Spencer, Cornelia (Yaukey). Song in the Streets.
John Day, 1960. A brief unbiased story of the
French revolution, its causes and results. (YA)

798. Sprague, Rosemary. Dance for a Diamond Star.
Walck, 1959. A novel about a dedicated ballerina,
in the late years of Louis XIV and the difficult de-
cision she has to make between her career and
marriage to a cousin of the king. (YA)

799. Trease, Geoffrey. Victory at Valmy. Vanguard, 1960.
An adventure story of the French Revolution in its
early stages. (YA)

800. Vance, Marguerite. Marie Antoinette, Daughter of an
Empress. Dutton, 1950. Ill. by Nedda Walker.
A biography of the Queen of Louis XVI (1755-93)
whose mother was the very dominating Empress
Maria Theresa of Austria. (YA)

800a. Webb, Robert N. Jean-Jacques Rousseau: The Father
of Romanticism. Watts, 1970. Map by Walter
Hortens. A short biography of Rousseau with a
chronology of his life (1712-78) and a list of his
major works. (YA)

801. Welch, Ronald. Escape From France. Oxford, 1960.
Ill. by William Stobbs. The adventures of a certain Richard Cary (of the Welsh-English Cary family whose members--of different generations--ap-
pear in various countries and periods), in his attempts to rescue his French relatives from the

guillotine, with suspense to the very end. (YA)
802. Wilson, Hazel. The Little Marquise, Madame Lafay-
     ette. Knopf, 1957. Ill. by Paul A. Sagsoorian.
     The love story of the Marquis and Marquise de
     Lafayette. (I)
803. Williamson, Joanne S. Jacobin's Daughter. Knopf,
     1956. Ill. by Charles Clement. An exceptionally
     good novel about the Revolution with particular at-
     tention to some of the leaders: Danton, Saint Just,
     Desmoulins and others, and to the conflict among
     revolutionary factions. (YA)
804. Wright, Constance. A Chance for Glory. Holt, 1957.
     A previously untold story of the rescue of Lafay-
     ette from prison in Olmutz in 1794, constructed
     from sources acknowledged in a section at the end.
     (A)

                    NINETEENTH CENTURY

          A.   Napoleonic Period and Aftermath

805. Brooks, Dame Mable. The St. Helena Story. London,
     1960. Ill. with paintings, photographs and a map
     of St. Helena. An exceptionally personal and in-
     timate story of the Emperor Napoleon in exile,
     written by a descendent of the Balcombe family
     whose young daughter, Betsy, became Napoleon's
     very good friend. (A)
806. Brown, Anthony. Dangerfoot. Meredith Press, 1966.
     Ill. by Jeanette Giblin. A spy story set in the
     time of Napoleon's threatened invasion of England
     on the Channel coast in 1801. (I and YA)
807. Carbonnier, Jeanne. Above All a Physician, A Biog-
     raphy of Theophile Laennec, Inventor of the Steth-
     oscope. Scribner, 1961. Laennec (1781-1826)
     grew up literally in the shadow of the guillotine,
     in Nantes, was a health officer at 15, and under-
     went many difficulties in order to fulfill his ambi-
     tion to become a physician. (YA)
808. Desmond, Alice Curtis. Marie Antoinette's Daughter.
     Dodd, Mead, 1967. Ill. with photographs, maps,
     diagrams and chronological tables. A book about
     one of the least known but very important charac-
     ters in French history, "Madame Royal, " as she
     was called, who was First Lady of France during

the reign of Louis XVIII and Charles X and who
was called by Napoleon, "the only man in her family." (A)

809. Doyle, Arthur Conan. The Glorious Hussar and Sabres
of France, ca. 1902; Walker edition, 1961, with
decorations. Two novels about the exploits and adventures of the Brigadier Gerard in the Napoleonic
campaigns. (YA)

810. Dumas, Alexander. The Count of Monte Cristo, 1844.
A novel about Edmund Dantes, unjustly imprisoned
on charge of aiding the exiled Napoleon. (A)

811. Eaton, Jeanette. Betsy's Napoleon. Morrow, 1936.
Ill. by Pierre Brissaud. Based on the memoirs of
Betsy Balcomb Abell published in 1844 under the
title "Recollections of the Emperor Napoleon During
the Time Spent by Him in her Father's Home in St.
Helena," and with a cover map of the island, the
novel has an authentic ring, though it is hard to
imagine that Betsy was truly that mischievous and
able to get away with it. (A)

811a. Gould, Linda. The Royal Giraffe. Dutton, 1971. Ill.
by Mircea Fasiliu. An entertaining story based
only slightly on fact and enriched with details un-
recorded in history, about a present from Mohammed
Ali Pasha of Egypt to Charles X of France (reign-
ing from 1824 to 1830). (E and I)

812. Komroff, Manuel. Napoleon. Messner, 1954. A biography (1769-1821). Like Winston Churchill, Napoleon was a two-century man, but his greatest impact on world history came in the nineteenth century. (I)

813. Maurois, André. Napoleon, A Pictorial Biography.
Viking, 1963. 175 illustrations and a chronology.
(YA)

814. Pringle, Patrick. Napoleon's Hundred Days. Warne,
1969. Ill. by Sheila Bewley. An account of the
period from Napoleon's escape from Elba to his
defeat at Waterloo. (YA)

815. Robbins, Ruth. The Emperor and the Drummer Boy.
Parnassus, 1962. Ill. by Nicolas Sidjakov. A
story of two young drummer boys on naval maneu-
vers under Napoleon. (I)

816. Vance, Marguerite. The Empress Josephine, From
Martinique to Malmaison. Dutton, 1956. Ill. by
Nedda Walker. This refers back mainly to the
eighteenth century, and is about her unhappy marriage to Alexander de Beauharnais before she mar-

ried Napoleon, with a quick summary of the French
Revolution and her life thereafter. (YA)

B. Mid-Century and Later

817. Curie, Eve. Madame Curie. Doubleday, 1937. Ill.
      with photographs. Translated by Vincent Sheean.
      A long personal biography of Marie Curie (1867-
      1935) by her daughter. (A)
818. DeGering, Etta. Seeing Fingers, The Story of Louis
      Braille. David McKay, 1962. Ill. by Emil Weiss.
      A short, warm biography (1809-52) of a man who
      had extreme difficulty in getting adopted the sys-
      tem which has brought the world of books to the
      blind. (I and YA)
819. Fox, Mary Virginia. Apprentice to Liberty. Abing-
      don, 1960. Ill. by Mel Silverman. A novel about
      the building and transportation of the Statue of Lib-
      erty from the viewpoint of an apprentice to the
      sculptor Bartholdi and about the tensions in France
      following the Franco-Prussian War of 1870. Good
      suspense. (I and YA)
820. Grant, Dr. Madeleine P. Louis Pasteur, Fighting
      Hero of Science. McGraw-Hill, 1959. Ill. with
      line drawings and photographs by Clifford Geary.
      A biography of the scientist, biologist and teacher
      (1822-1895). (YA)
821. Henriod, Lorraine. Marie Curie. Putnam, 1970.
      "A See and Read Beginning To Read Biography."
      Ill. by Fermin Rocker. Though Madame Curie
      was Polish born and raised, she studied, married,
      and made her great discoveries in Paris. She
      was born in 1867, received the Nobel Prize with
      her husband in 1903 for their joint discovery of
      radium, received a second as a widow in 1911,
      in chemistry, and died in 1935. (E)
822. Neimark, Anne E. Touch of Light, The Story of
      Louis Braille. Harcourt, Brace and World, 1970.
      Ill. by Robert Parker. A touching story indeed,
      lovingly but not sentimentally told, of the boy,
      blinded at the age of three, who invented the code
      which has come to be known by his name, opening
      the whole world of books to the blind. (I)
823. Nicolle, Jaques. Louis Pasteur; The Story of His
      Major Discoveries. Basic Books, 1961. A biog-
      raphy of the great scientist (1822-95) written by a

man whose father and uncle were members of
Pasteur's circle at the Pasteur Institute and who,
himself, lived at the Institute for a while.   (A)

824. Noble, Iris. Great Lady of the Theater, Sarah Bern-
hardt. Messner, 1960. Jacket by Rupert Fine-
gold. The long, exotic, often scandalous, always
courageous life (1844-1923) of the great actress
who, even when old and crippled, electrified au-
diences in France and abroad. (YA)

825. Pain, Nesta. Louis Pasteur. Putnam, 1958. Ill. by
Lili Rethi. A short biography (1822-95).   (I)

826. Pauli, Hertha. Bernadette and the Lady. Farrar,
Straus, 1956. Ill. by Georges Vaux. A biography
of Bernadette Soubirous, the Saint of Lourdes. (YA)

827. Peare, Catherine Owens. Jules Verne, His Life.
Holt, Rinehart and Winston, 1956. Ill. by Margaret Ayer. A timely book for the present day,
this is a biography of the science fiction writer
(1828-1905) who astounded his own world and our's
of today with his imaginative foresight in such books
as "From the Earth to the Moon" and "2,000
Leagues Under the Sea" and at least a hundred
others. (E and I)

828. Price, Willadene. Bartholdi and the Statue of Liberty.
Rand-McNally, 1959. Ill. with photographs. A
biography of Auguste Bartholdi (1834-1904) and how
he built the great statue and shipped it to New
York. (I and YA)

829. Raboff, Ernest Lloyd. Pierre-Auguste Renoir. Doubleday, 1970. A brief biography of the artist (1848-
1919) with color reproductions and analyses of his
works. An art book for children. (I and YA)

830. Ripley, Elizabeth. Rodin. Lippincott, 1966. Biography (1840-1917) with each page of text having a
facing page reproducing a specific work. (YA)

831. Rubin, Elizabeth. The Curies and Radium. Watts,
1961. Ill. by Alan Moyler. A "First Biography"
about both husband, Pierre (1859-1906) and wife
Marie (1867-1935), with a chapter at the end about
their daughter, Irene, and her husband, Frederic
Joliot, and radioisotopes. (I)

832. Schechter, Betty. The Dreyfus Affair. Houghton-
Mifflin, 1965. A story of the famous miscarriage
of justice in which Alfred Dreyfus, a French army
officer, was convicted of treason in 1894 and 1899,
and acquitted only in 1906. (YA)

833. Thorne, Alice. The Story of Madame Curie. Grosset,

1959. Ill. by Federico. A well arranged biography
of Marie Curie (1867-1935) with a chronology. (YA)

834. Werfel, Franz. The Song of Bernadette. Viking,
1942. A novel, translated by Ludwig Lewisohn,
about the Saint of Lourdes (1843-79). (A)

835. Werstein, Irving. I Accuse; The Story of the Dreyfus
Case. Messner, 1967. The case of the French
officer (1859-99) Alfred Dreyfus who was falsely
accused and convicted of treason in 1894 and 1899
but whose innocence was championed by Clemenceau
and the writer, Zola, so that he was fully exoner-
ated upon retrial in 1906. (YA)

835a. Wilson, Ellen. American Painter in France; A Life
of Mary Cassatt, 1844-1926. Farrar, Straus and
Giroux, 1971. Ill. with many reproductions of her
paintings. The story of an exceptionally liberated
woman, especially for the Victorian era, who, at
sixteen, startled her parents by begging permission
to go to Paris to study painting. She was granted
her wish at 22, and remained in France for the
rest of her life, gaining lasting fame as one of the
Impressionists. (YA)

TWENTIETH CENTURY

835b. Berna, Paul. They Didn't Come Back. Translated
from the French by John Buchanan-Brown. Pantheon, 1969. A novel based on a tragic period
before the liberation of France, about a band of
young men who left the shelter of a mountain hut
one August night to escape the Germans, and were
never seen again. (YA)

836. DeJong, Meindert. Journey From Peppermint Street.
Harper and Row, 1958. Ill. by Emily McCully.
A delicately amusing and, at the same time, exciting story of a little boy's excursion, with his
grandfather, into the night, across a swamp, encountering real and imaginary dangers. A little
historical background of Holland. (I)

837. Ellis, Leo R. Nights of Danger. Funk and Wagnalls,
1964. Ill. by Vic Donahue. A novel about a boy,
half French and half American, who aids the French
maquis (the underground) in destroying a radio
transmitter just before the Normandy landing. (I)

838. Frank, Anne. The Diary of a Young Girl. Random,
Modern Library, 1952. Translated from the Dutch

by B. M. Moorjaart and with an introduction by
Eleanor Roosevelt. A tragic book but remarkably
full of humor and even joie de vivre--the thoughts
of a young Jewish girl in hiding in Amsterdam from
June, 1942, to August, 1944, her own years being
from 13 to 15. She was murdered in the concentration camp at Bergen-Belsen in March, 1945.
(YA and A)

839.   Jablonski, Edward. Warriors with Wings. Bobbs-
Merrill, 1966. Ill. with photographs. A dramatic
story of the 38 men who served with the Lafayette
Escadrille before it was transferred to the Ameri-
can Air Force as the Lafayette Flying Corps in
World War I. (YA)

840.   Janssen, Pierre. A Moment of Silence. Atheneum,
1970. Ill. with photographs by Hans Samson. Translated by William R. Tyler, former U.S. Ambassa-
dor to the Netherlands, who says that its subject
"is the suffering and heroism of the dauntless people of the Netherlands in World War II." A deeply
sensitive story. (YA and A)

841.   Knight, Clayton and K. S. We Were There With the
Lafayette Escadrille. Grosset, 1961. Ill. by Clayton Knight. The true story of those early American fliers in France in World War I, with a list of
the volunteers in the Escadrille. (I)

842.   McKown, Robin. Patriot of the Underground. Putnam,
1964. Ill. by Edna Kaula. A tense story of the
part played by young boys in the French resistance
movement in the small mining towns of northeastern
France during the years of the German occupation
in World War II. (YA)

843.   _____. Janine. Messner, 1960. Jacket by Gerald
McCann. A novel set in the "black country," the
coal mining section of northeastern France, shortly
after its liberation from the Germans. The daughter of a miner, imprisoned by the enemy and pre-
sumed dead, has been receiving packages and mail
from a wealthy American girl who finally comes to
visit with her parents. The American is much at-
tracted to the young man rejected by Janine who
believes that his father betrayed her's. (YA)

844.   _____. She Lived for Science--Irene Joliot-Curie.
Messner, 1961. Jacket by Don Lambo. A biography of the elder daughter of Pierre and Marie
Curie who followed so successfully in their foot-
steps in the science of radiology, and who, with

her husband, made discoveries which won for them
the Nobel Prize in chemistry and also led to the
discovery of the neutron and the splitting of the
atom. (YA and A)

845. Nordhoff, Charles, and Hall, James Norman. <u>Fal-
cons of France</u>. Little, Brown, 1929. A novel
about the Lafayette Flying Corps in World War I.
(A)

846. Pease, Howard. <u>Heart of Danger</u>. Doubleday, 1946.
A "Ted Moran Mystery" set in France during and
after the end of World War II, in which two young
Americans (one, a Jew) try to join the French underground movement in order to obtain information
about German atomic research. (YA)

847. Rougé, Michel. <u>The Mystery of Mont Saint-Michel</u>.
Holt, Rinehart and Winston, 1955. Ill. by Peter
Spier. A "now and then" story of three boys, 10,
13, and 15, who, in exploring the Abbey of Mont
Saint-Michel, are trapped by the tide in an underground passage, and, while seeking escape, discover the remains of a Roman road and some pet-
rified wood--the remnants of an ancient forest.
Entirely fictional but, as explained in the epilogue,
such a place did actually exist thousands of years
ago. (I and YA)

848. Shemin, Margaretha. <u>The Little Riders</u>. Coward
McCann, 1963. Ill. by Peter Spier. The story
of a little American girl, visiting her Dutch grandparents, who is caught there in Holland by World
War II and the German occupation. How she saves
"the little riders" and learns not to hate all Germans. (I)

849. _____. <u>The Empty Moat</u>. Coward McCann, 1969.
Jacket by Peter Spier. A 16-year-old girl whose
family castle is occupied (with the exception of one
wing) by German soldiers, is faced with the choice
between her own safety and involvement with refugees from the Germans. (YA)

850. Tunis, John R. <u>His Enemy, His Friend</u>. Morrow,
1967. A serious novel about the inner conflict of
a German sergeant in the occupation forces in
France, when he is forced to order the execution
of six innocent hostages whom he has grown to
know and like. (YA)

851. _____. <u>Silence Over Dunkirk</u>. Morrow, 1962. A
suspenseful novel about two Englishmen left behind
in German occupied territory after the evacuation

of Dunkirk in 1940 and the important part played
by an airedale in their escape efforts. (YA)

852.   Van Rhijn, Aleid.   The Tide in the Attic.   Criterion,
1961.   Ill. by Marjorie Gill and translated by A.
J. Pomeraus.   A story of one of the greatest
storms in history, in 1953, and how one Dutch
family survived it.   (I)

853.   Van Stockum, Hilda.   The Winged Watchman.   Farrar,
Strauss and Cudahy, 1962.   Ill. by the author.   The
story of a valiant Dutch family during the German
occupation in 1944.   (YA)

854.   Vivier, Colette.   The House of the Four Winds.   Doubleday, 1969.   Jacket by Ann Grifalconi.   Translated and edited by Miriam Morton.   A book I
defy you to put down before the end, about the
French resistance in German-occupied Paris, 1943-
45, and a part played in it by a 12-year-old boy
who grows up mighty fast in the process.   (I)

855.   Werstein, Irving.   The Long Escape.   Scribner, 1964.
A harrowing and inspiring novel about a Belgian
nurse who managed to lead 50 small children through
the shambles of the Nazi blitz to Dunkirk and rescue.   Based on fact.   (YA)

856.   Whitehouse, Arch.   The Laughing Falcon.   Putnam,
1969.   Ill. by Albert Orbaan.   Whenever an airman
of the Lafayette Escadrille is threatened by an enemy plane, a mysterious flier appears to the rescue.   (YA)

857.   Wilhelm, Maria.   For the Glory of France; The Story
of the French Resistance.   Messner, 1968.   (YA)

PART IV: GREECE AND THE BALKANS

ARCHAEOLOGY, MYTHS AND LEGENDS

A. Greece

858. Aliki (Brandenberg). The Eggs, A Greek Folk Tale.
Ill. by the author. Pantheon, 1969. An amusingly
told and illustrated story and picture book. (E)

859. Baumann, Hans. Lion Gate and Labyrinth. The
World of Troy, Crete, and Mycenae. Pantheon,
1967. Ill. with drawings and color plates and
translated by Stella Humphries, from the German.
Ancient Greece and Greek mythology as presented
in the light of nineteenth century archaeology under
Heinrich Schlieman and Sir Arthur Evans, with a
glossary of terms and proper names used. (YA
and A)

860. Berry, Erick (Best, Allena). The Winged Girl of
Knossus. Appleton, 1933. Ill. with decorations
drawn from murals and decorations of Knossus and
other Minoan cities. A novel of Inas, daughter of
Daedalus, Princess Ariadne, and Theseus and the
final destruction of Knossus. (YA)

861. Bulfinch, Thomas. A Book of Myths. Macmillan,
1942. Ill. by Helen Sewell. Selections from his
long classic book and a good basic collection of
Greek myths. (I and YA)

862. Capon, Paul. Kingdom of the Bulls. Norton, 1962.
Ill. by Lewis Zacks. A suspenseful novel about a
young girl of Sarum, England, who is stolen by
Cretan traders to be taken as a sacrifice to the
Minotaur in the Knossus of King Minos. (YA)

863. Colum, Padraic. The Golden Fleece and the Heroes
Who Lived Before Achilles. Macmillan, 1921,
and 1949. Ill. by Willy Pogany. A blending of
myths into a continuous story. (I and YA)

864. Coolidge, Olivia. Greek Myths. Houghton-Mifflin,
1949. Ill. by Eduard Sandoz. (YA)

865. _____. The King of Men. Houghton-Mifflin, 1966.

Ill. by Ellen Raskin. A novel based on the Aga-
memnon legend about his struggle for power and
the conquest of Helen. (YA)

866. _____. The Trojan War. Houghton-Mifflin, 1952.
Ill. by Eduard Sandoz. The Homeric story with a
helpful table of characters. (YA)

867. _____. The Golden Days of Greece. Crowell, 1968.
Ill. by Enrico Arno. Historical tales and legends
of ancient Greece. (I)

868. Cox, Miriam. The Magic and the Sword. The Greek
Myths Retold. Row-Peterson, 1960. Ill. by Harold Price. The particular interest of this book is
in its telling of the many words and names from
Greek mythology we use in our contemporary speech
and writing. Glossary. (I)

869. D'Aulaire, Ingri and Edgar Parin. D'Aulaire's Book
of Greek Myths. Doubleday, 1962. Ill. by the
authors. A beautiful book to own. (I)

870. de Selincourt, Aubrey. Odysseus the Wanderer. Criterion, 1956. Ill. by Norman Meredith. A fine
retelling of "The Odyssey" with a handsome format.
(I)

871. Dolch, Edward and Marguerite P. Greek Stories for
Pleasure Reading. Garrard, 1955. Ill. by Marguerite Dolch and Robert S. Kerr. A book of stories rewritten using "the first thousand words,"
for beginning readers or those who find reading
difficult. (E and I)

872. Fadiman, Clifton. The Adventures of Hercules. Random, 1960. All the stories of the labors of Hercules in one short book. (I)

873. Faulkner, Nancy. The Traitor Queen. Doubleday,
1963. A well-constructed novel about Mycenean
plots against Crete and its King Minos, with a
useful map. (YA)

874. Galdone, Paul. Androcles and the Lion. Adapted and
illustrated by the author. McGraw, 1970. A retelling of the consequences following the meeting
of a slave, Androcles, with a wounded lion in the
forest. (E)

875. Galt, Tom. The Rise of the Thunderer. Crowell,
1954. Ill. by John Mackey. The ancient Greek
story of creation. (I)

876. Garfield, Leon and Blishen, Edward. The God Be-
neath the Sea. Pantheon, 1971. Ill. by Zevi
Blum. Here the dramas of the Greek legends have
been skillfully woven into a continuous narrative

that reads like a Greek tragedy. (YA and A)

877. Graves, Robert. Greek Gods and Heroes. Doubleday, 1960. Ill. by Dimitris Davis. Myths and legends retold by a poet. (YA)

878. _____. The Siege and Fall of Troy. Doubleday, 1962. Ill. by C. Walter Hodges. The stories of the Iliad and the Odyssey, supplemented with accounts of Latin and Greek authors. (YA)

879. Green, Roger Lancelyn. Mystery at Mycenae. Barnes, 1959. Ill. by Margery Gill. A detective story about the abduction of Helen of Troy. (YA)

880. _____. A Book of Myths. Dutton, 1965. Ill. by Joan Kiddell-Monroe. This book contains myths of other cultures many of which became the basis for Greek stories. (YA)

881. _____. Heroes of Greece and Troy. Walck, 1961. Ill. by Heather Copley and Christopher Chamberlain. In this retelling of the stories of ancient writers, Mr. Green has written a continuous narrative. (YA)

882. Gunther, John. The Golden Fleece. Random, 1959. Ill. by Ernest Kurt Barth. The story of the Argonauts. (I)

883. Hamilton, Edith. Mythology. Little, Brown, 1940. An adaptation of her longer definitive book. (YA)

884. Hawthorne, Nathaniel. Tanglewood Tales, 1853. Six Greek myths retold. (I)

885. _____. Pandora's Box, The Paradise of Children. McGraw-Hill, 1967. Ill. by Paul Galdone. The story of how troubles descended upon the world and their only remedy. (I)

886. Honour, Alan. Secrets of Minos: Sir Arthur Evans' Discoveries at Crete. McGraw-Hill, 1961. Ill. with photographs and line drawings. Jacket by P. A. Hutchinson and Foreword by Dr. John H. Young. A biography of the Englishman Evans (1851-1941) who brought the ancient Minoan civilization on Crete to life. (YA)

887. Johnson, Dorothy. Witch Princess. Houghton-Mifflin, 1967. Ill. by Carolyn Cather. A novel of the mysterious legend of Medea and the Argonauts, told from the viewpoint of a handmaiden to the princess. (YA)

888. King, Clive. The Twenty-Two Letters. Coward McCann, 1966. Ill. by Richard Kennedy. Though beginning and ending in a little Phoenician kingdom, there is enough of the action set in Minoan Crete to justify

its inclusion here. It is a scholarly, humorous
and imaginative reconstruction of the beginning of
celestial navigation, the introduction of cavalry,
and, most importantly, the invention of the alphabet. It contains a comparison of Egyptian hiero-
glyphics, Phoenician letters and modern letters.
(YA and A)

888a. Kingsley, Charles. The Heroes. Childrens' Press,
Chicago, 1968. Ill. by Ron King. Cover by Don
Irwin. A beautifully made book of Greek myths
with interesting marginal notes. (I and YA)

889. McLean, Mollie, and Wiseman, Anne. Adventures of
the Greek Heroes. Houghton-Mifflin, 1951. Ill.
by Witold T. Mars. Myths about Hercules, Per-
seus, Theseus, Orpheus, and the Argonauts. (I)

890. Miller, Katherine. Apollo. Houghton, 1970. Wood-
cuts by Vivian Berger. A retelling of the myths
about Apollo and other mythical characters such
as, Hercules, King Midas and Daphne. (I)

891. Petrovskaya, Kyra. The Quest for the Golden Fleece.
Lothrop, Lee and Shepard, 1962. Ill. by W. T.
Mars. The story of Jason and the Argonauts, retold with lively action and dialogue, and with a list
of the gods and people and places in the story. (I)

892. Picard, Barbara Leonie. The Odyssey of Homer.
Oxford, 1952. Ill. by Joan Kiddell-Monroe. A
translation of the epic for young readers. (I)

893. Pollack, Merrill. Phaethon. Lippincott, 1966. Ill.
by William Hofmann. A rhymed and rhythmical
retelling of the legend of the son of the Sun God
who aimed too high, and of the devotion of his
friend, Cygnus. (I)

894. Proddow, Penelope. The Spirit of Spring. Bradbury
Press, 1970. Ill. by Susan Jeffers. A tale of
the Greek god Dionysus when he lived on earth
before he went to live on Mt. Olympus with the
other gods. (I and YA)

895. _____. Dionysus and the Pirates. Homeric Hymn,
Number Seven, Doubleday, 1971. Ill. by Barbara
Cooney. A picture book for all ages. (P.B.)

896. Ray, Mary. Standing Lions. Meredith, 1969. Ill.
by Janet Duchesne. An exciting novel about the
growing in wisdom and patience of a 17-year-old
King of Argos, ten years before the Trojan war.
(I and YA)

897. Reeves, James. The Trojan Horse. Franklin Watts,
1969. Ill. by Krystyna Turska. The story re-

lated by a young Trojan boy escaping from the city
after the Greeks played their trick on the Trojans.
(E and I)

898. Schneider, Nina. Hercules, the Gentle Giant. Hawthorne, 1969. Ill. by Tomie de Paola. A humorously told and hilariously illustrated story of how
Hercules slew the fierce lion for the cowardly king.
(E)

899. Serraillier, Ian. A Fall From the Sky, The Story of
Daedalus. Walck, 1965. Ill. by William Stobbs.
A short story of the inventor and craftsman of
wings for man, and his son's flight toward the sun.
(I)

900. _____. Heracles the Strong. Walck, 1970. Wood-
cuts by Rocco Negri. Vividly told and illustrated,
the story of the mighty Greek hero of mythology
who performed miraculous labors in atonement for
murders he had committed under the spell of madness laid on him by Hera, queen of the gods.   (I)

901. Tomaino, Sarah F. Persephone, Bringer of Spring.
Crowell, 1970. Ill. by Ari Forberg. A beautiful
book of the legend. (I and YA)

902. Treece, Henry. The Windswept City. Meredith, 1968.
Ill. by Faith Jacques. A novel of the Trojan War.
(I)

903. Watson, James. The Bull Leapers. Crowell, 1970.
The story of Theseus who won the bull-leaping con-
test and the Kingdom of Crete. (YA)

904. Watson, Jane Werner. The Iliad and The Odyssey.
Golden, 1956. Ill. by Alice and Martin Provinsen.
Retold stories of Homer's epics. (I)

905. Weil, Lisl. King Midas' Secret and Other Follies.
McGraw-Hill, 1969. Ill. by the author. Greek.
mythology with an up-to-date humorous twist and
delightfully crazy drawings. (E and I)

B.   The Balkans

906. Kavčič, Vladimir. The Golden Bird, Folk Tales from
Slovenia. Translated by Jan Dekker and Helen
Lencek. World, 1969. Ill. by Mae Gerhard. In
this introduction to this attractive book, Mr. Kavčič
explains that though these stories were first written down in the latter half of the nineteenth century,
they had been told to many generations of children
and older people and reflect the life of the Slo-

venian people of long ago. (I)
907. Pridham, Radost. A Gift from the Heart. World,
      1966. Ill. by Pauline Baynes. Jacket by Suzanne
      Dolesch. A collection of amusing tales from the
      Balkans. (I)
908. Ure, Jean. Rumanian Folk Tales. Watts, 1960. Ill.
      by Charles Mozley. A book of stories about two
      rascals named Pacala and Tandala. (I and YA)

SIXTH CENTURY B.C.

909. Ray, Mary. The Voice of Apollo. Farrar, Straus
      and Giroux, 1964. Ill. by Enrico Arno. A novel
      about the burning of the temple at Delphi in 548
      B.C. and the Pythian games there and how two
      young men learned to accept fate and go on from
      there. (YA)

FIFTH CENTURY B.C.
(The Golden Age of Ancient Greece)

910. Coolidge, Olivia. Marathon Looks on the Sea. Hough-
      ton-Mifflin, 1967. Ill. by Erwin Schachner. A
      scholarly novel about the Greek-Persian wars, cul-
      minating in the Battle of Marathon which decided
      the supremacy of Athens, and in which Miltiades,
      the Greek, was opposed by his own son, Metiochos,
      who had been captured by the Persians and made a
      general by King Darius. (YA and A)
911. _____. The Maid of Artemis. Houghton-Mifflin,
      1969. A short poignant novel about a young Athe-
      nian girl who learns, by the time she is 14, that
      "growing is pain as well as pleasure, " the story
      inspired by an archaeological find of a small hand
      holding a bird. (I and YA)
912. _____. Men of Athens. Houghton-Mifflin, 1962.
      Ill. by Milton Johnson. A book about the Golden
      Age and some of the men who made it so. (YA)
913. Daringer, Helen. Yesterday's Daughter. Harcourt,
      Brace and World, 1964. Ill. by Michael A. Hamp-
      shire. A novel about Hesper, a young girl of De-
      los, whose father had ill luck in his shipping ven-
      tures and whose brother, therefore, could not af-
      ford a jockey to ride his horse in the races, until
      Hesper solves the problem. (YA)

914. Davis, William Stearns. _Victor of Salamis_. A Tale
      of the Days of Xerxes, Leonidas, and Themistocles.
      Macmillan, 1925. (A)
915. Goldberg, Herbert. _Hippocrates, Father of Modern_
      Medicine. Watts, 1963. A biography of the man
      who first said, "one man's meat is another man's
      poison." As little is known about his personal life,
      this book is mainly about the medical profession
      before and at his time (and some after, about Ga-
      len) and will especially interest those who are con-
      sidering medicine as a career. (YA)
916. Guillot, René. _The Champion of Olympia_. Reilly and
      Lee, 1968. Translated by Anne Carter. Ill. by
      Jaques Fromont and map. A brave Galatian boy
      endures enslavement by the Greeks until he triumphs
      in the Olympic chariot races and then flees for life
      and freedom. (YA)
917. Higgins, Dorothy. _Ring of Hades_. Parents' Magazine
      Press, 1969. Ill. by Mae Gerhard. A 12-year-
      old Greek boy comes face-to-face with danger as
      he tries to discover the secret of the ring his fa-
      ther sent back to him from the war with Sparta.
      (I)
918. Lawrence, Isabelle. _Niko, Sculptor's Apprentice_.
      Viking, 1956. Ill. by Arthur Marokvia. A story
      based on the building of the Parthenon, 447-432
      B.C. (I)
919. Mayer, A. I. _Olympiad_. Harper, 1938. Ill. by
      Cleveland J. Woodward. An exciting story, es-
      pecially interesting to wrestlers, about the 79th
      Olympiad, 464 B.C., with diagrams of a Greek
      house and a plan of Olympia. (YA)
920. Plowman, Stephanie. _The Road to Sardis_. Houghton-
      Mifflin, 1965. A fairly long novel about the Pelo-
      ponnesian War, 431-404 B.C. focussing on Alcibia-
      des (the main character), Euripedes, Socrates,
      Thucydides, Sophocles, and, very briefly, Pericles.
      Explanatory note and a chart of the relationships.
      (YA and A)
921. Renault, Mary. _The Lion in the Gateway_. Harper,
      1964. Ill. by C. Walter Hodges. A story of the
      heroic battles of the Greeks and Persians at Mara-
      thon, Salamis, and Thermopylae. (I)
922. Rockwell, Anne. _Temple on a Hill; The Building of_
      the Parthenon. Atheneum, 1969. Ill. by the au-
      thor. A clearly narrated and illustrated story of
      the battles of Thermopylae and Salamis, the glory

of Athens under Pericles, and the building of the
Parthenon. (I)

923. Silverberg, Robert. Socrates. Putnam, 1965. A biography (469-399 B.C.) stressing Socrates' thought
as given in the writings of Plato on which the book
is based. Only such words as are found in "The
Dialogues" are used. (YA)

924. Snedeker, Caroline Dale. Lysis Goes to the Play.
Lothrop, Lee and Shepard, 1962. Ill. by Reisie
Lonette. The story of a production of "Alcestis"
in the Theater of Dionysus, and a sister's sacrifice
so that Lysis might see it. (I)

925. _____ . The Perilous Seat. Doubleday, 1926. A
novel about Delhi and the Delphic Oracle at the
time the city was threatened by Xerxes. (YA)

926. Turlington, Bayly. Socrates, Father of Western Philosophy. Watts, 1969. Since so little is known
about Socrates' life, this is rather a "portrait"
which will set your mental wheels spinning as you
try to follow his method of reasoning. (YA)

FOURTH CENTURY B.C.

927. Aliki (Brandenberg). Diogenes: The Story of the
Greek Philosopher. Prentice-Hall, printed in Ja-
pan. Ill. by the author. Simply told and beautifully illustrated and presented, the story of the
great philosopher who lived from 412 to 323 B.C.
and is most remembered as the man who slept in
a tub and carried a lantern in search of an honest
man. (E)

928. Andrews, Mary Evans. Hostage to Alexander. Longmans Green, 1961. Ill. by Avery Johnson. A
story of Alexander the Great as narrated by a
young hostage from Rome, with a postscript identifying the historical characters and giving sources,
and a map of Alexander's conquests. (I)

929. Downey, Glanville. Aristotle, Dean of Early Science.
Franklin Watts, 1962. A biography of the philosopher and scientist (384-322 B.C.), pupil of Plato,
who tutored Alexander the Great. (YA)

930. Gunther, John. Alexander the Great. Random Landmark, 1953. Ill. by Isa Barnett. A biography of
the King of Macedon, conqueror of Asia (356-323
B.C.). (I)

931. Holm, Anne. Peter. Harcourt, Brace and World,

1958. Jacket by W. T. Mars. Translated from
the Danish by L. W. Kingland. The continuity of
history is the basic theme of this unusual time-
span book in which a boy in a portrait carries contemporary Peter back into ancient Greece, then
Norman England, and finally Cromwell's England.
(YA)

932. Household, Geoffrey. The Exploits of Xenophon. Random Landmark, 1955. Ill. by Leonard Everett
Fisher. A vividly, humorously told story of the
famous Athenian leader (435-355 B.C.) of 13,000
Greeks defeated by the Persians and forced to retreat 1,000 miles to their homeland. (I)

933. Mercer, Charles. Alexander the Great. American
Heritage, 1962. A Horizon Caravel book, illustrated with paintings, mosaics, sculptures, and
maps of the period. (I and YA)

934. Mitchison, Naomi. The Young Alexander the Great.
Roy, 1960. Ill. by Betty Middleton-Sanford. A
story of his early years. (I)

935. Skipper, Mervyn. The Fooling of King Alexander.
Atheneum, 1967. Ill. by Gaynor Chapman. A leg-
end of how a little boy foiled the plans of Emperor
Alexander to conquer China. (E)

936. Steele, Robert. The Story of Alexander. As published
by David McNutt, London, 1894 and by Xerox Mi-
crofilms in 1966. Ill. by Fred Mason. A romantic legend, probably Egyptian in origin, told in this
book as it might have been related in the middle
ages, and ending with a history of the many ver-
sions of the story down through the ages. (I and
YA)

937. Trease, Geoffrey. Web of Traitors. Vanguard, 1952.
An adventure story set in Athens at the time when
the Athenian democracy was nearing the end of its
struggle with Sparta. Socrates, Plato, Xenophon
and others included. (YA)

THIRD AND SECOND CENTURIES B.C.

938. Bendick, Jeanne. Archimedes and the Door of Science.
Franklin Watts, 1962. Ill. by the author. Biography (287-212). (I)

939. Coatsworth, Elizabeth. The Hand of Apollo. Viking,
1965. Ill. by Robin Jacques. A short dramatic
novel of the experiences and inner conflicts of a

lad of Corinth, in hiding after the destruction of
that city by the Romans, and their murder of its
men and enslavement of women and children. (YA)
940. Lexau, Joan M. Archimedes Takes a Bath. Crowell,
1969. Ill. by Salvatore Murdocca. A very funny
story about the way the great mathematician might
have made one of his important discoveries. (I)

FIRST CENTURY A.D.

941. Snedeker, Caroline Dale. Luke's Quest. Doubleday,
1947. A novel about Luke the physician, beginning
just before his conversion to Christianity. (YA)

SIXTH CENTURY A.D.

Byzantium (Constantinople) was the capital of the Byzantine or Eastern Empire after the fall of Rome in 476.

942. Downey, Glanville. Belisarius, Young General of Byzantium. Dutton, 1960. A biography of the general's first 30 years (505-535) concluding with his
African triumph. Contains a map of the Roman
world at this time, a long list of characters and
an afterword about sources. (YA)
943. Jacobs, David. Constantinople, City on the Golden
Horn. American Heritage, 1969. Ill. with reproductions of paintings, mosaics, statuary, architecture and maps. Consultant, Cyril Mango. A biography of a 2700-year-old city, now Turkish Is-
tanbul, which played such an important part in Eu-
ropean history, especially in the time of the Crusades. (YA)
944. Snedeker, Caroline Dale. Theras and His Town.
Doubleday, 1924 and 1961. Ill. by Dimitris Davis.
Information about Athens and Sparta presented
through the adventures of two boys escaping from
a brutal Spartan military camp. (I)

ELEVENTH THROUGH FOURTEENTH CENTURIES
(The Period of the Crusades)

945. Coolidge, Olivia. Tales of the Crusades. Houghton-
Mifflin, 1970. A collection of excellent short sto-

ries about the most dramatic events and characters
of the period 1095-1291. (YA)

946. Duggan, Alfred. The Story of the Crusades. Pantheon,
1964. Ill. by C. Walter Hodges' drawings, and by
photographs of major battle sites. A lively story
of all the crusades from 1095-1291 with an epilogue
and note on sources. (YA)

947. Hewes, Agnes Danforth. A Boy of the Lost Crusade.
Houghton-Mifflin, 1923 and 1951. Ill. by Gustaf
Tenggren. A story of the Childrens' Crusade
starting in France, and about the experiences of
a little boy in search of his father who falls into
Syrian hands. (I)

948. Knox, Esther Melbourne. Swift Flies the Falcon.
Hale, 1939. Ill. by Ruth King. A highly imagina-
tive story of the Crusades, based on Harold Lamb's
"Iron Men and Saints." (YA)

949. Suskind, Richard. Cross and Crescent. Norton, 1967.
Ill. by Victor Lazzario. A well-made short book
about the six (seven, counting St. Louis') crusades,
their causes, effects, and leaders. (I and YA)

950. Treece, Henry. The Crusades. Random, 1963. As
in all this late writer's books, violence and humor
combined with sound research. (A)

951. Welch, Ronald. Knight Crusader. Oxford, 1954. Ill.
by William Stobbs. A novel based on an actual
character whose adventures, however, are purely
imaginary. A clear map of medieval Europe and
the Kingdom of Jerusalem. (YA)

952. Williams, Jay. Knights of the Crusades. American
Heritage, 1962. Richly illustrated in color and
black and white with illuminating stories about the
Crusades. (I and YA)

FIFTEENTH AND SIXTEENTH CENTURIES

953. Faulkner, Nancy. Knights Besieged. Doubleday, 1964.
A strong novel about the downfall of the Knights of
St. John (Hospitalers) at Rhodes in 1522, and how
a young Englishman, well acquainted with both the
Knights and the conquering Turks, faced the truth
about men and war and his own soul. (YA)

954. Gladd, Arthur Anthony. Galleys East. Dodd, Mead,
1961. Ill. by Leonard Vosburgh. A sea story
about a young Greek sponge-diver in which the reader meets Cervantes (the author of Don Quixote),

Don Juan of Austria, Ali Pasha and other prominent characters. The Battle of Lepanto, 1571, pro-
vides the climax. (YA)

955. Kielty, Bernardine. The Fall of Constantinople. Random Landmark, 1957. Ill. by Douglas Gorsline.
This epic downfall of 1453 reads almost like a novel with its clearly drawn portraits of Constantine
XI (Paleologus) and Turkish Mohammed II. At the
end, the reader finds himself thinking with the author, "if only ... if only ... Constantinople might
have been saved." (YA)

SEVENTEENTH THROUGH NINETEENTH CENTURIES

956. Braymer, Marjorie. The Walls of Windy Troy; A Biography of Heinrich Schliemann. Harcourt, Brace,
1960. Ill. with photographs. The story of his life
(1822-90) and his discovery of the actual site of ancient Troy. An outline map and a time chart
adapted from Wallbank and Taylor's "Civilization,
Past and Present; Vol. I." (YA)

957. Dicher, Stefan. Rali. Stackpole Books, 1961. Ill.
by Liljana Dicheva and translated by Margaret Roberts. The time is the beginning of the uprising of
the Bulgarians against Turkish domination of their
country (1876) and the theme of the book is the in-
superable courage of the oppressed as personified
in a Bulgarian boy trying to escape from the Turks.
(YA)

958. Holberg, Ruth Langland. Michael and the Captain.
Crowell, 1944. Ill. by Sandra James. You may
be much surprised to find Captain John Smith as a
major character in this story of a Serbian boy who,
in attempting escape from impressment into the
Turkish Janizaries, falls into the hands of the Ta-
tars. A period (1603) and places (Serbia, Transyl-
vania, Russia) seldom encountered in historical fiction. (I and YA)

TWENTIETH CENTURY

A. Greece

959. Armstrong, Richard. Fight for Freedom. David

McKay, 1963. Ill. by Don Lambo. A novel of
adventure and escape from the Germans, based on
"Greece and Crete, 1941" by C. Cuckley. The
leading character is an 18-year-old apprentice of
a British merchantman who risks his own freedom
and life itself for the sake of others. (YA)

960. Forman, James. The Skies of Crete. Farrar, Straus,
1963. A novel about the Nazi invasion of Crete in
the spring of 1941, and the reactions of young and
old to aerial warfare. (YA)

961. _____. Ring the Judas Bell. Farrar, Straus, 1965.
A short terrifying novel about Greece in the late
1940s when the Andarte were fighting in the hills
and 10,000 Greek children were kidnapped by Communist Partisans. (YA)

962. _____. The Shield of Achilles. Farrar, Straus,
1966. A novel about the conflict between the Turks
and the Greeks on the island of Cyprus, and conflicting family loyalties. (YA)

963. Godden, Rumer. Operation Sippacik. Viking, 1969.
Ill. by Capt. James Bryan, R.A.E.C. One of
those books about the recent past which will soon
be historical--about the Blue Berets (British U.N.
forces on Cyprus) a Turkish boy whose father has
escaped from the Cypriots and is being hunted by
them, and an obstreperous donkey named Sippacik
who plays an important role in the exciting action.
(I)

964. Maclean, Alistair. The Guns of Navarone. Doubleday, 1957. A novel of suspense and adventure on
the island of Kheros during World War II. (A)

965. Zei, Alki. Wildcat Under Glass. Holt, Rinehart and
Winston, 1963. A story of humor, tragedy and intrigue about some Greek children during the beginning of the fascist regime in Greece, with a short
preface about "Greece and Freedom" which outlines a brief history of the country from the fall
of Constantinople in 1453 to modern times and maps
of the setting. (I and YA)

B. The Balkans

966. Archer, Jules. Red Rebel; Tito of Yugoslavia.
Messner, 1968. An exciting biography of a strong
man (1892-) who defied both Hitler and Stalin with
almost incredible narrow escapes. (YA)

967. Bridge, Ann (O'Malley, Mary Dolling). Illyrian Spring.
      Little, Brown, 1935. A novel set on the enchant-
      ing Dalmatian coast of Yugoslavia--the Illyria of
      the Roman Empire. (A)
968. _____. Singing Waters. Macmillan, 1946. A nov-
      el about Albania before World War II, giving a val-
      uable description of a country which is now com-
      pletely shut off from the western world by the Iron
      Curtain--history, economic and social conditions,
      and the people, their costumes and customs. (A)
969. Catherall, Arthur. Yugoslav Mystery. Lothrop, 1964.
      A thrilling story of pursuit and escape on a rocky
      island in the Adriatic, not far from Split, shortly
      after World War II. (YA)
970. Eton, Peter and Leasor, James. Wall of Silence.
      Bobbs, Merrill, 1960. A true mystery about the
      disappearance of World War II's greatest gold
      treasure, and the search that still goes on for it.
      (A)
971. Feuerlicht, Roberta Straus. The Desperate Act. Mc-
      Graw, 1968. Ill. with photographs and maps.
      About the assassination of Franz Ferdinand at Sara-
      jevo. Interviews with one of the two surviving as-
      sassins, give an account of the conspiracy which
      touched off World War I. (YA)
972. Franchere, Ruth. Tito of Yugoslavia. Macmillan,
      1970. Ill. with photographs. The story of Josip
      Broz (Tito, 1892---) born in Croatia, the man who
      has defied both Hitler and Stalin and has deter-
      minedly kept Yugoslavia united and independent of
      the Soviet Union. In spite of bitter poverty as a
      youth, inhuman imprisonment, frustration with the
      Royalists, or Chetniks led by Mihailovic, and Sta-
      lin, and through hairbreadth escapes from the Ger-
      mans in the mountains in World War II--he never
      lost this determination. (YA)
973. Held, Kurt (Klober). The Outsiders of Uskoken Cas-
      tle. Doubleday, 1967. Translated by Lynn Aubry.
      An action-packed story of Zora's Gang of five
      homeless kids, fighting and fending for themselves
      on the Dalmatian coast. Strong substance under-
      lies the humor and adventures. (I and YA)
974. Kusan, Ivan. The Mystery of Green Hill. Harcourt,
      Brace and World, 1962. Ill. by Kermit Adler and
      translated by Michael B. Patrovich. A detective
      story (20 days after the end of World War II) in
      which schoolboys are the detectives. (I)

975.   Miller, Elizabeth Cleveland.   Young Trajan.   Garden
       City, 1931.   Ill. by Maud and Miska Petersham.
       A love story, full of peasant lore and poetry and
       religious observations, complicated by a peasant
       uprising in Rumania in the early part of the cen-
       tury.   (I)
976.   Seuberlich, Hertha.   Annuzza, A Girl of Romania.
       Rand-McNally, 1962.   Ill. by Gerhardt Pallasch.
       A down-to-earth novel of a peasant girl in pre-
       World War II Romania.   (YA)
977.   Shannon, Monica.   Dobrey.   Viking, 1934.   Ill. by
       Atanas Katchamakoff.   An idealized picture of Bul-
       garian peasant life in the beginning of the present
       century.   (YA)

PART V: ITALY (ROME) AND SWITZERLAND

MYTHS, LEGENDS, FOLKLORE AND HISTORY

A. Italy

978. Behn, Harry. Omen of the Birds. World, 1964. Ill.
by the author. A novel based on archaeological
findings and legend about the Etruscan boy who finally became King Tarquin of Rome in A.D. 616,
and the young prophetess destined to become his
queen. The illustrations are based on Etruscan
tomb paintings. (YA)
979. Boldrini, Giuliana. The Etruscan Leopards. Pantheon
and Random, 1968. Ill. by J. C. Kocsis and translated by Eleanor Quigly. The story and illustrations of this reconstruction of Etruscan civilization
are based on a recently discovered mural and are
about the sea journey of a young merchant's son.
(YA)
980. Chubb, Thomas Caldecott. The Venetians, Merchant
Princes. Viking, 1968. Ill. with paintings, wood-
cuts and drawings by Laurel Toohey. Jacket by
Richard M. Powers. Definitely non-fiction, but included here as excellent background for fiction about
Venice and the Venetians, from ancient days until
the city state joined Italy in 1866. (YA)
981. Church, Alfred J. The Aeneid for Boys and Girls.
Macmillan, 1963. Ill. by Eugene Karlin. A retelling of Virgil's epic, with an Afterword by Clifton
Fadiman. (I)
982. Gerdes, Florence Marie, C. S. J. The Aeneid, A
Retelling for Young People. Ill. by George Ellen
Holmgren, C. S. J. St. Martin's, 1969. An attractive new version. (I)
983. Johnson, Dorothy. Farewell to Troy. Houghton-Mifflin, 1964. A novel of adventure and discovery,
based on the Aeneid of Virgil, with a postscript
giving the Fall of Troy as about 1183 B.C. (YA)
984. Suskind, Richard. Swords, Spears and Sandals. Knopf,

1941. Ill. by Enrico Arno. Here in a graphic, clearly organized short book is the whole history of Rome focussed on its fighting men, from about 800 B.C. to its fall in 476 A.D.

985. Taylor, N. B. The Aeneid of Virgil. Walck, 1961. Ill. by Joan Kiddell-Monroe. A fine prose translation for young readers. (YA)

986. Trease, Geoffrey. The Italian Story from the Earliest Times to 1946. Macmillan, 1963. Ill. with 31 plates and small clear maps. A pleasantly readable history. (YA)

B. Switzerland

987. Duvoisin, Roger. The Three Sneezes and Other Swiss Alpine Tales. Knopf, 1941. Ill. by the author. A collection of charming and humorous folk tales representative of various provinces of Switzerland. (I)

988. Huldschiner, Robert E. The Cow that Spoke for Seppl and Other Alpine Tales. Doubleday, 1968. Ill. by Carol Wilde. Original stories but told in the manner of folk tales and full of Alpine flavor and entertainment. (I)

989. Müller-Güggenbühl, Fritz. Swiss-Alpine Folk Tales. Oxford, 1958. Ill. by Joan Kiddell-Monroe and translated by Katherine Potts. (I)

ROME, THIRD CENTURY B.C.

990. Baumann, Hans. I Marched with Hannibal. Walck, 1962. Ill. by Ulrick Schramm. Translated by Katherine Potts. Fiction based on the life and times of Hannibal, with a map of his route, and a chronology of Carthaginian history, Hannibal's life, and the Punic Wars. (YA)

991. Houghton, Eric. The White Wall. McGraw-Hill, 1961. Ill. by Robin Jacques. A suspenseful novel about Hannibal's crossing of the Alps, based on "Alps and Elephants" by Sir Gavin de Beer, with an explanatory note. (YA)

992. Kellogg, Jean. The Rod and the Rose. Reilly and Lee, 1964. A rather complicated story of Hannibal's son, Hamilcar, based on the history of Carthage by Roman Livy and Greek Polybius. A

map would be helpful. (YA)

993. Kent, Louise Andrews. He Went with Hannibal.
Houghton-Mifflin, 1964. Ill. by W. T. Mars.
A good story and good history with a list of the
important dates of Hannibal's campaigns. (YA)

994. Merrell, Leigh. Prisoners of Hannibal. Nelson,
1958. A story of Hannibal, narrated by a young
Roman prisoner of war after the Battle of Canae
(216 B.C.). Map included. (YA)

995. Powers, Alfred. Hannibal's Elephants. Longmans
Green, 1944. Ill. by James Reid. A good story
with a particularly appealing portrayal of the human qualities of one old elephant. (YA)

ROME, FIRST CENTURY B.C.

996. Anderson, Paul L. Swords in the North. Biblo and
Tanner, 1935. Ill. by Norman Roberts. A novel
about Caesar's legions in Gaul and Britain, with
a list of characters and historical note. (YA)

997. _____. A Slave of Catiline. Biblo and Tanner,
1937. Ill. by Norman L. Roberts. A novel
about the Catiline Conspiracy in 63 B.C. (YA)

998. Coolidge, Olivia. Caesar's Gallic War. Houghton-
Mifflin, 1961. Ill. with decorations adapted from
old engravings. A good readable history based
on archaeology and classical research in addition
to Caesar's own Commentaries. (YA)

999. Gunther, John. Julius Caesar. Random Landmark,
1959. Ill. by Joseph Cellini. Biography (102?-
44 B.C.). (I)

1000. Houghton, Eric. They Marched with Spartacus. Mc-
Graw-Hill, 1963. Ill. by Robin Jacques. A novel
of the slave rebellion in 73 B.C. and a young
slave's perilous search for his mother who had
been captured by the Romans. (I)

1001. Isenberg, Irwin. Caesar. American Heritage, 1964.
Horizon Caravel Book, ill. with sculptures, mosaics and artifacts. (I and YA)

1002. Lawrence, Isabelle. The Gift of the Golden Cup.
Bobbs-Merrill, 1946. Ill. by Charles V. John.
An adventure story about a girl named Atia (who
grew up to be the mother of Caesar Augustus) and
her little brother, Gaius; the children are kidnapped
together and taken to Greece. (YA)

1003. _____. The Theft of the Golden Ring. Bobbs-

Merrill, 1948. Ill. by Charles V. John. A sequel to "The Gift of the Golden Cup" about a
treasure hunt in which Atia continues her hair-
raising adventures. (YA)

1004. Leighton, Margaret. Cleopatra, Sister of the Moon.
Farrar, Straus and Giroux, 1969. Jacket by
Catherine Smolich. An excellent biography of the
romantic Queen and a good history of Roman con-
quests in Egypt and of Rome at the time when
Cleopatra was married to Julius Caesar. (YA)

1005. Noble, Iris. Egypt's Queen, Cleopatra. Messner,
1963. A fairly long biographical novel about
Cleopatra, Julius Caesar, Brutus and Mark Antony. (YA)

1006. Shakespeare, William. Antony and Cleopatra. 1608?
A play. (A)

1007. _____. Julius Caesar. 1601? A play. (A)

1008. Snedeker, Caroline. The Forgotten Daughter. Doubleday, 1949. Ill. by Dorothy Lathrop. A novel
portraying the life of slaves during the second
century B.C. (YA)

1009. Webb, Robert. We Were There with Caesar's Legions. Grosset, 1960. Ill. by Fabian Zaccone.
Historical consultant, Major Gen. Courtnew Whitney, U.S.A. A story with a good plot built upon
the preparations for the Roman conquest of Britain. (I)

1010. Williamson, Joanne S. The Eagles Have Flown.
Knopf, 1957. Ill. by George Fulton. A novel
about the period following the murder of Julius
Caesar, the narrator a member of Brutus' household. (YA)

ROME, FIRST CENTURY A.D.

1011. Bulwer-Lytton, Edward George. The Last Days of
Pompeii, 1834. A romantic novel based on the
author's studies of the restoration of Pompeii.
(A)

1012. Coolidge, Olivia. Roman People. Houghton-Mifflin,
1959. Ill. by Lino Lipinsky. Short stories of
the lives of Romans of various classes and conditions during the rule of Caesar Augustus (27
B.C.-14 A.D.). (YA)

1013. Fosdick, Harry Emerson. The Life of Saint Paul.
Random Landmark, 1962. Ill. by Leonard Everett

Fisher. This biography of Paul of Tarsus, born
a Jew of Roman citizenship, carries the reader
throughout the Roman-dominated world (except for
Britain) of the first century A.D. to the time of
his death, about the year 67, and describes the
beginning and rapid growth of the Christian church
after his dramatic conversion. (I and YA)

1014. Gale, Elizabeth. Julia Valeria. Putnam, 1951. Ill.
by Bruno Frost. A novel about the early years
of the Christian era, during the reign of Caesar
Augustus. (YA)

1015. Latimer, John. The King's Rock. Meredith, 1969.
Jacket by Barry Martin. An adventure novel beginning in England where a young Roman centurion
stumbles upon a clue to a secret treasure buried
in a tomb somewhere in Egypt. In Rome, then
under the Emperor Domitius (51-96) where he goes
at risk of torture or death, he finds more clues
which finally take him to Egypt. (YA)

1016. Polland, Madeleine. City of the Golden House. Doubleday, 1963. Ill. by Leo Summers. A novel
about Nero's persecution of the Christians and the
death of Saint Peter. (YA)

1017. Sienkiewicz, Henryk. Quo Vadis. 1896. A romantic
novel about a young Roman in love with a Christian maiden during the reign of Nero (A.D. 54-
68). Among the historical figures are Paul of
Tarsus, Peter, Petronius, Seneca and Nero. (A)

1018. Speare, Elizabeth George. The Bronze Bow. Houghton-Mifflin, 1961. A novel set in Roman Palestine about some Zealots who looked for a military
Messiah but finally discover the Christian message
of the true Messiah. (YA)

1019. Wallace, Lew. Ben Hur, A Tale of the Christ. 1880.
A novel about a young aristocratic Jew finally converted to Christianity. (A)

1020. Wibberley, Leonard. The Centurion. William Morrow, 1966. A novel about Longinus, the Roman
soldier delegated to crucify Jesus--a book faithful
to the Gospels but enriched by the author's in-
sight and imagination. (A)

1021. Winterfelt. Detectives in Togas. Harcourt, Brace
and World, 1956. Ill. by Charlotte Cleinert and
translated from the German by Richard and Clara
Winston. A humorous, trickily plotted detective
story in which a group of Roman schoolboys rescue a schoolmate from imminent imprisonment and

the danger of being sent away as a galley slave.
(I and YA)

1022. _____. Mystery of the Roman Ransom. Harcourt,
Brace, Jovanovich, 1969-71. Ill. by Charlotte
Kleinert and translated from the German by Edith
McCormick. An hilarious sequel to "Detectives
in Togas" (though it can stand by itself) in which
the same Roman schoolboys foil an assassination
plot, with the help of a slave, their friendly
schoolteacher, and a friendly lion.   (I and YA)

ROME, SECOND THROUGH SIXTH CENTURIES

1023. Hays, Wilma Pitchford. The Story of Valentine.
Coward McCann, 1956. Ill. by Leonard Weis-
gard. Mostly imaginary, since little is known
about this saint, but he was a real person who
was thought to have performed miracles during
the times of persecutions of Christians.   (E and
I)
1024. Ish-Kishor, Sulamith. Drusilla, A Novel of the Emperor Hadrian. Pantheon, 1970. Ill. by Thomas
Morley. Hadrian's period as experienced by the
15-year-old daughter of the head of the Sacred
College of Augurs.   (YA)
1025. Williamson, Joanne. The Iron Charm. Knopf, 1964.
Ill. by Brian Wildsmith. A novel, like a tapestry
of dark colors, of a young Roman's ordeals, first
in the Constantinople of Justin and Justinian and
later in the Britain of heathenism and emerging
Christianity, with threads of the Arthurian legend
woven into it.   (YA)

THIRTEENTH CENTURY

1026. Benedict, Rex. Oh ... Brother Juniper. Pantheon,
1963. Ill. by Joan Berg. Some amusing stories
retold from "The Chronicles of Brother Juniper"
as they appear in "The Little Flowers of Saint
Francis."   (I)
1027. Buff, Mary and Conrad. The Apple and the Arrow.
Houghton-Mifflin, 1951. Ill. by Conrad Buff. The
interesting story of the beginning of Swiss independence as well as the well-known legend about
William Tell and his son.   (E and I)

1028. Byrne, Donn. Messer Marco Polo. Century, 1921.
Ill. by C. B. Falls. A poetic little book about
Marco Polo's romance with little Golden Bells in
the court of Kubla Khan, included here because
Marco Polo was a great Venetian traveler. (A)

1029. Doane, Pelagie. St. Francis. Walck, 1960. Ill. by
the author. The story of his life (1181?-1226).
(I)

1030. Evernden, Margery. Knight of Florence. Random,
1950. Ill. by Rafaello Busoni. The adventures
of a young apprentice to Giotto, near the end
of the century, with interesting material about
painting and Florentine politics. (I)

1031. Gies, Joseph and Frances. Leonard of Pisa and the
New Mathematics of the Middle Ages. Crowell,
1969. Ill. by Enrico Arno. A handsomely illustrated book about the author of the book, "Li-
ber Abaci," which introduced the Hindu-Arabic
numerals to the Latin World and which, in its
revised edition issued in 1228, has come down to
us. The appendices give some of its problems
for the reader to solve as well as other matters
of interest for the mathematically inclined of any
age. (YA and A)

1032. Holland, Cecelia. The King's Road. Atheneum, 1970.
Ill. by Richard Cuffari. Frederick II, Hohen-
staufen Emperor of the Holy Roman Empire from
1215-1250, was a poor little Sicilian King in his
boyhood and here is a story of an adventure he
might have had at the age of 12, in attempting to
escape from some who were trying to kill him
and how he learned a lesson that helped to make
him later known as "The Wonder of the World."
(I and YA)

1033. Hürlimann, Bettina. William Tell and His Son. Harcourt, Brace and World, 1967. Ill. by Paul
Nussbaumer and translated from the German by
Elizabeth D. Crawford. A picture book with a
text to read aloud to children not yet able to read
easily. (E)

1034. Jewett, Sophie. God's Troubadour. Crowell, 1910,
1940 and 1950. Ill. with reproductions of Giotto
paintings. A beautiful book about St. Francis
(Giovanni Francesco Bernardoni, 1181?-1226). (I)

1035. Kent, Louise Andrews. He Went with Marco Polo;
A Story of Venice and Cathay. Houghton-Mifflin,
1935. Ill. by C. Leroy Baldridge and Paul Quinn.

A fictional account of the adventures of a young
companion of Marco. (I and YA)

1036.   Knight, Ruth Adams. The Land Beyond. Whittlesey
House, 1954. Ill. by Wesley Dennis. A story of
the Childrens' Crusade in its travels through
Switzerland and the (fictional) part played by an
Egyptian mastiff known as the tiger dog. (I)

1037.   Knox, Esther Melbourne. The Flags of Dawn. Little,
Brown, 1944. Ill. by Marie A. Lawson. A nov-
el beginning in Salerno, Italy, with the problem
of obtaining bodies for dissection in anatomical
studies, and ending in England with the signing of
the Magna Charta by King John. (YA)

1038.   Komroff, Manuel. Marco Polo. Messner, 1952.
Ill. by Edgard Cirlin. A short biography of the
Venetian explorer (1254?-1324). (YA)

1039.   Llewellyn, Richard. Warden of the Smoke and Bells.
Doubleday, 1956. A novel about Marco Polo and
the early Italian Renaissance. (YA)

1040.   MacKaye, Loring. The Silver Disk. Longmans
Green, 1955. Ill. by Avery Johnson. A novel
of intrigue in which a band of young men (including one traitor) set out to protect the 7-year-old
King Frederick of Sicily and find for him the silver disk which, in his possession, "would give
him the world." He did, indeed, eventually become known as "The Wonder of the World" (Stu-
por Mundi) as Frederick II of the Holy Roman
Empire. (YA)

1041.   Politi, Leo. Saint Francis and the Animals. Scribner, 1959. Ill. by the author. Short stories
about the saint and his animal friends. (E)

1042.   Scherman, Katherine. William Tell. Random, 1960.
Ill. by Georges Schreiber. The legend of the ar-
row and the apple and other adventures of the
Swiss hero. (I)

1043.   Steffan, Jack (Alice Jaqueline). The Bright Thread.
Day, 1962. A novel of St. Clare of Assisi,
founder of the Poor Clares. (YA)

FIFTEENTH AND EARLY SIXTEENTH CENTURIES
(The High Renaissance)

1044.   Allen, Agnes. The Story of Michelangelo. Faber,
n.d. A short biography of the sculptor and
painter (1475-1564). (YA)

1045. Almedingen, E. M. Young Leonardo da Vinci. Roy,
       1963. Ill. by Azpelicueta. A biography of the
       youth of this great Renaissance figure whose whole
       life covered the period from 1452-1519, with an
       epilogue of known facts and legendary surmises.
       (I)
1046. Baker, Nina Brown. Amerigo Vespucci. Knopf,
       1956. Ill. by Paul Valentino. A biography (1451-
       1512) and map. (YA)
1047. Downer, Marion. Long Ago in Florence: The Story
       of the Della Robbia Sculpture. Lothrop, Lee and
       Shepard, 1968. Ill. with photographs and draw-
       ings by Mamoru Furnoi. The story of Luce della
       Robbia (ca. 1400-82) who created terra cotta
       sculptures with enamel glaze. (E and I)
1048. Eliot, George (Evans, Marianne). Romola. 1863.
       Oxford World's Classics, 1949. A novel about
       Savonarola and the Renaissance in Florence. (A)
1049. Gillette, Henry S. Leonardo da Vinci, Pathfinder of
       Science. Watts, 1962. Ill. by the author. A
       short biography (1452-1519). (I)
1050. Hahn, Emily. Leonardo da Vinci. Random Land-
       mark, 1956. Ill. by Mimi Korach. A biography.
       (I)
1051. Holland, Janice. The Apprentice and the Prize. Van-
       guard, 1958. Ill. by the author. A story of a
       sculptor's apprentice who, in competing for a
       prize of money for a statue of Saint Francis,
       finds a prize even greater than gold. (I)
1052. Kyle, Anne D. Apprentice of Florence. Houghton-
       Mifflin, 1933. Ill. by Erick Berry. A story set
       in Italy and Constantinople in the 1450s, with the
       artist Ghiberti, Cosimo and other Medicis, and
       the young Christopher Columbus, as historical
       figures. (YA)
1053. Mee, Charles L. (and the editors of Horizon Maga-
       zine). Lorenzo de Medici and the Renaissance.
       American Heritage, 1969. Horizon Caravel Book,
       ill. with paintings and drawings. A biography of
       the great Florentine patron of the arts (1449-
       1492). (YA)
1054. Meyer, Edith Patterson. First Lady of the Renais-
       sance, A Biography of Isabella d'Este. Little,
       Brown, 1970. Ill. with plates, portraits and a
       map. Jacket portrait by Leonardo da Vinci and
       design by Laine Roundy. A book so full of fa-
       mous names of artists and royalty, of wars and

shifting alliances, of popes and potentates, of
great collections of works of art, and, in general,
of the opulence of the High Renaissance, that it
would be difficult to read without the introduction
which the author gives us of "Some of the People
You Will Meet in This Book"--the Este, Gonzaga,
Borgia, and Sforza families, and others. Isabella (1474-1539), the wife of the Marquis of Man-
tua was indeed the First Lady of these fabulous
years. (YA and A)

1055.   Noble, Iris. Leonardo da Vinci, the Universal Genius.
        Norton, 1965. Ill. with paintings and da Vinci
        drawings. Biography (1452-1519). (YA)

1056.   Ripley, Elizabeth. Botticelli. Lippincott, 1960. Ill.
        by reproductions of Botticelli's paintings. A short
        biography (1444-1510) introducing the Medici fam-
        ily, Pope Sixtus, Michelangelo, Charles VIII of
        France and Savonarola. (I and YA)

1057.   _____. Leonardo da Vinci. Oxford, 1953. Ill.
        with drawings and paintings by Leonardo. A bi-
        ography. (I and YA)

1058.   _____. Michelangelo. Oxford, 1953. Ill. with
        drawings, paintings and sculptures by Michelangelo.
        Biography (1475-1564). (I and YA)

1059.   Rockwell, Anne. Filippo's Dome. Atheneum, 1967.
        Ill. by the author. The story of Filippo Brunel-
        leschi (1377-1446) and his works, climaxed by the
        dome of St. Mary of the Flower (the "Duomo" in
        Florence). The drawings will particularly interest
        budding architects. (I and YA)

1060.   Stone, Irving. The Great Adventures of Michelangelo
        [an abridged edition of "The Agony and the Ecsta-
        sy"]. Doubleday, 1965. Ill. by Joseph Cellini,
        and with black and white photographs. A bio-
        graphical novel that can stand by itself, not just
        as an abridgment. (YA)

1061.   Syme, Ronald. Amerigo Vespucci, Scientist and
        Sailor. Morrow, 1969. Ill. by William Stobbs.
        A biography of the man who first announced to the
        world the existence of the continent thought to be
        named for him (1454-1512). (I)

1062.   Thomas, John. Leonardo da Vinci. Criterion, 1957.
        With illustrations from the sketchbooks of Leo-
        nardo. A short biography (1452-1519). (I)

1063.   Williams, Jay. Leonardo da Vinci. American Heri-
        tage, 1965. Ill. with paintings, drawings and di-
        agrams of Leonardo's. A Horizon Caravel Book.
        (I and YA)

SIXTEENTH AND EARLY SEVENTEENTH CENTURIES

1064. Barr, Gladys. Master of Geneva, A Novel Based on
       the Life of John Calvin. Holt, Rinehart and Win-
       ston, 1961. Jacket by Ben Feder. A sympathetic
       biographical novel of John Calvin (1509-64) from
       the time he was 12, in 1521, until his Protestant
       authority became absolute in 1555. (A)

1065. Fermi, Laura and Bernardini, Gilberto. Galileo and
       the Scientific Revolution. Basic Books, 1961.
       Ill. with plates and diagrams. A biography (1564-
       1642) of the great astronomer, inventor of the as-
       tronomical telescope, who was condemned by the
       Roman inquisition for his revolutionary theories
       about the skies. (YA)

1066. Lauber, Patricia. The Quest of Galileo. Garden
       City, Doubleday, 1959. Ill. by Lee J. Ames.
       A simple pictorial biography of interest to all
       ages because of the drawings. (I)

1067. Lawrence, John. Pope Leo's Elephant. World, 1970.
       Ill. by the author. An elephant was a present
       from the King of Portugal to the Pope of Rome
       which makes for a good story. (I)

1068. Levinger, Elma Ehrlich. Galileo, First Observer of
       Marvelous Things. Messner, 1952. A short
       biography. (YA)

1069. Marcus, Rebecca B. Galileo and Experimental Sci-
       ence. Watts, 1961. Ill. by Richard Mayhew.
       A "First Biography" for very young readers.
       (E and I)

1070. Mincieli, Rose Laura. Pulcinella, or Punch's Merry
       Pranks. Knopf, 1960. Ill. by Joseph Law. A
       picture book with the story handed down from six-
       teenth century Italy about the forerunner of Punch.
       (E)

1071. Newcomb, Covelle. The Explorer with a Heart: The
       Story of Giovanni da Verrazzano. / McKay, 1969.
       An account of the great Italian's voyages to find
       a new sea route to Asia. (YA)

1072. Ripley, Elizabeth. Titian. Lippincott, 1962. Ill.
       with plates of paintings. A biography of the
       great painter (1487-1576), born in Cadore but
       living and painting mostly in Venice. (YA)

1073. Rosen, Sidney. Galileo and the Magic Numbers.
       Little, Brown, 1958. Ill. by Harve Stein. A
       biography (1564-1642) with illustrations of some
       of the magic numbers. (YA)

1074.   _____. Doctor Paracelsus. Little, Brown, 1959.
         Ill. by Rafaello Busoni. A biography of Philip
         Theophrastus Bombastus von Hohenheim, Swiss
         physician, alchemist, and chemist (1493?-1541).
         (YA)
1075. Susac, Andrew. Paracelsus, Monarch of Medicine.
         Doubleday, 1969. Jacket by Jules Maidoff. The
         story of a much misunderstood man, Theophrastus
         Bombastus von Hohenheim, (1493?-1541) a Swiss
         physician and alchemist who introduced (against
         the usual opposition met with by almost all inno-
         vators in the world of medicine) the concept of
         biochemistry, and who, way ahead of his time,
         believed in treating "the whole man." Written as
         fiction, but true to fact, a book for readers with
         a strong interest in, and stomach for, medical
         matters. (YA and A)
1076. Tamarin, Alfred. The Autobiography of Benvenuto
         Cellini. Edited, abridged and adapted from the
         translation by John Addington Symonds. Macmil-
         lan, 1969. Ill. with 70 photographs and jacket by
         S. A. Summit. This richly illustrated and read-
         able book vividly pictures the High Renaissance as
         well as the remarkable works and adventures of
         the great craftsman (1500-1571). (YA and A)
1077. Trease, Geoffrey. Shadow of the Hawk. Harcourt,
         1949. Ill. by Joe Krush. An exciting novel about
         a young Englishman, a student from Cambridge,
         on a search in Venice for a buried book of great
         value. (YA)

                        NINETEENTH CENTURY

1078. Baker, Nina Brown. Garibaldi. Vanguard, 1944.
         Ill. by Louis Slobodkin. A biography (1807-82)
         of the leader of unification for Italy. (YA)
1079. Davenport, Marcia. Garibaldi, Father of Modern
         Italy. Random Landmark, 1957. Ill. by Stuy-
         vesant Van Veen. Biography (1807-82). (I)
1080. Forsee, Aylesa. Louis Agassiz, Pied Piper of Sci-
         ence. Viking, 1958. Ill. by Winifred Lubell. A
         biography of the famous ichthyologist, zoologist,
         geologist, and, above all, teacher, born in Neu-
         chatel, Switzerland in 1807, where he was trained
         to be a physician but preferred the study of fish
         and glaciers. From 1846 on, he lived almost en-

tirely in America where he became the head of
the Lawrence School of Science at Harvard, and,
after a life of constant adventures and discoveries,
died in 1873. (YA)

1081. Hürlimann, Bettina. Barry, The Story of the Brave
St. Bernard. Harcourt, Brace, 1968. Ill. in
color by Paul Nussbaumer and translated by Elizabeth D. Crawford. A true story of a heroic dog
still remembered and loved by the Swiss. (E)

1082. Kaufmann, Helen. Anvil Chorus, The Story of Giuseppi Verdi. Hawthorne Books, 1964. Ill. by Vivian
Berger, endpapers by Frank Nicholas. An engrossing biography of the great composer focusing
on his operas, their composition and reception,
and outlines of the librettos. (YA)

1083. Malvern, Gladys. On Golden Wings. Macrae Smith,
1960. A biographical novel of Giuseppi Verdi
(1813-1901). (YA)

1084. Maynor, Eleanor. The Golden Key; A Story Biography of Nicolo Paganini. Criterion, 1966. Ill.
by Jack Gaughan. A dramatic biographical novel
of Paganini's boyhood, his immense self-confidence,
his driving father, his loyal friend, and his ex-
treme good fortune, with interesting material
about violins and violin music. (I and YA)

1085. Syme, Ronald. Garibaldi, The Man Who Made a Nation. Morrow, 1967. Ill. by William Stobbs. A
biography of the amazing Italian hero (1807-82)
who electrified the whole world (and quietly at-
tracted followers from many nations) with his
achievement of uniting Italy during a life of constant narrow escapes. (I and YA)

1086. Tharpe, Louise Hall. Louis Agassiz, Adventurous
Scientist. Little, Brown, 1961. Ill. by Rafaello
Busoni. See notes on his biography by Forsee
above, and read about Agassiz letting himself be
lowered 120 feet inside of a glacier, jumping over
crevasses on the way up the Jungfrau, and study-
ing sea life in the Magellan Strait. (YA)

1087. Trease, Geoffrey. Follow My Black Plume. Van-
guard, 1963. A novel based on "Garibaldi" and
"Defense of the Roman Republic" by G. M. Tre-
velyan, about a young Englishman involved in the
Italian fight for independence under Mazzini and
Garibaldi. (YA)

1088. _____. A Thousand for Sicily. Vanguard, 1964.
Ill. by Louis Slobodkin. A novel about a single

month in the Sicilian hills in 1860, full of humor,
romance and high adventure. (YA)

1089. Welch, Ronald. Nicholas Carey. Criterion, 1963.
Ill. by William Stobbs. A novel with a great deal
of detail about small arms and sword play, about
the adventures of a young Englishman in Italy,
Paris, and the Crimea in the turbulent mid-century. Historical preface. (YA)

1090. Wheeler, Opal. Paganini, Master of Strings. Dutton, 1950. Ill. by Henry S. Gillette. This book
should interest young violinists and composers.
Two short pieces with piano parts included. (I)

TWENTIETH CENTURY

1091. Archer, Jules. Twentieth Century Caesar, Mussolini.
Messner, 1964. A biography of the Italian dictator (1883-1945). (YA)

1092. Arthur, Ruth M. My Daughter, Nicola. Atheneum,
1965. Ill. by Fermin Rocker. A story of a
Swiss girl's dangerous adventure while trying to
prove to her father that a daughter is as good as
a son. (I)

1093. Bayne-Jardine, Colin Charles. Mussolini and Italy.
McGraw-Hill, 1968. Ill. with photographs and
maps. Foreword by William Jay Jacobs. A biography of the dictator (1883-1945) and the history of his times in Italy, continuing on beyond
his death until 1956 when Italy was admitted to
the United Nations. Excitingly, lucidly written.
(YA)

1094. Chamberlain, William. The Mountain. John Day,
1968. Jacket by Albert Orbaan. A World War
II novel about the campaign to liberate northern
Italy from the Germans and the difficult relations
of a young officer and his superiors. (YA)

1095. Daly, Maureen (McGivern). The Small World of Sergeant Donkey. Dodd, Mead, 1966. Ill. by Wesley Dennis. An endearing story of a 12-year-old
Italian boy, an American sergeant, and a donkey,
during the American campaign against the Germans in Italy in World War II. (I)

1096. Daniell, David Scott (Albert Daniell). Sandro's Battle. Duell, Sloane and Pearce, 1962. Ill. by
Colin Spencer. The adventures of a little Italian
boy collaborating with the Italian partisans during

World War II when the Germans occupied his castle home. (I)

1097. de Trevino, Elizabeth Borton. Turi's Poppa. Farrar,
Straus and Giroux, 1968. Ill. by Enrico Arno.
The happy story of a Hungarian violin-maker and
his son, the action set in Hungary, Yugoslavia
and Italy, based on a true incident of the Violin-
making Institute of Cremona which carries on the
traditions of that town's great violin-making families: the Amati, Guarneri and Stradivari. (I and
YA)

1098. Haugaard, Erik Christian. The Little Fishes. Houghton-Mifflin, 1967. Ill. by Milton Johnson. The
story of three little beggar children and their odyssey from Naples to Cassino in 1943. (YA)

1099. Henry, Marguerite. Gaudenzia, Pride of the Palio.
Rand McNally, 1960. Ill. by Lynd Ward. A
beautifully illustrated and narrated book about the
medieval pageantry and the exciting Palio races
in Sienna, in which a half-Arabian horse and her
rider are the focal characters. (I and YA)

1100. Leviton, Sonia. Journey to America. Atheneum,
1970. Ill. by Charles Robinson. Three little
girls and their frail mother, almost penniless
refugees from the Nazis in Switzerland, waiting,
waiting, waiting until their father, who has fled
to America can get the necessary papers and
money to send for them. Fiction, but the courage of the little family, the beastliness of the
storm troopers who made them leave their Berlin
home, and the kindness of a Swiss family, are
all true to life in that place and time just before
World War II. (I and YA)

1101. McGregor-Hastie, Roy. Pope John XXIII. Criterion,
1962. Ill. with photographs. This biography ends
before the crowning achievement of Angelo Joseph
Roncalli's life (1881-1963), the calling of the Ecu-
menical Council "Pacem in Terris." He was an
activist, exiled to Bulgaria, Turkey and Greece
during Mussolini's rule, and also a skilled diplo-
mat, but most important of all, he possessed a
loving, humble, delightful personality which
brought together people of all faiths. (YA)

1102. Sheehan, Elizabeth Odell. Good Pope John. Farrar,
Straus, A Vision Book, 1966. A short biography
of Pope John XXIII (1881-1963). (I)

1103. Werstein, Irving. The Battle of Salerno. Crowell,

1965.   Maps by Ava Morgan.   The story of the
Salerno landings in September, 1943.   (YA)

PART VI: RUSSIA AND POLAND

GENERAL HISTORY

1104. Almedingen, E. M. A Picture History of Russia.
Franklin Watts, 1964. Ill. by Clarke Hutton. (I)
1105. Hasler, Joan. The Making of Russia from Prehistory
to Modern Times. Delacorte, 1971. Ill. with
maps and photographs. A vivid, complete history
including eyewitness accounts, personality profiles,
and literary excerpts. (YA and A)
1106. Moscow, Henry. Russia Under the Czars. American
Heritage, 1962. A Horizon Caravel Book illustrated with many paintings, prints, engravings
and maps. (YA)
1107. Rice, Tamara Talbot. Czars and Czarinas of Russia.
Lothrop, 1968. Ill. with photographs and maps.
Profiles of the rulers of Russia from the expulsion of the Mongols to the beginning of the Soviet
regime. (YA)

LEGENDS AND FOLKLORE

1108. Borski, Lucia Merecka. Good Sense and Good Fortune and Other Polish Folk Tales. McKay, 1970.
Ill. by Erica Merecka Borski. Twenty-three delightful Polish folk tales showing the humor, wit
and cleverness of the Polish people. (I)
1109. Downing, Charles. Russian Tales and Legends.
Walck, 1956. Ill. by Joan Kiddell-Monroe. (I)
1110. Elkin, Benjamin. How the Tsar Drinks Tea. Parents'
Magazine Press, 1971. Ill. by Anita Lobel. An
original story but with folklore flavor, about a
poor Russian peasant who finds a brass samovar
and is brought, by a suspicious neighbor, before
the Tsar. (E)
1111. Guillet, René. Grishka and the Bear. Oxford, 1959.
Ill. by Joan Kiddell-Monroe. Translated by Gwen
Marsh. A "long ago story" about tribal customs
among the Tushkins of northern Siberia. (I)

1112. Konopnicka, Maria. The Golden Seed. Scribner,
       1962. Ill. by Janina Domanska. A Polish tale
       adapted by Catherine Fournier about a king who
       wished for gold but finally, in spite of himself,
       found something better. (E)
1113. Nathan, Dorothy. The Month Brothers. Dutton, 1967.
       Ill. by Uri Shulevitz and translated from the Rus-
       sian by Alexander Baksby in collaboration with
       Paul Nathan. A poetic version of a Russian leg-
       end about the months of the year, adapted from
       Samuel Marshk's play, "Twelve Months." (E)
1114. Ransome, Arthur. The Fool of the World and the
       Flying Ship. Farrar, Straus and Giroux, 1968.
       Ill. by Uri Shulevitz. Winner of the Caldecott
       Medal for 1969, this is a retelling of a Russian
       folk tale, originally published in 1916 as one of
       "Old Peter's Russian Tales," by Arthur Ransome,
       a book to seek out. (E)
1115. Singer, Isaac Bashevis. When Shlemiel Went to War-
       saw and Other Stories. Farrar, Straus and Gi-
       roux, 1968. Ill. by Margot Zemach and trans-
       lated by the author and Elizabeth Shuh. Some of
       these stories are based on traditional Jewish tales
       and others are Singer's own creations. (I)
1116. _____. Joseph and Koza--Or The Sacrifice to the
       Vistula. Farrar, Straus and Giroux, 1970. Ill.
       by Symeon Shimin and translated from the Yiddish
       by the author and Elizabeth Shuh. A large and
       beautiful book about how the word of God was
       brought to Poland and ended human sacrifice.
       (All Ages)
1116a. Tolstoy, Leo. Ivan the Fool and Other Tales. Se-
       lected and translated by Guy Daniels. Macmillan,
       1966. Ill. by Des Adniussen. With the excep-
       tion of "The Bear Hunt" these tales all carry
       Tolstoy's philosophy and messages of passive re-
       sistance, Christian love, and forgiveness, the
       virtue of manual labor, and equal distribution of
       wealth. (I and YA)
1117. _____. Russian Stories and Legends. Pantheon,
       n.d. Ill. by Alexander Alexeiff and translated
       from the Russian by Aylmer and Louise Maude.
       Stories with the common theme of brotherhood.
       (YA)

TENTH THROUGH FOURTEENTH CENTURIES

1118. Almedingen, E. M. The Knights of the Golden Table.
Ill. by Charles Keeping. Lippincott, 1964. Prince
Vladimir of Kiev assembled in the tenth century a
fellowship called the "Knights of the Golden Table,"
and around this group there grew up legends and
stories of magic similar to the British Arthurian
legends. (I and YA)

1119. Mills, Lois. So Young a Queen. Lothrop, Lee and
Shepard, 1961. A novel about Jadwiga, daughter
of Louis the Great of Hungary, who became queen
of Poland and married Jagielo, ruler of Lithuania,
converting him and all his people to Christianity.
(YA)

FIFTEENTH AND SIXTEENTH CENTURIES

1120. Bartos-Höppner, B. The Cossacks. Walck, 1963.
Ill. by Victor G. Ambrus. A novel about the
period (1580-84) when Yarmak captured the then
capital of Siberia (later Tobolsk) and the Stro-
ganovs ruled over a large part of Russia, the
time of the rise of Boris Godunov. Map, chronological table of events, and historical postscript.
(YA)

1121. _____. Save the Khan. Walck, 1964. Ill. by
Victor G. Ambrus and translated by Stella Humphries. A strong novel for older readers about
the conquest of Tatar Siberia by the Russians at
the end of the sixteenth century about 20 years
after the events in the novel "The Cossacks."
(YA)

1122. Kelly, Eric. From Star to Star. Lippincott, 1942.
Ill. by Manning de V. Lee. A novel about student life at the University of Krakow, Poland,
when Copernicus was a student there, and about
a hidden treasure which, when found, made possible the building of the university library. (YA)

1123. _____. The Trumpeter of Krakow. Macmillan,
1928 and 66. Ill. by Angela Prusznska in Krakow. The story of the Great Tarnov Crystal, set
in the time of King Casimir IV of the Jagielle
dynasty (1447-92). A Newbery Medal Book. (YA)

1124. Thomas, Henry. Copernicus. Messner, 1960. A
biography of the famous Polish astronomer. (I)

SEVENTEENTH CENTURY

1125. Baker, Nina Brown. Peter the Great. Vanguard,
      1943. Ill. by Louis Slobodkin. A biography of
      the Czar (1672-1725) who opened a window to the
      west for Russia when he had St. Petersburg built.
      (YA)
1126. Brodtkorb, Reidar. The Gold Coin. Harcourt, Brace
      and World, 1966. Ill. by W. T. Mars. Trans-
      lated by L. W. Kingsland. A novel about some
      children in search of their parents who had been
      carried off into slavery by a robber band, the
      search ending in Riga, Latvia. A brief introduc-
      tion explains some of the history of the Baltic
      provinces. (YA)
1127. Lamb, Harold. Chief of the Cossacks. Random
      Landmark, 1959. Ill. by Robert Frankenberg.
      A biography of Stenka Razin who rebelled against
      the Czar in 1670. (I)

EIGHTEENTH CENTURY

1128. Adams, Dorothy. Cavalry Hero, Casimir Pulaski.
      Kenedy, 1957. Ill. by Irena Lorentowiecz. A
      biography of the Polish soldier (1748-79) who be-
      came a military commander in the American
      Revolution. (I)
1129. Almedingen, E. M. The Young Catherine the Great.
      Roy, 1965. Ill. by Denise Brown. A biograph-
      ical novel about the Russian empress (1729-96),
      wife of Peter II, who was born Princess Sophia
      Augusta in the small German principality of An-
      halt-Zerbst--covering only the years before her
      marriage. (I and YA)
1130. _____. Young Mark. Farrar, Straus and Giroux,
      1967. Ill. by Victor G. Ambrus. The adven-
      tures of Mark Poltoratsky (1726-89) after running
      away from his home in the Ukraine to seek fame
      and fortune as a singer in St. Petersburg; based
      on his own diary and reconstructed as a novel by
      his great-great-granddaughter, with a biographi-
      cal note and a glossary of Russian and Ukrainian
      words. (YA)
1131. Bell, Margaret. Touched with Fire: Alaska's
      George William Steller. Morrow, 1960. Maps
      by Bob Ritter. Jacket by Walter Buehr. Though

Steller was born and brought up in Germany, this
exciting biography (1709-46) belongs in this Russian section because his accomplishments and discoveries were achieved as a member of Bering's
last Pacific expedition in 1741. As a scientist,
physician, and theologian, a member of Russia's
Academy of Science, he was frustrated at every
turn on that expedition by the bureaucracy, incompetence and professional rivalries of the Russian
courts. Fortunately many of his notes and speci-
mens did finally get back to St. Petersburg though
he himself did not. (I and YA)

1132.   Granberg, W. J. Voyage Into Darkness: To Alaska
with Bering. Dutton, 1960. Ill. by Gil Walker.
The story, from the viewpoint of 17-year-old
Laurentz Waxel, of the nine-year odyssey with
Bering which resulted in the discovery of Alaska
in 1741 and Russia's claim to it--a claim which
cost torturous hardships and many lives (including
Bering's), due largely to corruption, incompetence
and wrangling as well as to Bering's ill health and
lack of leadership qualities. (I and YA)

1133.   Kay, Mara. In Place of Katya. Scribner, 1963. Ill.
by Janina Domanska. A novel about a crucial
period in the reign of Catherine the Great when
a Pretender to the Throne threatened the town of
Kazan in 1774. (I)

1134.   Pushkin, Alexander. The Captain's Daughter. 1836.
Viking, 1928. Translated from the Russian by
Natalie Diddington with an introduction by Edward
Garnett. A short, humorous (in a rather grue-
some way) and exciting novel about the Pretender,
Pugachev, and his rebellion in 1773 and 1774. (A)

1135.   Scherman, Katherine. Catherine the Great. Random
Landmark, 1957. Ill. by Pranas Lape and with a
sketch map of Russia. A biography (1729-96) of
a powerful empress. (YA)

1136.   Sutton, Ann and Myron. Steller of the North. Rand-
McNally, 1961. Ill. by Leonard Everett Fisher.
Though Russia claimed Alaska because of Bering's
expedition in 1741, George William Steller, German born, was the first white man to set foot on
Alaskan soil. This is his biography (1709-1746)
and also the story of Bering's last voyage which
took nine years and the lives of half the members
of the expedition. (I and YA)

NINETEENTH CENTURY

1137.   Almedingen, E. M. Fanny, Frances Hermione de
        Poltoratzky. Farrar, Straus and Giroux, 1970.
        Ill. by Ian Ribbons. Compiled from sketches left
        by the author's aunt, this charming, nostalgic
        book is part autobiography and part period piece
        of nineteenth century Russia. (YA and A)

1138.   _____. Katia. Farrar, Straus and Giroux, 1966.
        Ill. by Victor G. Ambrus. A translation and re-
        vision of "The Story of a Little Girl" by the au-
        thor's great niece, giving a delightful picture of
        noble Russian family life in the Ukraine in the
        first half of the century. (I and YA)

1139.   _____. Retreat from Moscow. Warne, 1966. Ill.
        by Sheila Bowley. The story so graphically told
        in Tolstoy's "War and Peace" of Napoleon's dis-
        astrous invasion of Russia in 1812, and the agon-
        izing retreat of the French through the Russian
        winter. (I and YA)

1140.   Bartos-Hoppner, B. Storm Over the Caucasus. Walck,
        1968. Translated by Anthea Bell. A novel about
        the Moslem leader, Iman Shamyl's defense of his
        country, the Caucasus, against Russian imperial-
        ism in the mid-nineteenth century (a 60-year war).
        (YA)

1141.   Boucourechnev, A. Chopin, A Pictorial Biography.
        Viking, 1963. A Studio Book with notes on the
        pictures. Translated from the French by Edward
        Hyams, and with a chronology of the musician's
        life (1810-49) of which only the first 20 years
        were spent in his native Poland. (YA)

1142.   Breshkovska, Catherine. The Little Grandmother of
        the Russian Revolution. Little, Brown, 1918.
        Edited by Alice Stone Blackwell. An autobiography
        (1844-1934) and the letters of one of the leading
        revolutionists, idealistic and dedicated. (A)

1143.   Chekhov, Anton. Shadows and Light, Nine Stories.
        Selected and translated by Miriam Morton. Double-
        day, 1968. Ill. by Ann Grifalconi. Stories both
        sad and humorous which depict the life of the sim-
        ple folk of Russia. Includes an introductory biog-
        raphy of Chekhov (1860-1904). (YA)

1144.   Falstein, Louis. The Man Who Loved Laughter, The
        Story of Sholom Aleichem. Jewish Pub. Society
        of America, 1968. Ill. by Adrianne Onderdonk
        Dudden. The life of the loveable Yiddish writer

(1859-1916), born and raised in the Ukraine under
cruel limitations, who attained international fame
for his stories of the Human Comedy. (YA)

1145. Glasgow, Aline. The Pair of Shoes. Dial, 1971.
Ill. by Symeon Shimin. A pair of shoes teaches
a Polish boy the meaning of manhood on the eve
of his bar-mitzvah. (E and I)

1146. Janeway, Elizabeth. Ivanov Seven. Harper and Row,
1967. Ill. by Eros Keith. A humorous story of
a young man drafted from his mother's vineyard
in the Caucasus into the Czar's army where he
politely but firmly refuses to obey an order of
his superior officer, much to that person's em-
barrassment. (I and YA)

1146a. Jones, Adrienne. Another Place, Another Spring.
Houghton-Mifflin, 1971. Maps clearly outline the
almost year-long travels of Marya and her aristocratic mistress, from St. Petersburg across Siberia and Marya alone across the Pacific to Fort
Ross in California (soon to be sold to the U.S.
by Russia). It is a touching love story and also
a story of the exile system of the Czars in the
1840s and the exhausting hardships of travel
through Siberia, particularly harrowing as the
girls evade the Russian police who are on their
trail. (YA and A)

1147. Kay, Mara. Masha. Lothrop, Lee and Shepard,
1968. Ill. with photographs. Jacket by James
Barkley. Masha, a poor girl, goes to the Smolni
Institute for Noble Girls on a scholarship for
children of war casualties and finds herself beset
by all sorts of social and academic difficulties for
nine long years. Good period details of the early
nineteenth century. (YA)

1147a. _____. The Youngest Lady-in-Waiting. John Day,
1971. A novel of the Decembrist uprising in
Russia in 1825, during which the young lady-in-
waiting to the Grand Duchess is deeply troubled
by conflicting loyalties. (YA)

1148. Kennan, George. Tent Life in Siberia. N.Y. Times
Book Pub., 1971. An expensive reprint (but hope-
fully to be found in libraries) of a book published
100 years ago, in which young George Kennan
(1845-1924), nineteen when he set out, tells amusingly and vividly of his experiences and adventures
during the two years, 1865-67, with the Western
Union Russian-American Telegraph Expedition

when a small force of young Americans, headed
by a Russian engineer, surveyed, and began building, a telegraph line across Siberia, working often
without maps and with very few instruments, in
sub-Arctic temperatures. The reproduction of the
original illustrations and maps make this a unique
book about nineteenth century Siberia. (A)

1149. Mardus, Elaine. Man with a Microscope: Elie Metch-
nikoff. Messner, 1968. An engrossing biography
of a man whose life story (1845-1916) reads like
a novel and whose scientific explorations and discoveries are a regular detective story. A zoolo-
gist, bacteriologist, cellular embryologist, pioneer
gerontologist, and a friend of Pasteur. (YA)

1150. Philipson, Morris. The Count Who Wished He Were
a Peasant; A Life of Leo Tolstoy. Pantheon,
1967. Ill. with photographs. As the title indi-
cates, Tolstoy was a man of striking contradic-
tions, and the author's high estimate of him may
be disputed by some critics, but this biography
(1828-1910) is sure to interest those who have
read "War and Peace" and inspire those who
haven't to do so. (YA and A)

1151. Slobodkin, Florence. Sarah Somebody. Vanguard,
1969. Ill. by Louis Slobodkin. A charming and
touching story of a nine-year-old Polish Jewish
girl who, at the time when Poland was part of
Russia, and when Jews were strictly segregated,
and usually only the boys were educated, finds an
exceptional opportunity to learn to read and write
and become a "somebody." (E and I)

1152. Tolstoy, Leo. War and Peace, 1865-69. New American translation by Dunnigan, 1968; a Signet Classic.
An epic novel of Russia during the War of 1812
(Napoleon's invasion) in which a young girl's first
ball is described as being of as much importance
at least to her as a general's defeat or victory
on the battlefield. (A)

1153. _____. Nikolenka's Childhood. 1852. Pantheon,
1963. Ill. by Maurice Sendak. Translated by
Louise and Aylmer Maude. Largely fictional but
partly autobiographical, "Childhood," in 1852, was
Leo Tolstoy's first work to appear in print, and
is a sensitive portrayal of what life was like for
a little Russian boy of the upper classes growing
up in the early part of the century. (YA and A)

1154. Verne, Jules. Michael Strogoff, Courier of the Czar.

Scribner, 1923. Ill. by N. C. Wyeth. A wildly
imaginative story set in greater Russia and Siberia
in the years 1815-40. (A)

1155. Wheeler, Opal. The Story of Peter Tschaikowsky,
Part One. Dutton, 1953. Ill. by Christine Price.
About the musician's childhood and his abnormal
excitement aroused by music, his loving and understanding family, and his early sign of genius. (I)

TWENTIETH CENTURY

1156. Almedingen, E. M. My St. Petersburg. Norton,
1970. Ill. with photographs. This "reminiscence
of childhood, " with its detailed recollection of a
child's fresh impressions of pre-revolutionary St.
Petersburg, now Leningrad, will interest readers
of any age, especially any who plan to visit Leningrad. (YA and A)

1157. Archer, Jules. Man of Steel, Joseph Stalin. Messner,
1965. A short objective biography of Stalin (1879-
1953) covering the revolutionary movement in Russia and the rise of the U.S.S.R. (YA)

1158. Arsenyev, Vladimir. With Dersu the Hunter. (Adaptation by Anne Terry White.) George Braziller,
1965. Ill. with drawings and maps. The true
story of a naturalist-detective who saved the life
of a scientist in southeastern Siberia in the beginning of the century. (YA)

1159. Bartos-Höppner, B. Hunters of Siberia. Walck, 1969.
Jacket by Charles Robinson. Translated by Anthea
Bell. A stirring novel of the Siberian taiga
(swampy forest) in the beginning of the twentieth
century; about the efforts of a dedicated forestry
commissioner to institute and enforce game laws
with the help (at first unwilling) of a Caucasian
exile and his son, the opposition of the Siberian
natives to his interference with their way of life,
and the final conversion of the Caucasians to the
need for conservation of wild life and the abolition
of cruel methods of killing. (YA)

1160. Bloch, Marie Holun. Aunt America. Atheneum, 1963.
Ill. by Joan Berg. Older readers too may well
enjoy this story of the visit of an American aunt
to her family in the Ukraine (part of the U.S.S.R.
after World War II and quite isolated from the
outside world) and its effect upon her little niece

Lesya, who learns from her the meaning of freedom and the courage it takes to be free. (I)

1161. Burstein, Chaya. Rifka Bangs the Teakettle. Harcourt, Brace and World, 1970. Ill. by the author. A period piece of an impoverished Jewish village in Czarist Russia in 1904 and the story of Rifka, a boisterous, mischievous little girl with an intense desire to learn to read and write. (I)

1162. Coolidge, Olivia. Makers of the Red Revolution. Houghton-Mifflin, 1963. Ill. with photographs. Short biographies of Marx (1818-83), Lenin (1870-1924), Trotsky (1879-1940), Stalin (1879-1953), Tito (1892-), Khrushchev (1894-1971), and Mao Tse-Tung (1893-). (YA)

1163. Dubrin, Arnold. Igor Stravinsky, His Life and Times. Crowell, 1970. Ill. with photographs. Jacket by Jerome Snyder. Where to place this biography (1882-1971) and the story of Stravinsky's works, would be a problem if he had not himself said plainly, during his visit to Russia in 1962, "A man must have one birthplace, one fatherland, one country--he can have but one country--and the place of his birth is the most important factor in his life." He was born in Russia, and even though he left there forever (except for his 1962 visit) when he was about 28, he must surely be considered a Russian composer. Includes lists of books about him and his times, books by him, his works, and "pocket scores." (YA and A)

1164. Goldston, Robert. The Russian Revolution. Bobbs-Merrill, 1966. Ill. by Donald Carrick and photographs. (YA)

1165. Harr, Japp ter. Boris. Delacorte, 1969. Ill. by Rien Poortvliet. Translated from the Dutch by Martha Mearns. A poignant, realistic novel of a 12-year-old Russian boy who, by luck, bravery, and the help of a German soldier, manages to survive the siege of Leningrad by the Germans in 1942, learning not to hate even the enemy. (I and YA)

1166. Halliday, E. M. (and the editors of Horizon Magazine). Russia in Revolution. American Heritage Pub. Co., 1967. Ill. with paintings, cartoons and photographs. A good pictorial background for novels about the revolution. (YA)

1167. Harper, Theodore Acland. His Excellency and Peter. Doubleday, Doran, 1930. Ill. by Kurt Weise. Written in collaboration with Winifred Harper, this

is a novel to be enjoyed by older readers too,
about the relationship of Russia and China, following the Russo-Japanese War in 1904-05. The
young hero has a hard course to steer between
dedicated revolutionists and liberal government
officials. (YA)

1168.   Haskell, Helen Eggleston. Katrinka, The Story of a
Russian Child. Dutton, 1915 and 1943. Ill. but
no name. A comprehensive picture of life in
Russia before World War I, and how a little peasant girl became a ballerina in the Imperial Ballet.
Much Russian history woven into the story and
notes about the Russian words used. (I)

1169.   Hautzig, Esther. The Endless Steppe--Growing Up
in Siberia. Crowell, 1968. Autobiography of a
young Polish girl taken at the age of eleven, with
her family, from their gracious home in Poland
to a slave labor camp in cold, lonely Siberia
where, for five years, she endured incredible
hardships with indomitable courage and ingenuity
and even the ability to find beauty in the "endless
steppes." (YA)

1170.   Hume, Ruth and Paul. The Lion of Poland, The Story of Paderewski. Hawthorne, 1962. Ill. by Lili
Rethi. A biography of the musician-statesman
(1860-1941). (I)

1171.   Hunt, Mabel Leigh. Singing Among Strangers. Lippincott, 1954. Ill. by Irene Gibian. This heart-
rending novel about a Latvian family, first suffering from invading Russians, then from Nazi conquerors, and finally again from the pursuing Russians, is lightened by old Latvian songs woven
through the story like a golden thread in a black
shawl. A beautiful story of courage and hope
throughout their anguish as the family is first
taken to forced labor in Germany and then to a
refugee camp, and, finally to the United States.
(YA)

1172.   Kalashnikoff, Nicolas. The Defender. Scribner, 1951.
Ill. by Claire and George Douden. A Bambi-like
story about a Siberian tribesman and his friendship with wild mountain rams. (I)

1173.   _____. My Friend Yakub. Scribner, 1953. Ill.
by Feodore Rojansky. The story of a Tatar and
his life in a small Siberian town in the early part
of the century. (I)

1174.   Kellogg, Charlotte (Hoffman). Paderewski. Viking,

1957. A biography especially interesting for its
history of Poland during Paderewski's long life-
time (1860-1941). (YA)

1175. Kosterina, Nina. The Diary of Nina Kosterina.
Crown, 1968. Jacket and drawings by Ron and
Karen Bowen. Translated from the Russian and
introduced by Mirra Ginsburg. The diary covers
the years from 1936 to 1941, and Nina's age from
15 to 21, revealing her unswerving loyalty to the
Party and Communist ideology even though many
of her relatives (even her father, an early rev-
olutionist) are purged, and one of her best friends
is expelled from the Komsomol because she will
not repudiate her exiled parents. (YA and A)

1176. Lengyel, Emil. Ignace Paderewski, Musician and
Statesman. Watts, 1970. Ill. with photographs.
An absorbing biography of a man (1860-1941) who,
because of many obstacles in his youth (when Poland was divided between Russia, Prussia, and
Austria) had to learn his musical disciplines after
he was 21, but whose devotion and service to his
country was lifelong. Chronology and a final
chapter: "Paderewski on Piano Playing." (YA)

1177. Malvern, Gladys. Dancing Star, The Story of Anna
Pavlova. Messner, 1942. Ill. by Susanne Suba.
Not only the life story of the great, world re-
nowned ballerina (1882-1931) but also stories of
the Russian Imperial Ballet, famous musicians,
impressarios, choreographers, and other dancers
of the period. (YA)

1178. Massie, Robert K. Nicholas and Alexandra. Atheneum, 1967. Ill. with photographs and maps. This
long dual biography was inspired by the author's
experience with his own hemophilic son and his
consequent interest in the medical problem of the
disease and its impact on history, especially in
the case of the little Czarovitch of Russia. His
thesis is that history might have taken a different
turn if the heir to the Russian crown had been
normally healthy. (A)

1179. Mirvish, Robert F. The Last Capitalist. Sloane,
1963. A novel about a lad of Murmansk during
World War II and the Russian Revolution; how he
used his keen wits and the free enterprise system
to keep himself and a group of "lost children" fed
and clothed and out of reach of the Soviet officials
who were trying to round them up. (A)

1180.   Plowman, Stephanie. _Three Lives for the Czar._
        Houghton, 1969. Ill. with maps and genealogical
        chart. The narrator in this fine historical novel
        is a close companion to the Czar's four daughters,
        his father being equerry to Nicholas II, and his
        mother, lady-in-waiting to the Czarina Alexandra.
        The story commences in 1894 with the accession
        of Nicholas II and ends with the beginning of World
        War I. (YA and A)

1181.   _____. _My Kingdom for a Grave._ Houghton, 1970.
        A powerful sequel to "Three Lives for the Czar"
        telling of the disastrous Russian advance into East
        Prussia in the summer of 1914, the disintegration
        of the Russian army and final collapse, followed
        by the revolution of February, 1917, the November
        revolution, abdication of the Czar and the murder
        of him and his family--all this tragic story nar-
        rated by the same young narrator of the preceding
        book which makes it a human as well as historic
        tragedy. Map and genealogical charts. (YA and
        A)

1182.   Rossif, Frederick and Chapsal, Madeleine. _Portrait_
        of a Revolution, Russia, 1896-1924. Little, Brown,
        1969. A photographic panorama, with explanatory
        text. (YA)

1183.   Sammis, Edward R. _The Last Stand at Stalingrad._
        Macmillan, 1966. Ill. by photographs and a map.
        The story of the battle that lasted from September
        13, 1942, to February 2, 1943. (YA)

1184.   Seraillier, Ian. _The Silver Sword._ Criterion, n.d.
        Ill. by C. Walter Hodges. A harrowing story of
        a family of Polish children during World War II,
        their struggle to survive, and to find their par-
        ents. (YA)

1185.   Singer, Isaac Bashevis. _A Day of Pleasure._ Farrar,
        Straus and Giroux, 1969. Ill. with photographs by
        Roman Vishniac. Stories rich in folklore, comedy
        and tragedy, courage and human frailties, of a
        Hasidic boy growing up in Russian Warsaw (until
        World War II when Germans and Austrians took
        over) and of the author's Poland of over half a
        century ago. (YA and A)

1186.   Trease, Geoffrey. _The White Nights of St. Peters-_
        burg. Vanguard, 1967. Ill. by William Stobbs.
        A novel of the 1917 revolution, bringing in the
        principal figures of the time--Rasputin, Kerensky,
        Lenin, Stalin and Trotsky--as encountered by a

young American who has been sent by his father
to Russia to study the people and business oppor-
tunities. (YA)

1187. Wayne, Kyra Petrovskaya. Shurik. Grosset and
Dunlap, 1970. Ill. with photographs and maps.
The author's own story of the days when she was
a nurse in Leningrad during the 900-day siege and
of a lost boy whom she befriended. Introduction
by Harrison Salisbury. (I and YA)

1188. Werstein, Irving. The Uprising of the Warsaw Ghetto,
Nov. 1940-May, 1943. Norton, 1968. Ill. with
photographs. Few Jews survived to tell this
proud, tragic tale of resistance to Hitler's orders
for total destruction of the Warsaw Ghetto. (YA)

1189. Wilkinson, Winifred. Even in the Depths. Reynal,
1965. A strong, poignant novel of a boy of fif-
teen, struggling to keep alive in the rubble of
postwar Warsaw, and a wise old woman who
comes to his rescue. (A)

1190. Wuorio, Eva-Lis. Venture at Midsummer. Harcourt,
1967. When the province of Karelia is captured
by Russia after the Russo-Finnish War, three
men decide to smuggle a botanist's plants out to
Finland. (I and YA)

1191. _____. Code Polonaise. Holt, Rinehart and Winston, 1971. Jacket by Herbert Danska. A novel
of the hardships, dangers, courage and ingenuity
of some Polish children during the varied occupa-
tions of their country in the 1940s. (I and YA)

PART VII: SCANDINAVIA
(Norway, Sweden, Denmark, Finland, Iceland)

MYTHS, LEGENDS AND FOLKLORE

1192.   Asbjornsen, P. C. and Moe, Jorgen E. Norwegian
        Folk Tales. 1845. Viking, 1960. Ill. by Erik
        Werenskiold and Theodore Kittelsen. Translated
        by Shaw Iversen and Carl Norman. (I)
1193.   . East of the Sun and West of the Moon.
        Dover, 1970. Translated by George Webbe Da-
        sent (1817-96). A republication of Popular Tales
        from the North, 3rd edition, 1888: 59 Norwegian
        folk tales with 77 pictures added. (I)
1194.   Behn, Harry. The Faraway Lurs. World, 1963.
        Ill. by the author. A love story, based on the
        discovery of a primitive coffin (from about 1000
        B.C.) in Egtved, Denmark, in 1921, about a girl
        of the Forest People and the chief's son of a war-
        rior tribe of pastoralists. (I and YA)
1195.   Bosley, Keith. The Devil's Horse; Tales from the
        Kalevala. Pantheon, 1971. Beautiful adventure
        stories from Finland's great epic poem, retold
        in prose. (I and YA)
1195a. Boucher, Alan. Mead Moondaughter and Other Ice-
        landic Tales. Chilton, 1967. Ill. by Karoluia
        Larusdottir. Tales, based on Icelandic sagas,
        adapted and translated by Alan Boucher, with in-
        teresting notes. (I, YA and A)
1196.   Bowman, Dr. James C. and Bianco, Margery.
        Tales from a Finnish Tupa. Whitman, 1958.
        Ill. by Laura Bannon. Translated by Aili Kaleh-
        mainen, with a glossary of Finnish names, let-
        ters and sounds, and appendix about Finnish folk-
        lore. (I and YA)
1197.   Colum, Padraic. The Children of Odin: The Book
        of Northern Myths. Macmillan, 1920 and 1948.
        Ill. by Will Pogany. (I)
1198.   Dahl, Borghild. The Cloud Shoes. Dutton, 1957.
        Ill. by Hans Helweg. An amusing original story,
        though told as a legend, about how skis first came

into use in Norway and why they were called
skis. (E and I)

1199. D'Aulaire, Ingri and Edgar Parin. East of the Sun
and West of the Moon. Viking, 1969. Ill. by the
authors. Twenty-one Norwegian folk tales. (I)

1200. _____. Norse Gods and Giants. Doubleday, 1967.
Ill. by the authors. A beautiful picture book of
Norse myths. (E and I)

1201. Deutsch, Babette. Heroes of the Kalevala. Messner,
1932 and Holt, 1949. Ill. by Fritz Eichenberg.
Finnish legends. (I and YA)

1202. Feagles, Anita. Autun and the Bear. Young Scott
Books, 1967. Ill. by Gertrude Barrer-Russell.
A retelling of an old Icelandic legend from the
tenth century. (E)

1203. _____. Thor and the Giants. Scott, n.d. Ill.
by Gertrude Barrer-Russell. An old Norse legend retold. (E and I)

1204. Hosford, Dorothy G. Sons of the Volsung. Macmil-
lan, 1932 and Holt, 1949. Ill. by Frank Dobias.
An adaptation of "Sigurd the Volsung" by William
Morris. (I and YA)

1205. King, Cynthia. In the Morning of Time: The Story
of the Norse God, Balder. Four Winds, 1970.
Ill. by Charles Mikolaycak. Based on the Norse
myths contained in the Poetic Edda and the Prose
Edda. (YA)

1206. Lauring, Palle. The Stone Daggers. Macmillan,
1964. Ill. by Ib Spang Olsen. Translated by
Ruth M. Herberg and with an introduction by
Walter A. Fairservis. The scary adventures of
13-year-old twins in fearfully dangerous Denmark
in the Bronze Age. (I)

1207. Shideler, Rose. Staffan. Parnassus, 1970. Ill. by
Nicolai Sidjakov. A favorite Swedish folk song
(the music of the carol included) about a stable
boy who became Sweden's patron saint of horses.
(E)

1208. Sutcliffe, Rosemary. Beowulf. Dutton, 1962. Ill.
by Charles Keeping. An excellent retelling of the
sanguinary Anglo-Saxon epic, which was based on
Norse legends and historical events in sixth century Denmark. (YA)

FIRST THROUGH SIXTH CENTURIES

1209. Garthwaite, Marion. The Locked Crowns. Double-

day, 1963. Ill. by Herman B. Vestal. A novel
built upon the dangers besetting Havelock the Dane,
whose story first appeared in epic verse around
1280 but was probably told and sung long before--
as gory as all the old sagas and equally poetic.
(I and YA)

1210. Knudsen, Poul E. The Challenge. Macmillan, 1963.
Translated by L. W. Kingsland, with a note. A
novel whose Cimbri hero travels to Rome and
back, in the first decade of the Christian era,
encountering perilous adventures on his way through
central Europe. (YA)

1211. Walsh, Gillian Paton. Hengest's Tale. St. Martin's,
1966. Ill. by Janet Margrie. The story of the
first Saxon conqueror of Kent, England (fifth century), the action taking place in Scandinavia before the conquest. Fragments of old English poetry, skillfully placed together into a novel. (YA)

EIGHTH THROUGH ELEVENTH CENTURIES
(The Viking Period)

1212. Best, Herbert. The Sea Warriors. Macmillan, 1959.
A novel about Viking exploits in Greenland and
Leif Ericson's Vinland, the Fruitful. (YA)

1213. Bond, Susan McDonald. Eric, the Tale of the Red-
Tempered Viking. Grove, 1968. Ill. by Sally
Trinkle. A very funny story with equally amus-
ing drawings, about Eric the Red, father of Leif
Eriksson. (E)

1214. Boucher, Alan. The Land Seekers. Farrar, Straus
and Giroux, 1964. A Viking tale about two boys
who made the dangerous voyage in the 800s from
northern Scotland to Iceland where they managed
to make their homes under the guidance of the
grandmother of one who owned the other as a
thrall. Based on Icelandic books written 200
years later, the leading characters of this novel
were real people. (I and YA)

1215. _____. The Sword of the Raven. Scribner, 1969.
Ill. by Doreen Roberts. A compelling novel based
on an Icelandic saga, about a boy whose childhood
friendships and loyalties have been broken by a
family feud. (YA)

1216. Bulla, Clyde Robert. Viking Adventures. Crowell,
1963. Ill. by Douglas Gorsline. A story of

courage and high adventure about a boy who sailed
to Vinland. (E)

1217. Coblentz, Catherine Cate. The Falcon of Eric the
Red. Longmans Green, 1942. Ill. by Henry C.
Pitz. A lovely white falcon is given to Jon, a
castaway lad, by Eric the Red, and Jon takes it
with him from Greenland to Vinland (possibly Nova
Scotia). An endearing story of a boy and his beloved falcon and the true meaning of freedom. (I
and YA)

1218. D'Aulaire, Ingri and Edgar Parin. Leif the Lucky.
Doubleday, 1941. Ill. by the authors. A biography of Leif Eriksson (whose name is spelled in
so many ways). (E)

1219. Haugaard, Erik Christian. Hakon of Rogen's Saga.
Houghton-Mifflin, 1963. Ill. by Leo and Diane
Dillon. A novel based on Icelandic sagas, about
the end of the Viking period. (YA)

1220. _____. A Slave's Tale. Houghton-Mifflin, 1965.
Ill. by Leo and Diane Dillon. A sequel to "Hakon
of Rogen's Saga." (YA)

1221. Johansen, Margaret Alison. Voyagers West. Washburn, 1959. Ill. by William Ferguson. A novel
about the Vikings led by Eric the Red in 982 and
the discovery of Vinland by his son, Leif Ericson.
(YA)

1222. Jonsson, Runer. Viki Viking. World, 1968. Ill. by
Ewert Karlsson. Translated from the German by
Birgit Rogers and Patricia Tracy Lowe. Hilarious
adventures of a little boy with more brains than
brawn. (E and I)

1223. Liljencrantz, Ottilie. The Thrall of Leif the Lucky.
McClurg, 1902. The story of a son of an English
earl serving Leif Ericson on his voyage to the
new world. (I)

1224. Mowat, Farley. Westviking. Little, Brown, 1965.
Maps and drawings by Claire Wheeler. A long
book for serious readers of Viking lore, based
on the sagas and the author's "on the spot" research. A chronology of western voyages. (A)

1225. Newman, Robert. Grettir the Strong. Crowell, 1968.
Ill. by John Gretzer. Retelling of an ancient Icelandic saga based on the translation of E. Magnus-
son, 1869, and G. A. Hight, 1914, about a strong-
willed, short-tempered outlaw. (I)

1226. Pohl, Frederick J. The Viking Explorers. Crowell,
1966. Contains drawings, photographs, maps (in-

cluding the new Yale map of Vinland from 1440),
illuminations from ancient manuscripts and diagrams of archaeological discoveries. Rhoda Tupp
was the illustrations editor. (YA)

1227. Polland, Madeleine. Bjorn the Proud. Holt, Rinehart and Winston, 1961. Ill. by William Stobbs.
The story of a Viking boy and his Irish captive
who converts him to Christianity. (YA)

1228. Ritchie, Rita. Ice Falcon. Norton, 1963. A good
story of falconry in the days of Haaken the Good
of Norway. (I)

1229. Schaff, Louise E. Skald of the Vikings. Lothrop,
Lee and Shepard, 1965. A story of a 13-year-
old boy taken on a voyage from Greenland to Vinland and the colony established there, later at-
tacked by the Indians. (I)

1230. Schiller, Barbara. The Vinlander's Saga. Holt,
Rinehart and Winston, 1966. Ill. by William
Bock. Inspired by the Yale Vinland map, a story
about the early Norsemen, beginning with Eric
the Red. (I)

1231. Schroeder, Mary. The Hunted Prince. Coward-Mc-
Cann, 1969. Jacket by W. T. Mars. A tremen-
dously exciting story about Olaf Tryggvason (later
King of Norway 995-1000), who, as a baby escapes with his queen mother from a usurper to
the Norwegian throne, and, guarded by a courageous and loyal son of a noble, survives capture
by pirates and slavery in Eastland. (I)

1232. Sellman, R. R. The Vikings. Roy, 1957. Ill. by
the author and various Norwegian artists. A
splendidly arranged history of the Viking period,
their way of life, their conquests and defeats,
with maps, the Runic alphabet and a chronology
of explorations. (YA)

1233. Shippen, Katherine B. Leif Eriksson, First Voyager
to America. Harper and Row, 1951. Biography.
(I)

1234. Shura, Mary Frances. The Valley of the Frost Giants. Lothrop, 1971. Ill. in color and black
and white by Charles Keeping. Two Viking children who become separated from their parents,
befriend an abandoned baby and courageously
stand by him in this stirring tale. (E and I)

1235. Sprague, Rosemary. A Kingdom to Win. Oxford,
1953. Ill. by Eleanor Curtis. A romantic novel
about Olav Trygvison, taken as a slave to the

kingdom of Gardarik (part of present Russia),
showing the contrast between the Scandinavian
and Byzantine cultures in the tenth century. (YA)

1236. _____ . Heroes of the White Shield. Oxford, 1955.
Ill. by Eleanor Curtis. A sequel to "A Kingdom
to Win," about Olaf's Christianization of Norway.
(YA)

1237. Treece, Henry. The Burning of Njal. Criterion,
1964. Ill. by Bernard Blatch. A Viking story
of the period from 874 to 1017. (YA)

1238. _____ . Horned Helmet. Criterion, 1963. Ill. by
Charles Keeping. A story based on the finding
of an ancient helmet in the Thames. (I)

1239. _____ . The Last Viking. Pantheon, 1966. Ill.
by Charles Keeping. A story of Harald Hardrada
and his youthful adventures in the Russia of his
cousin Jaroslav. (YA)

1240. _____ . Viking's Dawn. Criterion, 1956. Ill. by
Christine Price. The first of a series about a
Harald Sigurdson and his Viking voyages about
A.D. 780 before the first invasions of Britain.
A map and introduction set the stage. (YA)

1241. _____ . The Road to Miklagord. Criterion, 1957.
Ill. by Christine Price. The second book (a sequel to "Viking's Dawn") carries Harald Sigurdson
to Ireland, Moorish Spain, and Constantinople.
(YA)

1242. _____ . Viking's Sunset. Criterion, 1960. Ill. by
Christine Price. The last of the Harald Sigurdson
series in which Harald voyages to North America
via Iceland and Greenland. (YA)

1243. _____ . Swords from the North. Pantheon, 1967.
Ill. by Charles Keeping. Originally published in
Britain as "The Northern Brothers" this is the
fourth novel about Harald Hardrada when he lived
in Constantinople as captain of the Greek Emper-
or's guard. There were three emperors at that
time, the three husbands of Empress Zoe. (YA)

1244. _____ . Westward to Vinland. S. G. Phillips,
1967. Ill. by William Stobbs. From the Icelandic sagas, this is the story of Eric the Red,
Leif Erikson, and the voyages to America 500
years before Columbus. (YA)

1245. Weir, Ruth Cromer. Leif Eriksson, Explorer.
Abingdon Press, 1951. Ill. by Harve Stein. A
biographical story. (I)

THIRTEENTH THROUGH SIXTEENTH CENTURIES

1246. Coatsworth, Elizabeth. Door to the North. Winston,
       1950. Ill. by Frederick Chapman. A story based
       on the discovery in Minnesota of a stone on which
       the date of 1364 has seemed to some scholars to
       indicate that Scandinavians might have settled
       there and intermarried with a now extinct tribe
       of Indians. (I)

1247. Evernden, Margery. Simon's Way. Walck, 1948.
       Ill. by Frank Newfeld. The story of a boy caught
       up in a struggle for the throne of Norway in which
       he aided Haaken Haakenson in 1223. (I)

1248. Polland, Madeleine. The White Twilight. Holt, Rine-
       hart and Winston, 1965. Ill. by Alan Cober. A
       novel about a young girl whose father is commis-
       sioned to rebuild the castle of King Frederick II
       of Denmark, and about her life at court where
       she meets a young page who is suspiciously know-
       ing about a certain pirate. Mystery and adven-
       ture. (YA)

1249. Trease, Geoffrey. The Secret Fiord. Harcourt,
       1950. Ill. by Joe Krush. A novel of suspense
       about the Hanseatic League, one of whose ware-
       houses has been preserved as a museum on the
       quayside at Bergen, Norway. The author's note
       gives the history of the Hanseatic League. (YA)

SEVENTEENTH AND EIGHTEENTH CENTURIES

1250. Haugaard, Erik Christian. The Untold Tale. Hough-
       ton-Mifflin, 1971. Ill. by Leo and Diane Dillon.
       A haunting, melancholy novel of love and hate in
       the time when Denmark was at war with Sweden,
       with the recollections of a steward of King Chris-
       tian IV of Denmark, about some children who needed
       him and whom he deserted. (YA)

1251. Silverstein, Alvin and Virginia. Carl Linnaeus, The
       Man Who Put the World of Life in Order. John
       Day, 1969. Ill. by Lee J. Ames. A well-or-
       dered (as indeed it should be) biography of the
       man (1707-78) who was the prime arranger in the
       field of natural history, and many of whose clas-
       sifications are still in use. (I and YA)

1252. Stoutenburg, Adrien and Baker, Laura Nelson. Be-
       loved Botanist: The Story of Carl Linnaeus.

Scribner, 1961. A biography of the founder of
modern systematic botany (1707-78). (I)

NINETEENTH CENTURY

1253. Benet, Laura. Enchanting Jenny Lind. Dodd, Mead,
1961. Ill. by George Gillett Whitney. A long,
full biography of the Swedish singer (1820-87)
with interesting material about the Sweden of that
time. (YA)
1254. Berry, Erick (Allena Best). A World Explorer:
Fridtjof Nansen. Garrard, 1969. Ill. by William
Hutchinson. This biography (1861-1930) empha-
sizes Nansen's physical stamina. Even as a boy
he would ski in the bitter cold without warm
wraps. It also relates his extraordinary achievement with his ship the Fram (still to be seen in
Oslo, Norway) and his scientific discoveries and
humanitarianism. (I)
1255. Cavanah, Frances. Two Loves for Jenny Lind.
Macrae Smith, 1956. A biography largely con-
cerned with the singer's American tour under the
auspices of P. T. Barnum. (I and YA)
1256. Coatsworth, Elizabeth. Jon the Unlucky. Holt, Rinehart and Winston, 1964. Ill. by Esta Nesbitt.
Intrigued by reports of two settlements (fifteenth
century) that completely vanished from Greenland,
the author has built a story around an imagined
solution of the puzzle, in which an orphaned Danish boy in the late nineteenth century, finds the
isolated descendants of the vanished settlers. (I)
1257. Hall, Anna Gertrude. Nansen. Viking, 1940. Ill.
by Boris Artzybasheff. A beautiful book in every
way--illustrations, maps, and especially the story
telling about the great Norwegian Arctic explorer,
scientist, statesman, and humanitarian (1861-1930),
whose ship the Fram may be seen today in Oslo.
(I and YA)
1258. Kyle, Elizabeth (Dunlop, Agnes Mary Robertson).
The Swedish Nightingale, Jenny Lind. Holt,
Rinehart and Winston, 1964. A biographical
novel about the singer's youthful career, introducing Queen Desideria (Desirée Clary of France,
wife of Count Bernadotte, later King of Sweden)
and Hans Christian Andersen who was in love
with Jenny. (YA)

1259. _____. Song of the Waterfall; The Story of Ed-
       ward and Nina Grieg. Holt, Rinehart and Win-
       ston, 1970. Jacket by Michael Lowenstein. More
       nearly a biographical novel than straight biography,
       this is a love story as well as the life story of
       the Norwegian composer (1843-1907), and among
       other famous figures in it are Ole Bull, the great
       Norwegian violinist, and Henrik Ibsen. (YA)

1260. Manning-Sanders, Ruth. The Story of Hans Andersen,
       Swan of Denmark. Dutton, 1906. Ill. by Astrid
       Walford. Biography mainly concerned with Ander-
       sen's "ugly duckling" youth and told in the manner
       of one of his own universally loved fairy tales.
       (I)

1261. Mattson, Olle. Mickel and the Lost Ship. Watts,
       1955. Ill. by R. M. Sax and translated from the
       Swedish by Anna Spruge and Elizabeth Sprigg. A
       mystery story set in rural Sweden in 1892, about
       a boy's search for his father who left years before
       for the Klondike. A Nils Holgersson Award book.
       (I and YA)

1262. Meyer, Edith Patterson. Dynamite and Peace. The
       story of Alfred Nobel. Little, Brown, 1958. Bi-
       ography of the Swedish chemist and inventor, man-
       ufacturer of explosives, and originator of dynamite,
       and founder of the Nobel Peace prize. (I and YA)

1263. Myers, Elisabeth P. Jenny Lind, Songbird from Swe-
       den. Garrard, 1968. Ill. by Frank Vaughn and
       with photographs. A biography (1820-87) with em-
       phasis on Jenny's insecure childhood and rejection
       by her mother and other later difficulties which
       she splendidly overcame. (YA)

1264. Noel-Baker, Francis. Fridtjof Nansen, Arctic Ex-
       plorer. Putnam, n.d. Ill. by Robert Doremus.
       A biography (1861-1930) of the Norwegian explorer,
       scientist, sportsman, and diplomat statesman who
       is best remembered for his polar explorations at
       the end of the century. (I and YA)

1265. Sommerfelt, Aimee. No Easy Way. Criterion, 1967.
       Ill. by Theresa Prudi and translated by Patricia
       Crampton. A stagestruck girl and her adamant
       archduke father finally come to an understanding
       in this tense novel about the theater in Oslo in
       1867 when Ibsen was a beginning playwright. (I
       and YA)

1266. Turngren, Annette. Flaxen Braids. Prentice-Hall,
       1937 and 1939. Ill. by Polly Jackson. A simple

story of a happy warm Swedish family on the move
to northern Sweden, where the father hopes to obtain work, who find friendly folk and happy events
on the way. (I)

1267.   . The Copper Kettle. Prentice-Hall, 1939,
revised, 1961. Ill. by Polly Jackson. Another
pleasant story of Swedish life and customs on the
little island of Oland in the late 1800s. A visit
to Stockholm brings Jenny Lind into the story. (I)

1268. Unnerstad, Edith. Journey to England. Macmillan,
1961. Ill. by Ulla Sundin-Wickman. Jacket by
Eric Blegvad. The adventures of two Swedish
children searching for their mother in 1885, with
a map of their journey. Introducing Jenny Lind.
(I)

1269. Wheeler, Opal. Hans Andersen, Son of Denmark.
Dutton, 1951. Ill. by Henry Pitz. A biography
of the Danish writer (1805-75) with a little Danish
history of the period. (I)

TWENTIETH CENTURY

1270. Arnold, Elliott. A Kind of Secret Weapon. Scribner, 1969. Jacket by Ilse Koehn. A gripping
novel about a 12-year-old boy involved, with his
parents, in putting out an underground newspaper
and other activities of the Danish underground
movement during World War II. The "secret
weapon" is only one of the many tricks the Danes
played on the Germans. Grim as it is, the story
also contains some gentle humor among the members of the little Andersen family. (I and YA)

1271. Balderson, Margaret. When the Jays Fly to Barbmo.
World, 1968. Ill. by Victor G. Ambrus. A novel of a young girl, half-Norwegian and half-Lapp
and her years from age 15 to 18, on a small
Norwegian island above the Arctic Circle; of the
German invasion during World War II and her escape to her Lapp family; and the conflict she
feels within herself between the two cultures,
Norwegian and Lappish. The story with its evoc-
ative description of the far north during the Dark
Time, starts slowly and quietly but builds up to
a stunning climax. (YA and A)

1272. Bernhardsen, Christian. Fight in the Mountains.
Harcourt, Brace and World, 1968. Jacket by

W. T. Mars and translated from the Danish by
Franey Sinding. A serious, somber novel about
two brothers escaping from the Gestapo after an
unsuccessful attempt at sabotage, to join the free
Norwegian forces in the mountains and finding
great difficulty in discovering friend from foe.
(YA)

1273. Catherall, Arthur. Lapland Outlaw. Lothrop, Lee
and Shepard, 1966. Ill. by Simon Jeruchim. An
exciting story, historical only in the sense of portraying a culture and economic system which may
soon be history, about two young Laplanders pitted
against a crooked reindeer trader and the power
of the Finnish police. (YA)

1274. DeLeeuw, Cateau. Roald Amundsen, A World Explorer. Garrard, 1965. Ill. by George I. Par-
rish. The exciting story of Amundsen's explorations and discovery of the South Pole in 1911.
(E and I)

1275. Holm, Anne. North to Freedom. Harcourt, Brace
and World, 1965. Translated from the Danish by
L. W. Kingsland. A blend of realism and alle-
gory about a 12-year-old boy's long trek home to
Denmark from a concentration camp somewhere
in eastern Europe, in constant terror of being re-
captured. (YA)

1276. Howarth, David. We Die Alone. Macmillan, 1955.
Ill. with photographs and a map on the inside cover. A true survival story about young men escaping from the German invaders of Norway in
World War II. The appendix gives the German
version of what they (the Germans) called "mis-
led Norwegians," and there is a chronology of the
escape of the lone survivor. (A)

1277. Levin, Jane Whitbread. Star of Danger. Harcourt,
World and Brace, 1966. A documentary novel
(with fictitious names of actual characters) about
two Jewish boys escaping to Sweden from the Nazis, and the help given them by the Danes. (YA)

1278. Levine, L. E. Champion of World Peace, Dag Ham-
marskjöld. Messner, 1962. A biography of the
Swedish and United Nations statesman (1905-61).
(YA and A)

1279. Lindgren, Astrid. Emil's Pranks. Follett, 1971.
Ill. by Bjorn Berg. The story of a little boy so
mischievous that the neighbors offer to buy him a
one-way ticket to America--set in rural Sweden

in the early part of the century.   (I)

1280.   Ruthin, Margaret (Catherall).   Elli of the Northland.
Farrar, Straus and Giroux, 1968.   About a young
Lapp girl, shortly after World War II, who wants
to stay with her Lapp friends and herd reindeer
against the wishes of her wealthy father in Hel-
sinki who sends a sheriff after her.   (I)

1281.   Senge, Sigurd.   Escape.   Harcourt, Brace and World,
1964.   Jacket by Charles McCurry.   Translated
by Evelyn Ramsden.   A novel of the Norwegian
underground, and the risks taken by two young
Norwegians (a boy and girl) to rescue a Russian
prisoner of war from his brutal Nazi captor.   (YA)

1282.   Werstein, Irving.   That Denmark Might Live.   Macrae, Smith, 1967.   Ill. with photographs.   Jacket
by James Johnston.   A dramatic account of the
indomitable courage of the Danes, greatly assisted
by the R. A. F., their almost incredible feat of
whisking most of their 8,000 Jews out from under
the Germans' very noses and getting them to Sweden, and their dogged resistance to the very end
of the war.   (YA)

GENERAL HISTORY AND GEOGRAPHY

1283. Lodor, Dorothy. <u>The Land and People of Spain</u>.
Lippincott, 1955. Ill. with photographs and maps.
Portraits of the Nations Series. (I and YA)

1284. Wohlrabe, Raymond and Krusch, Werner. <u>The Land</u>
<u>and People of Portugal</u>. Lippincott, 1960. Por-
traits of the Nations Series. Both these books
provide good background for fiction and biography
of this area. (I and YA)

MYTHS AND LEGENDS

1285. DeVivanco, Maria. <u>El Cid, Soldier and Hero</u>. Gold-
en, 1968. Ill. by Lazlo Gal. A dynamically illustrated, finely made book, with the complete
story and historical background of the Spanish hero who died and became a legend, in 1099. (I
and YA)

1286. Goldston, Robert. <u>The Legend of the Cid</u>. Bobbs-
Merrill, 1963. Ill. by Stephane. A novel about
the conflict between the Moors and the Christians
in the time of Fernando I, King of Castile and
Leon, from 1032-1065. The Cid, whose real
name was Ruy de Vivar, fought both Moors and
Christians and became a legendary figure. (I and
YA)

1287. _____. <u>Tales of the Alhambra</u>. Bobbs-Merrill,
1962. Ill. by Stephane. Adaptation of nine of
Washington Irving's tales. (I)

1288. Gunterman, Bertha L. <u>Castles in Spain and Other</u>
<u>Enchantments</u>. David McKay, 1928 and 1956.
Ill. by Mahlon Blaine. An unusually attractive
compilation of legends. (I)

1289. Irving, Washington. <u>The Alhambra</u>. Selected and
arranged by Mabel Williams. Macmillan, 1953.
Ill. by Louis Slobodkin. When Irving went to
Spain in 1829, as an attaché at the American le-

gation in Madrid, he took advantage of his position
to live for a time in the great Moorish palace (be-
gun in the thirteenth century and completed in the
fourteenth), and later wrote up his experiences and
the legends he discovered there, in "Legends of
the Alhambra," 1832 and 1852. (YA)
1290. Lauritzen, Jonreed. Blood, Banners and Wild Boars.
Little, Brown, 1967. Ill. by Gil Mirat. Tales
based on legends about the Roman invasion of the
second century B.C., the French invasion under
Charlemagne and Roland in the eighth century A.D.,
and Viking invasions in the twelfth century. (YA)
1291. Sherwood, Merriam. The Tale of the Warrior Lord
El Cid. Longmans Green, 1930. Ill. by Henry
C. Pitz. A prose translation based on "Cantor de
Mio Cid" by Ramon Menendez Pidal, 1908-1911.
The first manuscript of the ballads was probably
made in 1307 by a monk in a Spanish monastery
who signed himself "Per Abbot" or "Pedro Abad."
(YA)

EIGHTH THROUGH THIRTEENTH CENTURIES

1292. de Trevino, Elizabeth Borton. Casilda of the Rising
Moon. Farrar, Straus and Giroux, 1967. Saint
Casilda was a real person in the eleventh century
and this story is built on chronicles and legends
about her. (YA)
1293. Fon Eisen, Anthony. The Prince of Omeya. World,
1964. The introduction sets the stage for this
story which takes place almost entirely in the
eighth century Moslem world of Syria, Egypt, and
Africa, but its climax comes in Cordoba, Spain.
It is about the thrilling escape from the Caliph of
a rival house, of the last of the Ommiad dynasty
of Syria, and was suggested to the author by Washington Irving's "Spanish Papers." (YA)
1294. Marcus, Rebecca. Moses Maimonides, Rabbi, Philosopher, Physician. Watts, 1969. A biography
of a great scholar (1135-1204) whose influence is
still felt in Jewish, Christian, and Moslem thinking. Though he lived most of his life in Egypt,
he always considered himself a Spaniard. A list
of important events in his life, a glossary, and
an appendix, giving the Thirteen Articles of Faith,
are especially useful in a book about a man of so
long ago. (YA)

1295. Trease, Geoffrey. The Red Towers of Granada. Van-
       guard, 1966. Ill. by Charles Keeping. A novel
       about a young Englishman and a Jewish doctor
       searching, in Spain, for a remedy for the illness
       of Queen Eleanor of England. Exciting to the end.
       (YA)

                          FIFTEENTH CENTURY

1296. Anderson, Helen Jean. Henry the Navigator, Prince
       of Portugal. Westminster, 1969. The importance
       to world history of this Portuguese prince has
       been sadly understated and can hardly be overes-
       timated, for his promotion of science above super-
       stition lay the groundwork for the great discoveries
       of his age and the years following his death in
       1460. (YA)

1297. Bailey, Bernardine. Christopher Columbus, Sailor
       and Dreamer. Houghton-Mifflin, 1960. Ill. by
       Cheslie D'Andrea. An easy to read story of Co-
       lumbus' life, adventures, discoveries, and disap-
       pointments (1446?-1506). (I)

1298. Baumann, Hans. The Barque of the Brothers. Walck,
       1958. Ill. by Ulrich Schramm and translated by
       Isabel and Florence McHugh. A tale of the days
       of Henry the Navigator (1394-1460), particularly
       the disastrous expedition against Tangiers and the
       Moors in Africa in 1436. A chronology of histor-
       ical events from 1328 B.C. to 1460 A.D. (YA)

1299. Burt, Olive W. I Challenge the Dark Sea. John Day,
       1962. Map. A novel based on the life of Henry
       the Navigator. (YA)

1300. Criss, Mildred. Isabella, Young Queen of Spain.
       Dodd, Mead, 1941. Ill. by Mark Siniont. A rel-
       atively long novel requiring considerable historical
       knowledge about Castille. A genealogical chart and
       map would have been helpful. (YA)

1301. D'Aulaire, Ingri and Edgar Parin. Columbus. Dou-
       bleday, 1955. Ill. by the authors. As in all the
       D'Aulaire's books the text and pictures supple-
       ment each other perfectly. (E and I)

1302. Judson, Clara Ingram. Christopher Columbus. Fol-
       lett, 1960. Ill. by Polly Jackson. A "beginning
       to read" book intended for second graders. (E and I)

1303. Kent, Louise Andrews. He Went With Vasco da Gama.
       Houghton-Mifflin, 1938. Ill. by Paul Quinn. A

good story about the sailing to the Indies around
the Cape of Good Hope in July, 1497, written with
humor and conveying a good measure of Portuguese history. (YA)

1304. Kidwell, Carl. Granada! Surrender! Viking, 1968.
An exciting novel about the struggle to drive the
Moors out of Spain, and one young man's dream
of sailing across the ocean with Columbus. (YA)

1305. McKendrick, Malveena. Ferdinand and Isabella.
American Heritage, 1968. Ill. with a great va-
riety of prints, portraits, paintings, genealogical
charts, etc. Queen Isabella's dates were 1451-
1504, and Ferdinand's 1452-1516. They ruled together from 1474 until Isabella's death, and, during their reign, with the conquest of Granada,
Spain became, in the main, a united country. She
extended her power to the west, first with Columbus, and then with others, the Jews were expelled,
and the Inquisition was enforced. (YA)

1306. Polland, Madeleine. Alhambra. Doubleday, 1970.
A historical romance set in Spain during the era
just before the final expulsion of the Moors by
Ferdinand and Isabella. A brother and sister are
captured by Moorish invaders and escape being
sent as slaves to the Barbary coast by entering
one of the inner courts of the Alhambra. Romantic entanglements with Moors ensue, and finally
the brother captures a luxurious palace for Queen
Isabella. (YA)

1307. Sperry, Armstrong. The Voyages of Christopher Columbus. Random Landmark, 1950. Ill. by the
author. Written in exciting narrative form, this
is a story of the trials and triumphs of the man
(1446?-1506) who, though born in Genoa, Italy,
spent most of his life when not at sea in Portugal, first, and later Spain, where he finally died,
sadly neglected by King Ferdinand. (I and YA)

1308. Syme, Ronald. Vasco da Gama, Sailor Toward the
Sunrise. Morrow, 1959. Ill. by William Stobbs.
A biography of the man who first sailed around
the Cape of Good Hope to India from Portugal,
(1497-99) but who made serious mistakes in his
relations with the Arabs, causing long enmity
between them and the Portuguese. He became
very wealthy and acquired the title of Count of
Vidigueira. (I)

SIXTEENTH CENTURY

1309. Baker, Nina Brown. Ponce de Leon. Knopf, 1957.
       Ill. by Robert Doremus. A biography of the
       Spanish explorer (1460-1521) who discovered Flor-
       ida in 1513. (YA)
1310. Barret, Leighton. Don Quixote de la Mancha [An
       adaptation from the Matteux translation of the
       text of Miguel de Cervantes]. Little, Brown,
       1939. Ill. by Warren Chappell. Don Quixote,
       of course, was a purely imaginary character but
       Cervantes' creation of him, first printed in 1605,
       makes him seem historical. (YA)
1311. Baumann, Hans. Son of Columbus. Oxford, 1957.
       Ill. by William Stobbs. Translated by Isabel and
       Florence McHugh. A story about Ferdinand Colum-
       bus and how he went on his father's last voyage
       to the West Indies on which they experienced se-
       vere storms, shipwreck and mutiny. (YA)
1312. Blassingame, Wyatt. Ponce de Leon, A World Ex-
       plorer. Garrard, 1965. Ill. by Russ Hoover.
       A bridge book to the New World. (I)
1313. Busoni, Rafaello. The Man Who Was Don Quixote,
       The Story of Miguel Cervantes. Prentice-Hall,
       1958. Ill. by the author. A finely written and
       illustrated biography (1547-1616) of the creator
       of Don Quixote, who led almost as adventurous
       a life as his fictional hero. (YA)
1314. Cohen, Florence. Freedom Next Time. Messner,
       1971. Jacket by Don Lambo. A frightfully ex-
       citing novel about a rich Portuguese family who
       were Morranos (Jews forced to convert to Chris-
       tianity) at the time of the spreading Inquisition,
       based on facts and legends about an actual rich
       merchant family. (YA)
1315. Diaz-Plaja, Fernando. Cervantes, the Life of a
       Genius. Scribner, 1970. Translated by Sue
       Matz Soterakos. A biography of Spain's, and
       one of the world's, greatest writers, his life,
       his struggles, and his dream; also the story of
       Spain during his tempestuos lifetime (1547-1616),
       with a list of his literary works. (YA and A)
1316. Engle, Eloise. Sea Challenge, The Epic Voyage of
       Magellan. C. S. Hammond, 1962. Ill. by Herb
       Mott. A fictional account of Magellan's circum-
       navigation of the globe (1519-22), soundly based
       historically on the writings of Pigafetta, a mem-

ber of the expedition. (I and YA)

1317. Heyer, Georgette. Beauvallet. Dutton, 1969. Bantam Book, paperback, 1969. A swashbuckling
romance of an Elizabethan pirate and a Spanish
heiress. Just the ticket for a rainy day in the
country. (A)

1318. Israel, Charles E. Five Ships West, The Story of
Magellan. Macmillan, 1966. Ill. with prints and
maps. Jacket by Arthur Shilstone. This excitingly narrated story of the first navigator of the
globe, might well be titled "The Frustrations of
Magellan," for it tells of continuous threat of mu-
tiny. (YA)

1319. Lobdell, Helen. Golden Conquest. Houghton-Mifflin,
1953. Ill. by Seymour Fleishman. The story of
Cortez' expedition to Mexico, in 1519, based on
Prescott's "Conquest of Mexico." (I)

1320. Nevins, Albert J. St. Francis of the Seven Seas.
Farrar, Straus, 1955, a Vision Book. A biography of St. Francis Xavier (1506-52), a founder,
with St. Ignatius de Loyola, of the Society of Je-
sus, who spent eleven years in India and the Far
East. (YA)

1321. Parry, Judge Edward Abbott. Don Quixote of La
Mancha. Dodd, Mead, 1919. Ill. by Walter
Crane. A retelling of the first part of Cervantes'
book. (YA)

1322. Plaidy, Jean (Hibbert). The Spanish Bridegroom.
Putnam, 1971. A novel of Philip II, King of
Spain from 1556 to 1598, beginning with his unhappy boyhood and youth as Prince Philip, and
ending with the death of his third wife, Elizabeth
of France. Mary Tudor was his second wife, so
there is a section about England, but it is mainly
set in Spain, the Spain of the Inquisition, in
which, alas, Philip devoutly believed. (A)

1323. Pond, Seymour Gates. Ferdinand Magellan, Master
Mariner. Random Landmark, 1957. Ill. by Jack
Coggins. Biography (1480-1521). (I)

1324. Porter, Elizabeth Cannon. Cortez the Conqueror.
Dorrance, 1944. For very young readers. (E)

1325. Reeves, James. Exploits of Don Quixote. Walck,
1960. Ill. by Edward Ardizonne. Some of the
adventures of the knight of the mournful counte-
nance. (YA)

1326. Syme, Ronald. Magellan, First Around the World.
Morrow Jr. Books, 1953. Ill. by William Stobbs.

Born in Portugal in 1480, Magellan first sought
the support of the king of that country in financing
a voyage west to India, but when he refused, he
became a Spanish citizen and procured the support
of the king of Spain. The voyage took two perilous years before he was killed by hostile Asians,
but one of his ships returned to Spain in 1522,
mission fulfilled. (I)

1327. Welch, Ronald. Ferdinand Magellan. Criterion, 1956.
       Ill. by William Stobbs. A fictionalized biography.
       (YA)

1328. Williams, Jay. The Spanish Armada. American
       Heritage, 1967. Richly illustrated. The exciting
       events at sea during the period of approximately
       1568 to 1588, in which year the great Armada
       sailed out against England. (YA)

SEVENTEENTH CENTURY

1329. de Trevino, Elizabeth Borton. I Juan de Pareja. Far-
       rar, Straus and Giroux, 1965. A novel about the
       Negro slave of the painter, Velázquez, who, him-
       self, became a respected artist at the time of
       King Philip IV of Spain (reigning 1641-65). An
       afterword explains the factual basis of the book.
       (YA)

1330. Ripley, Elizabeth. Velázquez. Lippincott, 1965.
       Ill. with pictures of his paintings. A biography
       of the artist who spent most of his life (1599-
       1660) at the court of King Philip IV in Madrid,
       but whose paintings also depict peasants and
       homely scenes. One wishes that some of the
       pictures were in color and that there was more
       about Velázquez' assistant, Juan de Pareja. (YA)

NINETEENTH CENTURY

1331. Heyer, Georgette. The Spanish Bride. Dutton, 1965.
       A novel of the Peninsular War, 1808 to 1814--
       based on the diarists of the period, the works of
       Napier and Sir Charles Oman, and Wellington's
       dispatches--a war of the French against the Bri-
       tish who were aided by Spanish and Portuguese
       volunteers. The plot concerns a young Spanish
       lady married to a British soldier, but the main

interest of the book is in Wellington's military strategy. (A)

1332.   Mackay, Margaret. The Wine Princes. John Day, 1958. A novel about the Portuguese wine industry during the Napoleonic War and how that war affected the English wine merchants. (A)

1333.   Sprague, Rosemary. Fife and Fandango. Walck, 1961. A novel about a high-born Spanish señorita who marries an English soldier in Wellington's army. (YA)

1334.   Styles, Showell. Greencoats Against Napoleon. Vanguard, 1960. Jacket by Albert Orbaan. A derring-do novel about a 16-year-old ensign fighting the French under Napoleon in northern Spain, using his skill in rock climbing and foot racing to rescue a maiden in distress and playing a crucial part in the British victory of Corunna, with the help of a Yankee backwoodsman and a couple of Cockney riflemen. (YA)

1335.   Welch, Ronald. Captain of Foot. Oxford, 1959. Ill. by William Stobbs. Reprint, 1963. A novel of military action during the Peninsular Campaign of Wellington. The young hero is a member of the same fictional Cary family whose members have appeared in several other books, and his actions are based on the records of a real Captain John Hopkins. Most of the background material is true. A map, Cary family tree, and historical note. (YA)

TWENTIETH CENTURY

1336.   Bridge, Anne (O'Malley). Portuguese Escape. Macmillan, 1958. A novel of adventure, history, nature, architecture, etc. in Portugal. (A)

1337.   _____. Frontier Passage. Little, Brown, 1942. A novel of espionage and sabotage on the Spanish-French border in which an 18-year-old English girl plays an important role. Also a love story. (A)

1338.   Goldston, Robert. The Civil War in Spain. Bobbs-Merrill, 1966. Ill. with photographs and drawings by Donald Carrick. A good, solid, readable history of the Spanish Civil War (1936-39). (YA)

1339.   Greenfeld, Howard. Pablo Picasso. Follett, 1971. Ill. with fine reproductions of Picasso's works in

black and white and color. The first half of this
fine book gives an account of the artist's early
years (born 1881), and the second his development as an artist. (YA and A)

1340. Ripley, Elizabeth. Picasso. Lippincott, 1959. Ill.
with reproductions of the painter's works, one
picture opposing each page of text. Born in Spain
in 1881, Picasso has spent almost all of his life
since the age of 20 in France where he still lives
and works. (YA)

1341. Wojciechowska, Maia (Rodman). Shadow of a Bull.
Atheneum, 1964. Ill. by Alvin Smith. Though
not historical in the usual sense, this short poetic
novel about bull fighting and fighters describes an
historic tradition. (YA)

AUTHOR INDEX

187

TITLE INDEX

BIOGRAPHICAL INDEX